ARMS CONTROL:
THE MULTILATERAL ALTERNATIVE

UNA-USA POLICY STUDIES BOOK SERIES

The United Nations Association of the USA is a private, non-profit organization dedicated to broadening public understanding of the activities of the United Nations and other multilateral institutions. Through its nationwide membership and network of affiliated national organizations, UNA-USA conducts a broad range of programs to inform and involve the public in foreign affairs issues. The UNA-USA Policy Studies Program conducts projects involving research and analysis of a wide spectrum of policy issues of concern to the international community. The Program brings together panels of interested and knowledgeable Americans to study and make recommendations on specific problems of U.S. foreign policy and multilateral activities. As part of this process, a number of papers are commissioned from leading specialists. The UNA-USA Policy Studies Book Series contains books based on rewritten and edited collections of some of these papers. UNA-USA is responsible for the choice of the subject areas and the decision to publish the volumes, but the responsibility for the content of the papers and for opinions expressed in them rests with the individual authors and editors.

Already published:
Disaster Assistance: Appraisal, Reform and New Approaches, edited by Lynn H. Stephens and Stephen J. Green.
The New International Economic Order: A U.S. Response, edited by David B. H. Denoon.
The Politics of Human Rights, edited by Paula R. Newberg.
The Future of US-China Relations, edited by John Bryan Starr.
The US, the UN, and the Management of Global Change, edited by Toby Trister Gati.

ARMS CONTROL: THE MULTILATERAL ALTERNATIVE

Edited by

EDWARD C. LUCK

New York University Press

New York *and* London

1983

JX
1974
.A76 926
1983

Library of Congress Cataloging in Publication Data
Main entry under title:

Arms control: the multilateral alternative.

(UNA-USA policy studies book series)
Bibliography: p.
Includes index.
Contents: Foreword / Elliot L. Richardson—
Introduction / Edward C. Luck—The rise and fall of
multilateral arms control / Alan F. Neidle—[etc.]
1. Arms control—Addresses, essays, lectures.
I. Luck, Edward C.   II.   Series.
JX1974.A76926   1983   327.1'74   82-22587
ISBN 0-8147-5005-2
ISBN 0-8147-5006-0 pbk.

Clothbound editions of New York University Press books are Smyth-
sewn and printed on permanent and durable acid-free paper.

CONTENTS

LIST OF ABBREVIATIONS

ABM	Anti-Ballistic Missile
ASAT	Anti-Satellite Weapons
AMs	Associated Measures
BWs	Biological Weapons
CANDU	Canadian Deuterium Uranium Reactor
CBWs	Chemical and Biological Weapons
CD	Committee on Disarmament, United Nations, Geneva
CCD	Conference of the Committee on Disarmament, United Nations, Geneva
CSCE	Conference on Security and Cooperation in Europe, Helsinki (1975), Belgrade (1977), and Madrid (1980), unless specified
CPD	Comprehensive Programme for Disarmament
CART	Conventional Arms Control Reduction Talks
ENDC	Eighteen Nation Disarmament Committee, United Nations, Geneva
EURATOM	European Atomic Energy Community
EURODIFF	Eurodiffusion Consortium
EEC	European Economic Community
FNLA	Front for the National Liberation of Angola
GCD	General and Complete Disarmament
GSP	Generalized System of Preferences
ICBM	Inter-Continental Ballistic Missile
INF	Intermediate Nuclear Forces

IAEA	International Atomic Energy Agency, Vienna
INFCE	International Nuclear Fuel Cycle Evaluation Conference—1977–80
IPS	International Plutonium Storage System
LDCs	Less Developed Countries
LRTNF	Long Range Theatre Nuclear Forces
LEU	Low Enriched Uranium
MAC	Multilateral Arms Control
MIRV	Multiple Independently Targetable Re-entry Vehicle
MBFR	Mutual and Balanced Force Reduction Talks
NATO	North Atlantic Treaty Organization (also referred to as the Atlantic Alliance)
NFU	No First Use of Nuclear Weapons
NPT	Treaty on the Non-Proliferation of Nuclear Weapons, 1968
OMs	Operational Methods
OAU	Organization of African Unity
SSOD–I	First Special Session on Disarmament of the United Nations General Assembly, 1978
SSOD–II	Second Special Session on Disarmament of the United Nations General Assembly, 1982
SALT	Strategic Arms Limitation Talks
SALT I	First Strategic Arms Limitation Treaty, 1972
SALT II	Second Strategic Arms Limitation Treaty, 1979
START	Strategic Arms Reduction Talks
SLBM	Submarine-Launched Ballistic Missile
UNITA	Union for the Total Independence of Angola
UN	United Nations
UNGA	United Nations General Assembly

FOREWORD

ELLIOT L. RICHARDSON

This book addresses one of the most exasperating, vital, and least understood aspects of world politics: how the international community attempts to tame the global and regional arms races. The history of multilateral negotiations has been a frequently frustrating mixture of success and failure, characterized both by seemingly endless rhetoric and by a series of useful agreements. Over the last year for example, the second UN Special Session on Disarmament failed to make any headway, while negotiations on European security gained momentum. For most Americans, arms control is still perceived to be a Soviet-American affair, with other countries invited to watch but not to participate.

As the spread of advanced conventional arms and nuclear weapons potential has accelerated in recent years, however, it has become painfully apparent that the arms competition is no longer a two-party exercise. While the United States and the Soviet Union remain by far the leading actors, they cannot and will not stem the proliferation of conventional, chemical, and nuclear weapons without the active involvement and cooperation of their allies and the countries of the third world.

The superpowers, with their vast nuclear arsenals and global military reach, bear the primary responsibility for easing tensions and bringing their arms competition under control. But their responsibilities have not ended with the welcome revival of serious bilateral negotiations. Their central, yet often neglected, task is to provide leadership in stimulating the international community to act more decisively and vigorously in limiting the broader aspects of the arms race. Without strong leadership, 157 nation states cannot possibly move in a coherent, purposeful direction, as demonstrated in the second Special Session.

Some degree of Soviet-American comity is a prerequisite for progress at the multilateral level, though the US should take the lead in proposing new ideas and innovative answers to old problems. The US, with its more vibrant and pluralistic system, is more capable than the USSR of exercising vigorous and imaginative leadership. Despite the defensiveness that has too often hampered American diplomacy over the past decade, many nations still look to the US as the engine of ideas and initiatives. It will require a dynamic and strategic vision of the future to break the diplomatic stalemate that presently hinders efforts to resolve this and other interrelated problems on the international agenda. President Reagan, by choosing to address the second Special Session in June 1982, demonstrated his personal interest in multilateral disarmament efforts.

Now the United States faces the greater challenge of developing realistic, feasible, and far-reaching proposals to put before the peoples and nations of the world. If the US does not rise to this challenge, no other nation will. Multilateral negotiations are inherently slow and frustrating; their payoffs are long-term and often not immediately visible. Yet the political and security risks for the US in seizing the initiative are low, certainly lower than in having to react repeatedly to Soviet and non-aligned proposals that have a propaganda twist. Even if global discussions were only a diplomatic game, as cynics sometimes claim, it would behoove the US to play the game better than the other players. The stakes involved in failing to organize international efforts to limit nuclear and conventional proliferation, however, are both real and high.

Over the past year, western public opinion has reappeared as a major factor in the disarmament equation. Although the largest demonstration of all was timed for the opening of the second Special Session, the American public—like many officials—lacks a clear conception of the history, accomplishments, weaknesses, and potential of multilateral forums. There are no widely accepted yardsticks for assessing their results or the US performance in them. The public is bound to become disillusioned with the slow and uncertain pace of multilateral efforts if there is no understanding of their nature and purposes. For example, it is difficult to explain why events like the second Special Session are designed more for discussion than action. To those with unrealistically high expectations, the meager results may only serve to confirm their suspicions that the UN is unable to handle central security issues. The serious ongoing work of the Committee on Disarmament in Geneva, on the other hand, rarely gets any public attention at all.

If the public movement is to have influence over the long term, it must go beyond generalities and begin to address the hard issues of why arms control progress has been relatively modest despite two decades of determined effort and what alternative proposals are feasible, negotiable, and desirable. It should also broaden its concerns to include conventional and chemical weapons as well as nuclear weapons and to encompass multilateral as well as bilateral issues. The United Nations Association, with its dual purposes of policy analysis and public outreach, seeks to contribute to public understanding of international policy issues. These papers are designed to give the public, professionals, and students of foreign policy a richer appreciation of the complexities and possibilities of multilateral arms control. Since this book is the first major American study of the subject, it is hoped that its publication will stimulate others to pursue the issues further and to build upon its analysis and conclusions.

This volume suggests a range of possible strategies and initiatives for the United States, based on an extensive analysis of the history, functioning, and politics of multilateral arms control forums. It is based on the premise that international arms control efforts have some untapped potential and deserve more serious study than they have received in the past, but its tone is more analytical than hortatory. The papers have been reviewed by a Study Group composed of leading American arms control experts from within and outside of the government, but they represent the views of the individual authors and not necessarily those of the Study Group members or of the United Nations Association. The Association is indebted to Ambassador James F. Leonard, a distinguished diplomat with broad experience in arms control and UN affairs who very ably chaired the Study Group sessions, and to its members for their excellent substantive contributions.

The project was supported by a contract from the US Arms Control and Disarmament Agency and a grant from the Ford Foundation. While neither organization is responsible for the final product, the Association greatly appreciates the breadth of vision both institutions displayed in supporting an intensive study of an aspect of arms control that has traditionally been seen as outside the mainstream of policy concerns and as a lesser priority. It has been especially satisfying for the Association to organize and participate in a cooperative governmental-private sector enterprise. In our view, this kind of direct interaction has great potential for addressing US policy choices realistically and for enriching the perspectives of both sides of the dialogue.

ARMS CONTROL:
THE MULTILATERAL ALTERNATIVE

INTRODUCTION

EDWARD C. LUCK

This book is the chief product of a study project undertaken by the United Nations Association of the USA from October 1981 through July 1982, a period in which many Americans were questioning the utility of international negotiations as a means of addressing vital issues of US and international security. There was growing frustration with the slow pace and bewildering complexity of the negotiating process and an eagerness to test new approaches and to find simpler answers to complex problems. Unfortunately, very little of this attention and creativity was devoted to multilateral efforts, once again the neglected dimension of arms control.

With this backdrop in mind, the project had several purposes:

1. To initiate a dialogue within the United States between government officials and non-governmental specialists concerning both the future US role in multilateral disarmament discussions and possible multilateral approaches to certain arms limitation problems;

2. to identify and explore a broad range of alternative American policies toward, and within, multilateral disarmament mechanisms;

3. to commission a number of leading American arms control experts, including some who have not previously worked on multilateral aspects of disarmament, to do some innovative thinking and writing on these issues; and

4. to fill a vacuum in serious analytical research and writing in this field by combining these research papers in the present book.

The objective of fostering a governmental-private dialogue was embodied in the creation of the UNA-USA Study Group on Multi-lateral Approaches to Arms Control. Under the able Chairmanship of Ambassador James F. Leonard, this group of distinguished specialists from within and outside the US government held a series of five meetings from February through July 1982 to discuss the issues raised in the papers. (A list of the Study Group members is included as Appendix B.) Each author presented an earlier draft of his essay to the Study Group for discussion and then revised his draft based on the group's comments. The papers represent the personal views of the authors, however, and do not necessarily reflect the views of any members of the Study Group.

The discussions dealt equally with the regional and global dimensions of multilateral arms control. Considerable attention during the earlier meetings, however, was devoted to policy alternatives for the United States as it prepared for the second UN Special Session devoted to disarmament, which was held during the course of the project.

The ten authors of this volume represent an unusually wide range of interests, perspectives, and professional experiences. Charles William Maynes, for example, was Assistant Secretary of State for International Organization Affairs in the Carter Administration and played a principal role in US policymaking at the first UN Special Session on Disarmament in 1978; W. Scott Thompson served as an official advisor for the Reagan Administration at the second Special Session in 1982. Alan Neidle's chapter is his first public reflection on what he learned in over twenty years as an American diplomat in multilateral forums. Gregory F. Treverton has closely followed US-allied relations from both inside and outside the government. Steven Canby, on the other hand, brings a professional military perspective to bear on a subject that has generally been addressed from political and diplomatic points of view. George Quester, Michael Nacht, Michael Brenner, and Richard Bissell have been among this country's leading security and arms control analysts, yet they bring fresh insights to this volume because relatively little of their previous work has been on multilateral issues.

The papers are policy oriented and most of them recommend specific policy directions, but the volume as a whole is intended to present a range of alternatives, rather than advocating a particular point of view. There is considerable discussion of the history, politics, and functioning of multilateral arms control forums in order to give both students and specialists a larger understanding of the environment in which these policy choices must be made. The rarely told story of multilateral efforts provides, in our view, an excellent introduction to the postwar history of arms control and international security. The scope of the book is ambitious, encompassing all postwar arms control efforts involving three or more countries, so a number of important topics have not been treated in detail. It addresses multilateral forums of a regional, functional, or global character.

The book is divided into three sections, each with a brief introduction. The first focuses on the historical and political evolution of multilateralism, and outlines several alternative strategies for the United States. The second analyzes the major international political forces with which US policies must cope, concentrating on the interests and policies of US allies, the Soviet Union, and the nonaligned countries. The third section looks at specific policy areas—nuclear non-proliferation, conventional arms control, and confidence-building measures and verification—and draws some conclusions about the future of multilateral approaches.

In organizing the project and preparing this book, the editor received invaluable support from many quarters. Enid Schoettle of the Ford Foundation and Eugene Rostow, Director of the US Arms Control and Disarmament Agency, demonstrated unusually broad vision in deciding to provide support for an area of study that has been accorded a low priority by most scholars and officials. James F. Leonard proved once again to be a skillful chairman and a delightful colleague. The authors and Study Group members confirmed that they all deserve to be called scholars and professionals. John McGrath was a diligent and competent Rapporteur and Research Associate throughout the project. As always, Patricia Addeo was at all times a dedicated, hard-working, well-organized and somehow cheerful Administrative Assistant. My indebtedness to Dana, my wife, in this enterprise, as in all other things, is endless.

I. STRATEGIES FOR THE US: THREE VIEWS

The three chapters in this section discuss possible strategies for the United States based on a review of the history and functioning of multilateral arms control forums. While the US has been actively engaged throughout the postwar era in a wide variety of international discussions and negotiations aimed at limiting armaments, it has lacked a clear and consistent strategy for advancing US and international security through multilateral bodies. As these chapters point out, the US has tended to focus on tactical and procedural issues, rather than integrating its multilateral policies into a broader strategic framework. This tendency has been nurtured by the low priority given to multilateral, in comparison with bilateral, approaches and by substantial ambivalence in the minds of key officials about the utility of multilateral efforts. The authors of these chapters share some of this skepticism about the effectiveness of multilateral bodies, based on past experience, but they all conclude that a more ambitious US approach would both advance US interests and improve the performance of the multilateral mechanisms themselves.

Alan Neidle, who spent many years as a US diplomat in these bodies, traces the rise of multilateralism, from 1963 to 1976, and its subsequent fall as a productive means of attaining arms control agreements. In analyzing the reasons for this decline, he focuses on the decisive role of the Soviet-American political relationship. Multilateral bodies have atrophied and soured, he concludes, and cannot be revived without an improvement in East-West relations.

The next two papers, written from fundamentally different political perspectives, outline possible strategies for the United States in global forums. Interestingly, despite beginning their analyses from different premises, both papers conclude that it is in the US interest to adopt an innovative, activist posture in multilateral bodies. W. Scott Thompson and Richard Bissell contend that an activist approach is necessary because the US must take the diplomatic offensive in a period of relative military weakness. They urge US policymakers to approach multilateral discussions from a broad strategic perspective rather than to continue focusing on narrow tactical issues. Charles William Maynes, on the other hand, argues that this is needed to bolster the non-proliferation regime and to promote larger arms control goals. He suggests several specific policy directions that would forward these objectives.

THE RISE AND FALL OF MULTILATERAL ARMS CONTROL: CHOICES FOR THE UNITED STATES

ALAN F. NEIDLE

INTRODUCTION

The recent surge in American public interest in arms control and disarmament was manifested in the massive demonstration attending the opening of the June–July 1982 UN Special Session on Disarmament. Rather than reflecting interest in multilateral arms control, however, the demonstration underlined growing public anxiety about the risk of nuclear war and a desire to see the US and the Soviet Union limit their nuclear arms competition. Demonstrations in Europe, as well as in the US, have been preoccupied with bilateral arms control. Multilateral arms control has for a good part of the last decade been very much overshadowed.

Of course, no one in favor of arms control would want the two leading powers to cut back their bilateral efforts. If anything, they should be made more serious and more productive. Bilateral talks between the two leading nuclear powers are central to achieving major arms control objectives. The question remains, nevertheless, can multilateral arms control, which was productive in the 1960s and the early 1970s, but which has been singularly unproductive in recent years, be reinvigorated? Is there a significant and realistic future role for multilateral arms control in strengthening the overall fabric of international peace and lessening the likelihood of war, including nuclear war?

The future of multilateral arms control depends upon the nature of the relationship between the US and the Soviet Union. In brief, if these two nations wish to work seriously for basic improvement in their relations, it is possible that multilateral arms control measures, in addition to serving their ostensible arms control purposes, can support even larger goals in strengthening a structure of international peace and cooperation. Conversely, it is difficult to see how multilateral arms control can prosper without the determined leadership and cooperation of the US and the Soviet Union.

But even if the two countries wish to give renewed priority to multilateral arms control, the difficulties in achieving significant concrete results will be formidable. Some idea of the depth of these difficulties will be seen in the section of this essay which describes the present decline of multilateral arms control. But first, it will be helpful to look at a brief historical summary of the rise of multilateral arms control which will reveal how past arms control efforts interacted with the course of US-Soviet relations. The final sections of the essay will elaborate on the policy choices for the United States, bearing in mind larger US interests in promoting international peace and security.

THE RISE OF MULTILATERAL ARMS CONTROL, 1963–76

Between 1963 and 1976 seven multilateral treaties were negotiated, and all of them entered into force. Some were of great significance, such as the Limited Test Ban of 1963 prohibiting nuclear testing in the atmosphere and the Non-Proliferation Treaty of 1968 limiting the spread of nuclear weapons to more nations. At least one was trivial from the standpoint of its impact on weapons development and deployment—the Seabed Arms Control Treaty of 1971, which prohibited emplacement of nuclear weapons or launchers on the ocean floor beyond twelve miles from coasts—a course of action no nuclear power had any intention of pursuing. And some were patently flawed, such as the Biological Weapons Convention of 1972, which prohibited production and possession of all biological weapons but did not contain effective verification provisions.

The exceptionality of the arms control output between 1963 and 1976 can be appreciated by looking at what took place before this period, as well as afterwards. Between the end of World War II and the 1963 test ban, a period when arms control efforts were almost totally dominated by the all-encompassing political struggle between East and West, the international community negotiated only one treaty containing significant arms control provisions, the Antarctic Treaty of 1959. Since 1976, when negotiations of the Treaty Prohibiting Military Use of Environmental Modification Techniques were completed, there have been a plethora of negotiations—on chemical weapons, on ending all nuclear testing, on radiological weapons and on mutual and balanced force reductions—but it has not been possible to carry any multilateral project through to completion.

In searching for a logical and meaningful explanation for the rise and fall of multilateral arms control, it is inadequate to assert simply that progress depends on the "political will" of the superpowers. This notion is often expressed in the form of complaints by persons who are understandably frustrated in their inability to move the superpowers through exhortations to demonstrate greater "political will." But, analytically, the concept is merely a truism—a statement that if countries sufficiently desire to do something they will do it, and vice versa. The significant question remains why, at different times, countries did or did not have the requisite "political will."

What was the driving force which generated the rise of multilateral arms control? It was nothing less than a desire by both the United States and the Soviet Union to change the nature of their relationship. In brief, arms control was the principal vehicle through which both sides found it possible to move from a relationship in which it was widely believed that there existed no substantial mutual interests—indeed, that because of the nature of their conflict none could exist—to a relationship in which it was possible to explore, develop, and even register in treaties, important common interests. This basic shift came about not in a smooth progression, but almost in fits and starts, and there were often doubts within each side about whether what was happening was a good thing.

During the late 1940s through the early 1960s, US-Soviet relations were in the grip of the Cold War with only a few brief and partial respites, based mainly on the Eisenhower summits. But overall, this period was dominated by what has come to be known as a zero-sum game relationship. On the US side, for example, every gain of any sort by the Soviet Union, it was generally feared, meant a corresponding loss by the United States. If the United States was condemned to an unending struggle with the Soviet Union, then anything which gave the latter comfort, eased any of its problems, added to its strength in any way, was harmful and should be avoided or prevented.

The public posture of the United States, at least in the disarmament field, was to seek agreement with the Soviet Union, but most senior officials believed that agreement on anything significant was impossible. After all, if the Soviet Union decided that it wanted to reach agreement, and on anything resembling US terms, it must have decided that there was some advantage to be gained, and if that was the case then obviously it would be a mistake for the US to proceed. Why should it confer an advantage on the adversary?

Such thinking actually intruded into the negotiation of the Antarctic Treaty—although it did not thwart the project—which had as its purpose ensuring the use of Antarctica for peaceful purposes through the prohibition of military activities. The negotiation began in 1957 with Soviet obstructionism typical of the Cold War era. The Soviet Union, through many preparatory meetings, insisted that the negotiation was invalid because the German Democratic Republic, then East Germany (a country conducting no Antarctic activities), had not been invited to participate by the US government. But in mid-stream the Soviets dropped this objection and began to negotiate seriously. When this happened, the question was raised within the US side whether it would not be better to excoriate the Soviets for their past behavior, let the negotiations stall, and return to the more conventional assumption that there could not be mutual interests with the Soviet Union. This point of view did not prevail. In the end, final negotiation at the formal conference in Washington in 1959 was greatly facilitated by Khrushchev's instruction to the chief Soviet negotiator, which was conveyed to the US delegation, to demonstrate that the Soviets knew how to conduct serious business.

US-Soviet cooperation in negotiating the Antarctic Treaty was regarded as something of an oddity. Its positive lessons were neither absorbed nor even perceived by most of the US bureaucracy. The possibility of giving a new and more hopeful direction to US-

Soviet relations through arms control did not become widely apparent for several more years. After the US and the Soviet Union had passed through the most acute crisis of the nuclear era, the October 1962 Cuban missile crisis, there was increasing recognition that the prior pattern of virtually total confrontation was extraordinarily perilous and that new efforts should be made to moderate it. It had, after all, led to civilization's closest brush with nuclear war. President Kennedy, it will be remembered, called for a reexamination of attitudes toward the Cold War and arms competition in his commencement address at American University in June 1963.

It was not obvious at the time that the subject of nuclear testing would be amenable to swift agreement in any form. Nuclear testing had come to symbolize, almost to embody, the nuclear arms race in the Cold War era. Moreover, there had been years of dispute over central issues. Both sides had shifted positions many times throughout this convoluted history—not only on the politically sensitive requirements for inspection but on the basic conditions of agreement, such as whether a test ban need be linked with other arms control measures or whether an atmospheric ban could be separated from a complete ban. Nevertheless, agreement was reached swiftly on an atmospheric nuclear test ban in the summer of 1963. The explanation was the desire to build a better relationship. In the immediate aftermath of the missile crisis, senior US and Soviet officials had discussed whether there might be a new opening for conciliation, and the nuclear test ban was raised specifically in this context.[1] After negotiation of the treaty, opponents in the US feared that an improvement in relations would be a delusion and that it would be dangerous to limit US weapons programs in the course of the struggle with the Soviet Union.

The next serious effort of the United States and the Soviet Union to find common interests in arms control came in the negotiation of the Non-Proliferation Treaty (NPT), roughly between 1966 and 1968. Since the purpose of the negotiation was to prevent the spread of nuclear weapons to countries which did not already possess them, rather than to limit the nuclear arsenals of the US and the Soviet Union, one might have assumed it would be fairly easy for the two main nuclear powers to reach agreement. However, the first years of negotiation, 1964–66, were dominated by sharp East-West conflict. The Soviet Union urged treaty proposals aimed at preventing the Federal Republic of Germany, the "Nazi revanchists," from getting a finger on the nuclear trigger through a possible NATO Multilateral Force (MLF) of nuclear-armed ships.

Throughout the negotiation, US representatives bore down on their Soviet counterparts repeatedly in informal conversations. They pointed out that the Soviet Union had a great deal to gain from successful negotiation of the treaty, for if the project failed and proliferation accelerated, the most likely proliferators would be technologically advanced countries of the West, most of whom would regard the Soviet Union as the adversary. Once it became clear in 1966 that NATO's MLF would not materialize, the Soviet Union and the United States were able to work out remaining problems in a non-polemical fashion and they maintained an effective common front in dealing with issues posed by the non-nuclear countries. Despite this, there were signs that full collaboration with the United States was not wholly natural for the Soviet Union. For example, after the two countries had worked out common provisions, the Soviet Union insisted that each country submit separate, but identical, texts to the conference. Apparently, a joint document was too much for Moscow to swallow.

The non-proliferation treaty remains the most important and far-reaching project embodying mutual interests of the two countries in the field of multilateral arms control. Down through the years, the Soviet Union appears to have been guided by this perception. At times it has sought greater common effort with the United States than the latter has been ready to accord, as in Soviet initiatives to strengthen the inspection capabilities of the International Atomic Energy Agency, the body charged with implementing inspection safeguards under the NPT.

The conclusion of the NPT in 1968 provided a strong impetus to US-Soviet arms control efforts, especially, of course, to SALT. Agreement to begin SALT was announced by President Johnson at the signing of the NPT in July, but the Soviet Union's invasion of Czechoslovakia in August led to an indefinite postponement. Multilateral arms control, however, was not stalled by the invasion of Czechoslovakia.

In this period, Soviet diplomats often talked of the desirability of finding multilateral subjects which would be relatively easy to negotiate and which would permit the momentum of US-Soviet cooperation in multilateral arms control to continue. They privately urged that the best candidate for this role was the idea of preventing emplacement of nuclear weapons on the seabeds, a denatured version of an initiative by Malta in the UN General Assembly in 1967 to reserve the ocean floors exclusively for peaceful purposes.

The main importance of the Seabed Arms Control Treaty which was then negotiated was obviously not its infinitesimal contribution to the body of substantive arms control restraints. Rather, its negotiation, immediately following the Soviet invasion of Czechoslovakia in 1968, served as a demonstration that normal and serious business could be done with the Soviet Union. This seemed somewhat surprising and puzzling, and perhaps slightly reassuring, to some of the highest officials of the new US administration. Serious US-Soviet negotiations on the Seabed Treaty thus had their significance in providing a connecting link between the NPT and the opening of the historic SALT negotiations in November 1969.

The force of the motivation to reach agreements between the United States and the Soviet Union had gathered great strength by the early 1970s—the time of President Nixon's "era of peace." This force almost certainly was a factor that helped make it possible to pursue and achieve a major agreement, despite the fact that it contained significant defects. This was the Biological Weapons (BW) Convention of 1972, with its inadequate precision in defining the quantities of biological agent that could be retained for peaceful purposes and with its totally non-obligatory provisions for verification.

There were, however, good reasons to negotiate a BW treaty, even with its significant imperfections. It will be recalled that US support for a BW treaty followed President Nixon's 1969 declaration that the US unilaterally renounced possession of biological weapons whether or not other nations possessed them. No one in the US government, including the military, disagreed that in these circumstances it was in the US interest to have a multilateral treaty prohibiting biological weapons even if effective verification could not be obtained. The Senate also agreed when it approved the treaty unanimously in 1974. (The significance for future arms control negotiations of the verification and enforcement problems created by the outbreak of anthrax in Sverdlovsk in 1979 is discussed later in this chapter.)

A few general observations should be added to this brief summary of the rise of multilateral arms control. As indicated above, the main motivating force behind the rise of multilateral arms control—the force without which there would not have been a series of successful negotiations—was the mutual desire of the US and the Soviet Union to change the nature of their relationship. But as in all large and complex stories in history, there were undoubtedly many significant factors at work.

A facilitating factor was the predominance of overall power which the United States enjoyed over the Soviet Union, at least when the rise of multilateral arms control began. Even as the period wore on, the US never had to face all of the policy implications of full military parity with the Soviet Union and the consequent rise in expectations by that country for treatment as a political equal, conditions with which it has been so difficult for the US to cope in recent years.

But this margin of military power which the US enjoyed was mainly a psychological factor—a tranquilizer, as it were, making the US less nervous about the whole enterprise—as opposed to a hard operative factor. For, in multilateral arms control, relative positions of military power measured in traditional terms, such as the number and quality of troops and armaments, can lose much of their pivotal importance as a great many other large political factors come into play.

It is often thought that arms control requires parity of military power between the major participants. But this has not always been so in multilateral arms control. In the case of the atmospheric test ban, for example, the Soviet Union was certainly in a much weaker position than the US. Not only had the US conducted a great many more tests, from which it surely had a greater bank of knowledge, but it also doubtless had greater technological sophistication for moving to underground testing. It would be extraordinarily difficult to portray the Soviet Union as having negotiated from "parity." If any slogan can be said to apply, the Soviet Union "negotiated from weakness."

Another general point regarding the causes of the rise of multilateral arms control is the relatively *unimportant* role played by traditional arms control goals. These are usually thought of as making war less likely, making it less destructive if it occurs, and saving money.[2] US officials were, of course, conscious of these goals. But with the possible exception of the negotiation of the NPT they were never dominant. Officials with direct influence over decisions seldom if ever said to each other: "This proposed measure would contribute greatly to arms control goals and therefore we must do everything we possibly can to achieve it." Nor did they say: "That measure is trivial in advancing arms control goals and therefore we should not waste time on it." Instead, they usually said things like: "This measure is probably achievable; it is pretty safe for us; it may do a little good; it is better than not having it at all; it will keep up the arms control process with the Soviet Union; it will help in showing the non-nuclear countries that we are trying." It may be surprising or disappointing to some people that traditional arms control goals were not more central, but it should not be—assuming it is accepted that the main driving force behind multilateral arms control was improvement in US-Soviet relations. This, in turn, lessened the overall risk of nuclear war.

Finally, to close this historical review a word should be said about the relationship between multilateral arms control and bilateral arms control. In fact, as suggested by the preceding discussion, the two efforts have often been in what might be called a symbiotic relationship. Multilateral arms control was a major stimulus of bilateral arms control. For example, the NPT, which called for negotiation between the nuclear powers to control and reduce their nuclear arsenals, was clearly a stepping stone to SALT. This provision could only have been helpful in persuading the Soviet Union, at a time when the Vietnam War continued and when the practice of bilateral negotiations with the chief capitalist enemy was not firmly established, to undertake with the US the historic collaborative enterprise of SALT.

Conversely, bilateral arms control—that is, direct US-Soviet negotiation—was always a central feature of multilateral arms control. The NPT would not have been possible without domination and massive pressure from the US and the USSR. The large number and intensity of regional security anxieties, combined with the understandable reluctance of many nations to undertake the unnatural act of formally renouncing a major weapon while some countries retained it, would have overwhelmed the project. As with the NPT, almost all other successful multilateral arms control negotiations have been based on initial US-Soviet formulation and acceptance of the core prohibitions.

The 1967 Treaty for the Prohibition of Nuclear Weapons in Latin America has been the only exception. It was negotiated in 1965–66 without direct participation of the US and the USSR. But the negotiation was almost stillborn as a result of the reluctance of the largest South American countries. It succeeded only because of the phenomenal diplomatic skill and tenacity of its main Mexican proponent, Ambassador García Robles, who constructed an amazing and unique structure of conditional undertakings. This negotiation surely was the exception that proved the rule that US-Soviet leadership is needed for successful multilateral arms control.

The most important phase of bilateral arms control—strategic nuclear arms control or SALT—was separated and cut off completely from multilateral arms control in 1969. This was both inevitable and understandable, given the need for privacy, the limited knowledge and lack of responsibility of third parties, the great stakes and sensitivity for the US and the Soviet Union, and their consequent desire not to permit any additional complications from multilateral exposure to be added to an already nearly impossible task.

But the new modus operandi was not without its costs. Ironically, as pointed out by George Rathjens, the bilateral SALT process—with its emphasis on counting and balancing numbers and types of weapons systems between two parties—tended to revive zero-sum-game bargaining.[3] It was just this aspect of every gain for one side being a corresponding loss for the other that had been such an impediment to the arms control process getting off the ground in the first place. One might say that some of the seeds for the subsequent severe deterioration of US-Soviet cooperation in arms control, as a whole, can be found in the very essence of the SALT process—that process which also made possible the most significant nuclear arms control restraints between the US and the Soviet Union in the postwar era.

THE FALL OF MULTILATERAL ARMS CONTROL

Present and recent multilateral arms control efforts have been unproductive, contentious, and deeply frustrating for almost all concerned. They have generally consumed, rather than created, international understanding and good will. There are several reasons for this bleak characterization.

First, the persistent lack of success warrants this description. The main multilateral disarmament forum, the Committee on Disarmament (CD) which meets regularly in Geneva, has been stupefyingly unproductive. For example, for some five years the CD has labored without success to produce a modest treaty to ban radiological warfare. When the US and the Soviet Union submitted for multilateral consideration a draft treaty about three years ago, it was chewed up by the non-aligned with a pirhana-like fury. The end of the negotiation is not yet in sight. Other more meaty subjects, like a comprehensive test ban or the control of chemical weapons, have foundered on the inability of the US and the Soviets to achieve a basic framework of agreement. Still other subjects, like assurances against the use of nuclear weapons and formulation of a comprehensive disarmament program, have stimulated endless and repetitious disputation.

In addition, a more general factor has made it more difficult for multilateral forums to find suitable and promising subjects on which to negotiate. Since the 1960s, many third world countries have become major regional powers with formidable military forces. Their disputes and their security concerns have increased in relative importance on the world stage. Indeed, the arms and security aspects of many of the world's greatest conflicts have regional origins, such as the Arab-Israeli conflict, and cannot be dealt with in worldwide disarmament forums. The powers directly concerned may sometimes make general statements about their conflicts in a worldwide forum. But they simply will not permit a body whose composition includes many outsiders to deal with sensitive elements of the conflict, such as the arms control aspects.

As a consequence, there is a search for armaments problems that can be dealt with on a global basis, like the effort to ban radiological warfare. But when the task is as peripheral as that one, there is an understandable tendency by lesser powers to rebel, to charge that the superpowers are feeding them trivia in order to keep them away from the problems that really count. On the other hand, dealing with major weapon systems, like chemical weapons or nuclear weapons in a comprehensive test ban, is utterly dependent for any real progress on the cooperation and political will of the two greatest powers, the US and the Soviet Union. But these countries, as the CD continues to degenerate, show less and less disposition to conduct their important negotiations within its confines. The abstract, and increasingly politicized, debate that ensues at the CD only deepens the impression that it is not a forum for serious substantive negotiation.

But the most profound cause of the present decline in multilateral arms control lies not in a general disarray or unruliness of the multilateral forum. It lies in the sharp deterioration of US-Soviet relations that has taken place since the mid-1970s. This is not the place to chronicle why that deterioration took place.[4] Suffice it to say that the original driving force behind multilateral arms control, US-Soviet rapprochement, is exhausted. No East-West political structure now supports arms control, multilateral or bilateral. As William Hyland has pointed out about bilateral arms control, SALT I was supported by political agreements, like the German treaties, but SALT II was not, and was therefore highly vulnerable.[5]

The attempt to pursue serious multilateral arms control without any political underpinning may be futile and frustrating, or worse. The dénouement of the US-Soviet Conventional Arms Transfer Talks (CAT) in Mexico City in 1978 illustrates how bad a fate can befall a project under which there is no policy framework. (While these talks were conducted bilaterally, the application of the agreement would have been multilateral.) These negotiations, initiated at US urging in 1977, were based on American concepts of restraint and responsibility. Soviet representatives, in the view of US participants, demonstrated a serious approach to the negotiation. The Soviet side had accepted a US proposal to discuss arms transfers to various regions and, specifically, to Latin America and sub-Saharan Africa. But when the Soviet Union said it wished to discuss the regions of East Asia and West Asia also, the US government, fearful of the impact on US relations with China and Iran, instructed the US delegation to inform the Soviet delegation just prior to the opening of the fourth round of the talks in December 1978 that the US side would walk out if the Soviets brought up these regions. In other words, after pressing for discussion of restraints on a regional basis, the US side would not agree to hear what the Soviet Union wished to say about specific regions in which it was interested.[6]

The US behavior was a throwback to the days of the deepest Cold War when agenda disputes were all-consuming and paralyzing. This type of catatonic rigidity had been left behind in the course of decades of disarmament negotiations in which it became understood that any participant could raise any subjects or views it wished without creating presumptions of "legitimacy" for those subjects or views. Surely the US performance at the end of the CAT talks must constitute a nadir for US diplomacy. What caused this debacle was the absence of a policy framework in which the US saw it in its interests to pursue limited forms of cooperation with the Soviet Union regarding the third world.

CURRENT REALITIES AND CHOICES FOR THE UNITED STATES

Is there any reason to believe that a mutual US and Soviet desire to build better relations is less needed as a supporting structure for multilateral arms control than it has been in the last two decades? If anything, there is probably more need for such an underpinning now than before.

There are a variety of reasons for this. Uncomplicated multilateral arms control measures and ones that are relatively painless for the US and the Soviet Union will be increasingly difficult, if not impossible, to find. It is hard to imagine new measures like the NPT, which inhibited mainly the non-nuclear nations, or the Seabed Treaty, which prohibited no real military plans, or the Biological Weapons Convention, which contained no serious verification provisions.

The principal multilateral arms control measures now on the world's agenda are of awesome complexity. For example, the negotiation of a treaty to prohibit chemical weapons will require detailed definitions of a variety of substances, and a range of different verification procedures for destruction of weapons, monitoring of shut-down plants, policing of permitted production, and checking out suspicious activities at other locations. A comprehensive nuclear test ban would involve similar complexities, with its requirements for installation of automatic seismic stations, complex arrangements for exchange of seismic data, and procedures for on-site inspections.

To resolve problems like these the US and the USSR would need to have an unusually strong motivation to succeed and a readiness to compromise. As in all major negotiations, they would have to be willing to adopt solutions that satisfy neither side completely. It is hard to imagine that two governments sustaining this type of effort—knocking heads together within bureaucracies to achieve the necessary compromises—against a backdrop of general confrontation and against an expectation that relations will continue to deteriorate.

Even if agreement could be reached during such a period of confrontation—which is probably not possible—it is even harder to imagine the successful implementation of a chemical weapons convention or a comprehensive test ban without a continuing commitment of both countries to cooperation and compromise. The capability of verification equipment would have to be checked against technical standards; there would have to be practical and flexible cooperation in installation and maintenance of equipment; arrangements for visits of national or international verification personnel would have to be supplemented or modified to meet the inevitable unforeseen contingencies; both sides would have to resist temptations to exploit ambiguities to demonstrate the unreasonableness of the other side. All of this would have to be done not only between the US and the Soviet Union but with some degree of involvement or review by a wide variety of non-nuclear nations, some patient and flexible, others suspicious and resentful. Nothing like this has ever been done before.

It may also be asked whether it is possible for non-aligned countries to play a role of bridge-building between East and West so that, even in the present state of deteriorating US-Soviet relations, multilateral arms control can again begin to be productive.[7] Some may recall that in the 1960s moderation of the US-Soviet conflict seemed a paramount goal in international affairs and, indeed, there was prestige to be acquired by third countries in being seen to be effective in helping to bring together the two superpowers. This was surely reflected, for example, in India's proposal that the US and the Soviet Union should be co-chairmen of the Eighteen Nation Disarmament Committee when it was founded in 1962.

However, the situation is very different today. Over the past two decades, there has been a remarkable diffusion of power, resulting in rapid technological and military development by many non-aligned countries. They are no longer prepared to play the role of neutral catalysts seeking patiently to promote progress by more "important" powers. Of course, many are deeply concerned that further deterioration of US-Soviet relations may lead to a world conflagration. But so far as promotion of nuclear arms control goes, theirs is an attitude of the "demandeur," based on the perception that the two superpowers have not made good on their promise in the NPT to limit their nuclear armaments. On top of all this, there is undoubtedly a feeling on the part of third countries, not wholly unwarranted, that there is little they can realistically do to move the two superpowers forward, beyond continuing exhortations. In recent years, the US and the Soviet Union have pretty well insulated their serious arms control negotiations from global forums, conducting them bilaterally and secretly. In sum, the key to progress in achieving significant multilateral arms control remains in the hands of the US and the Soviet Union.

If the above analysis is correct, it follows that by far the most significant choice for the United States affecting the prospects for multilateral arms control is the choice of a strategy to pursue in its overall relations with the Soviet Union. To oversimplify somewhat, one possible strategy has been to try to "defeat" the Soviet Union, to exploit the grave economic and social weaknesses of its system, and to try to sustain a variety of pressures against it which would force fundamental change in its external behavior and its internal system. The main alternative strategy has been to seek gradual improvement in US-Soviet relations, while pursuing necessary competitive elements in the relationship, and to encourage a long-range favorable evolution in the Soviet system through efforts to engage the Soviet Union in an expanding network of constructive international projects from which it would gain benefits and which would thereby increase its stake in a cooperative and interdependent order.

The first strategy has been generally rejected through most of the last quarter of a century because it is predicated on unprovable and doubtful assumptions—that the Soviet Union can be "defeated" by economic and other pressures—and because it has seemed too dangerous. If this strategy becomes the core of US policy, then the question of how multilateral arms control fits in becomes rather simple. It really does not. For the reasons described above, there could not be a realistic expectation of serious multilateral arms control achievements involving the US and the Soviet Union. The main tasks would be diplomatic and political: to limit damage to the American image; to attempt to deprive the Soviet Union of propaganda advantage; to minimize strains within the western alliance. These would be serious challenges, but hardly of primary importance in an atmosphere of general Soviet-American confrontation.

It is the second strategy, of trying gradually to expand the area of common interests with the Soviet Union and encouraging evolution in its external and internal behavior, even while competition continues, that has provided an overall continuity for American policy as well as a supporting structure for arms control. If this strategy is adopted by the Reagan Administration—it remains uncertain as of mid-1982 whether it will be—or if it is again pursued by a successor administration, then significant multilateral arms control will become possible, though by no means certain.

The choice of a strategy for the US to pursue with the Soviet Union is, of course, a question of vast dimensions. It should include consideration of arms control, but must go far beyond that, to basic judgments about American goals in world affairs, the nature of the Soviet Union and the seriousness of particular threats it poses, the potential utility and costs of exercising a wide variety of forms of American power, the interaction and relative priorities among many diverse international issues like alliance solidarity, resolution of various regional disputes, economic cooperation, promotion of human rights, and many others.[8] Perhaps of greatest importance, and difficulty, in formulating an effective strategy is the need to blend and balance in a coherent fashion contrasting elements: on the one hand, efforts to deter and contain Soviet actions prejudicial to the basic interests of the US and its friends, and steadiness in maintaining the necessary strength for this purpose; and, on the other hand, continuing readiness to seek ways to reduce tensions, and persistence and boldness in developing areas of common interest that can gradually be enlarged. To expand on these matters would be beyond the scope of this essay, but there is a large and readily available literature that may be helpful to the reader.[9]

A positive and effective general strategy toward the Soviet Union, should this be deemed in the national interest, can make arms control more likely; arms control, in turn, can support broader goals of the strategy. The possibility of achieving a multilateral agreement that would reduce the level and limit the deployments of military forces of NATO and the Warsaw Pact in Europe provides an interesting illustration. As Jonathan Dean, a former US representative to the Vienna Mutual and Balanced Force Reduction negotiations, has pointed out, achievement of an agreement

. . . that would entail Western acceptance of continued participation by Poland and the Eastern European countries in the Warsaw Pact, could provide some assurance to Soviet leaders that the West would not seek to convert political and economic change in Eastern Europe to the military disadvantage of the East and to challenge Soviet security interests in the area. Consequently such an agreement might make Soviet leaders less unwilling to accommodate internal pressures for change.[10]

An agreement limiting the increase of Soviet forces in Central Europe would thus provide an additional factor that, in a particular crisis, could contribute to a balance of considerations tipping the scales against Soviet military intervention in Poland. Such a factor could influence Soviet behavior in an area where it possesses overwhelming military power and where, accordingly, every possible additional contribution to restraint is especially valuable.

Another example of how multilateral arms control can promote broader goals is the slow but steady progress that has been made in pushing the Soviet Union toward greater openness. In the comprehensive test ban negotiations of 1977–80, the Soviet government demonstrated what appeared to be a genuine readiness to install automatically-recording seismic stations within its territory, and to negotiate detailed procedures for on-site inspection of ambiguous events. In June 1982 at the second UN Special Session on disarmament (SSOD–II), Foreign Minister Gromyko announced that the Soviet Union would permit inspection of Soviet peaceful nuclear facilities by the International Atomic Energy Agency, a step which the US had itself accepted and had long urged on the Soviet Union as being supportive of the NPT regime. Gromyko also announced readiness of the Soviet Union to accept, in a chemical weapons treaty, some forms of on-site inspection that had previously been rejected.[11]

The type of multilateral arms control now on the world's agenda would involve extensive participation by the Soviet Union in detailed verification arrangements, both outside and inside the Soviet Union. It is by no means certain that these can be achieved in the foreseeable future. But if they could, with Soviet officials working with those of the US and other nations to implement verification procedures and to solve practical problems, it would become significantly more difficult, or virtually impossible, for the Soviet Union to maintain the same degree of rigidity about access to the truth that it has in the past.

Another way in which positive and active US participation in multilateral arms control efforts can bring dividends beyond those strictly related to arms control involves the building of closer ties with other governments, both allied and non-aligned. While it is probably true that there are many governments in today's world that are barely, if at all, interested in arms control, there still remain many others that set great store by these goals. These governments will be important not merely in supporting any significant multilateral arms control that the US may find, now or in future years, to be in its security interests. They are also important in much more basic ways, since a great many of them share traditional US views about the rules against force and the standards of restraint that ought to prevail in the international community. Given the continuing resort to force, contrary to the UN Charter, that has taken place in recent years, there is good reason for all these countries to intensify their efforts to promote both respect for basic standards of conduct and greater limitation of the means of violence through effective arms control. If the US were able to demonstrate in this broad realm of international security that it can be part of the solution rather than the problem, this would enhance what Professor Alan Henrikson has described as the "emanation of power."[12] The US will strengthen its repute, enlarge the potential of its leadership, and add to its power, if it shows that its policies and diplomacy are important in bringing about progress in the realization of shared goals.

THE SIGNIFICANCE OF POSSIBLE SOVIET TREATY VIOLATIONS

The question may certainly be asked whether these goals and progress toward their achievement are more theoretical than real in the light of recent incidents that indicate Soviet disregard for several multilateral treaties. Does an incident like the 1979 outbreak of anthrax in the Soviet city of Sverdlovsk,[13] which raised a serious US concern that biological weapons may have been retained by the Soviet Union contrary to the Biological Weapons convention, indicate that genuine arms control progress with the Soviet Union is illusory, that it is only prudent to conclude arms control agreements with the Soviet Union when there is iron-clad verification and enforcement procedures which, of course, can almost never be achieved? Does the very strong evidence that the Soviet Union has used chemical and biological agents (toxins), and has assisted its North Vietnamese allies to do so in wars in Asia, contrary to multilateral treaties, mean that the Soviet Union will abide by its undertakings only so long as it is convenient to do so, that the arms control structure is in reality built on sand?

These are, of course, serious and important questions. But they are not the most relevant questions. They tend to confuse two rather different issues: whether the Soviet Union is capable of perpetrating outrages and whether the treaties are worthwhile nevertheless. Much more relevant questions would be: are the US, and other like-minded nations, better off with the treaties or without them? Did the US give anything up or limit itself in some way prejudicial to its security in order to get the treaties? Are there ways that the situation can be improved, whether through diplomacy or through amendments, to lessen the treaty's deficiencies? Viewed in the light of these questions, the situation is far from perfect, but it is not bad for the United States.

The US gave up nothing to achieve the essentially unverifiable prohibition of biological weapons. It sees no advantage in possessing these weapons even now. But it is better off under present circumstances with the biological weapons treaty remaining in force. Its existence provides a solid legal and political basis for denouncing Soviet possession and use of toxin weapons. The same considerations hold true for the Geneva Protocol of 1925, which prohibits use of chemical and biological weapons and which the Soviet Union appears to have violated in Asia. The United States obviously gave up nothing because of this treaty, which it belatedly ratified only in 1975. Regrettably, it must be said that use of chemical weapons, except in World War I, has always taken place in remote corners of the world against defenseless populations that cannot retaliate. The United States has retained its stockpile of chemical weapons for deterrence. And now, as a party to the Geneva Protocol, the US has solid standing for pressing the UN to investigate Soviet violations. The overall objective should certainly be to reduce the likelihood that these weapons will be used again in the future. Surely no one can believe that the Russians, or anyone else, would be less likely to use the weapons if the treaties did not exist.

Can anything be done in the future to improve this far from satisfactory situation? Regarding the evidence of the use of toxins and chemical weapons, the US and other nations have done the best possible thing in launching a UN investigation. That will not, of course, guarantee against future use, but it will raise the costs in terms of worldwide opprobrium and thus decrease somewhat the chances of future use.

In the case of the Biological Weapons Convention of 1972, it should be possible to seek an amendment to the treaty that improves its procedures for enforcement. One of the shortcomings of the treaty was its failure to provide for automatic or mandatory establishment of an investigative committee to look into questions of compliance. After the Biological Weapons Convention's negotiation in 1972, it was possible to include, with the consent of the Soviet Union, such a procedure in the 1977 Treaty Prohibiting Military Use of Environmental Modification Techniques. It is always easier for the Soviet Union to agree to a provision that it has accepted in an earlier treaty. But for the improved provision to be added to the Biological Weapons Convention as an amendment, which requires Soviet assent, it would probably be necessary to assure the Soviet Union that the provision would not be used ex post facto to attempt to investigate the Sverdlovsk incident. This would not be much of a loss, since Sverdlovsk is not likely to be further elucidated under present or foreseeable circumstances, and there would be a net gain in improving the enforceability of a major global treaty.

The Sverdlovsk incident and the serious charges of use of chemical and toxin weapons by the Soviet Union in Asia will certainly contribute to a more difficult public and Congressional climate in the US for the approval of multilateral arms control treaties. But, in logic, they do not negate the general value of these treaties for the US, provided there is adequate verification given all the relevant circumstances surrounding the particular treaty, and provided the US will not suffer significant harm to its security if the treaty is not observed.

FORUMS AND PROCEDURE

Several important and difficult questions regarding forums and procedure remain to be addressed. First, if it is not possible or is deemed undesirable for the US to seek an improving US-Soviet relationship that includes close collaboration in multilateral arms control, could significant measures still be achieved through multilateral forums in which others take the lead, in which the US and the Soviet Union keep their distance, in which they participate by providing views, redrafting the proposals of others, and so forth? In other words, could there be a reversion (or perhaps progression) to an earlier form of multilateral diplomacy, one that treats the participants more as equals, one in which a key role is played by a respected chairman who finds compromises and develops consensus? One wishes this could be so, but unfortunately it probably cannot.

The US and the Soviet Union will continue to have very great stakes in the outcome of any multilateral arms control negotiation affecting their comparative power or their global reach. In the past, the US and the Soviet Union have shown extraordinary sensitivity about formulating all the key provisions in such negotiations. Reaching compromises has usually been agonizingly difficult. It is as unlikely in the future, as it has been in the past, that the leaders and bureaucracies of these two countries will be willing to entrust to a non-aligned chairman, no matter how respected, the crucial role of steering toward consensus on the most sensitive issues affecting US and Soviet power. That is not to say that third parties will not be able to make valuable proposals or have important influence through their advocacy or criticism of proposals. It is rather to stress that the US and the Soviet Union, if they want to do important and sensitive arms control business, will almost surely continue to insist on doing it themselves.

If this is so, other questions naturally follow. Is it possible in today's world for the US and the Soviet Union to dominate totally the framing of key provisions in a treaty, say the comprehensive test ban, and to expect the necessary support and adherence from third world countries so that the treaty will fulfill its multilateral purposes? If the US and the Soviet Union acquiesce in full multilateral participation by the current Committee on Disarmament, are the careful compromises they formulated likely to be trampled over in a roughhouse of non-aligned politics and resentment? These questions reflect the inevitable tension between the need to preserve bilateral accord, which is essential for ultimate success, and the desirability of allowing third countries to participate, which may or may not be conducive to ultimate success.

The 1977–80 trilateral negotiations between the US, the Soviet Union and the UK on a comprehensive test ban, although they collapsed with the deterioration of US-Soviet relations, provide an interesting illustration. In the first half of 1978, it appeared to many that these three nuclear powers would be able to reach agreement on key provisions. Had they been able to do so, a very tough diplomatic and procedural question would have faced them: to what extent should they then have permitted multilateral negotiation to take place with the possibility of the unravelling of key provisions, or long delays as different groups stonewalled? A question such as this is worth considering for its general and long-range implications even though, as reported in July 1982, the Reagan Administration has decided to defer pursuit of a comprehensive test ban.

The main reason for permitting a relatively full and "democratic" multilateral participation would have been to build up support for a final product in which many countries, including key "near-nuclear" nations, would have felt a stake, since they would have contributed to its formulation. However, viewed realistically, there would probably have been a number of aspects of the draft of the three nuclear powers that it would have been vital for them to preserve, such as special verification procedures to cover the nuclear powers, but that would have been displeasing to many nonnuclear countries and might therefore have provoked very difficult pressures for renegotiation. Moreover, it is uncertain, at best, whether an opportunity to improve a nuclear power draft would have been used solely for this purpose. It is at least as likely that some countries would have attempted to stall the negotiations in the hope that they would never be faced with the reality of a completed comprehensive test ban that they would be urged to sign. Given the general enfeeblement of the Geneva forum in recent years, it is not unreasonable to fear that such tactics might have had high potency.

No single prescription will suffice for how to handle this problem in the future. There will be significantly different factors affecting each major arms control enterprise. For example, the degree of multilateral negotiation needed for a treaty prohibiting chemical weapons may well be greater than that needed, or manageable, for a comprehensive test ban. Nevertheless, there is one general principle that should be followed: the impact on substantive results must take precedence over procedural considerations. This means that if the US, the Soviet Union, and the UK, for example, in the case of the comprehensive test ban, were able to work out a treaty in the future and were to decide, after full deliberation and perhaps after consultation with selected other countries, that minimal, or virtually no, multilateral negotiation on their draft treaty was the only prudent course to ensure relatively prompt realization of a treaty acceptable to them, then that is the course they should follow.

Such a decision would be extraordinarily difficult. To some extent, it would involve a diminution of the benefits sought in multilateral arms control discussed earlier in this essay, such as the strengthening of working relationships with other countries that desire to participate in constructive negotiations. There would also be a risk of significant defections from the ranks of those prepared to sign the treaty, at least initially. However, the balance of considerations—given the circumstances postulated—would seem clear. For those who favor significant progress in nuclear arms control, it would be far more important to have the breakthrough of a major treaty put into force, even with a shortened list of initial accessions and with some diplomatic bruises, than to run serious risk of losing the achievement. Many responsible non-nuclear countries, although disappointed about the procedure, might well be brought around to the same conclusion.

A final question about procedure should be asked. Can the difficulties involved in multilateral arms control negotiations be alleviated by making basic changes in the multilateral machinery, or by reforming or restructuring the negotiating forum? There are two types of reforms that can be envisioned. The first would promote greater "democratization," strengthening the role of the non-aligned and non-nuclear nations, with the purpose of increasing pressures on the superpowers to move forward more rapidly. The second, which is nearly the opposite of the first, would involve cutting back on the role of lesser powers, decreasing the "disorderliness" of the Geneva committee, with the purpose of increasing the willingness of the US and the Soviet Union to do more of their serious business under multilateral auspices. Neither of these approaches to reform would be logical or practical under present circumstances.

The first approach, greater "democratization," was the motive force behind the reforms instituted at the first UN Special Session in 1978. Third world states, seeking a greater voice in disarmament negotiations, successfully pushed for an enlargement of the Committee on Disarmament and abandonment of the US-Soviet co-chairmanship of the Committee. These reforms did not lead to progress in arms control. If anything, they further encouraged the trend toward greater separation of serious US-Soviet negotiations from the Committee. At the 1982 Special Session, there was little impetus for further changes to promote "democratization."

The second approach to reform, greater "orderliness" and the reflection of actual power, would require considerable leverage on the part of those desiring these changes. This is because those participating countries that felt that their role and prestige would be lessened could be counted upon to resist the changes. Leverage of sufficient potency to effect results might possibly exist if leading countries, like the US and the Soviet Union, were able to convince others that they were prepared to move forward decisively in a major multilateral project, but would agree to the participation of others only if the relevant forum or its procedures were changed. But these conditions do not seem likely in the near future. One cannot escape the underlying reality: the fundamental reasons that multilateral arms control efforts prosper or decline relate to political and security considerations, not to procedure.

CONCLUSION

The prospects for serious multilateral arms control in the near future cannot be rated as anything other than slim. There are many reasons for this but the main one is the severe deterioration of US-Soviet relations.

Those who favor arms control, bilateral or multilateral, usually argue that arms control should be kept separate from the ups and downs of the US-Soviet relationship, that arms control is too important to be held hostage to politics, that the US should try to realize the security benefits from arms control whatever the international climate. After all, is not arms control needed most to help control an adversary's military strength, and especially when there are dangerous tensions?

These arguments are relevant when dealing with the issue commonly known as "linkage," that is, in opposing the idea that the US should, as a general practice, interrupt or not begin arms control negotiations with the Soviet Union when it is conducting highly objectionable activities in other spheres. However, these ideas do not capture the full reality. They do not explain why or when there can be reasonable prospects of success in the extraordinarily difficult job of reaching agreement on sensitive arms control issues.

The explanation seems clear, both from logic and practice. The US and the Soviet Union must desire what is inherent in the close collaborative effort to work out arms control, in the ceremonies that accompany successful conclusion of a major negotiation, and in the cooperation required for implementation—namely, improvement in their overall relationship. There has never been a successful arms control negotiation and entry into force of the agreement when relations have been declining, only when they have been improving. To fail to face up to this is to evade a critical reality.

There is thus the necessity of a choice. It is the choice of what type of relationship the American people and their government want with the Soviet Union. If the choice is made for gradual improvement and evolution, to be pursued patiently, while at the same time continuing to maintain firmness where competition is inevitable, then there should be at least a possibility for achieving both bilateral and multilateral arms control.

The possibility will also depend on whether the Soviet Union has the desire and the capacity to improve relations and to make the necessary compromises required for arms control.[14] This is difficult to predict. It does seem significant, however, that the Soviet government has given every sign of continuing to attach very great importance to the pursuit of arms control, even while relations have been deteriorating. However, the Soviet Union faces a succession crisis that may paralyze its policymaking process. Strong leadership, in any direction, may be impossible for some time to come. On the other hand, new opportunities for cooperation could emerge.

The difficulties in achieving important multilateral arms control will, in any event, be numerous. The issues are often nearly intractable. The existing multilateral forum, the Committee on Disarmament, has both atrophied and soured. But success is not impossible. If it can be achieved, the benefits can extend beyond the strict confines of the arms control measures themselves. There can be an accretion in the repute and power of the United States, greater solidarity with friends and allies, and even the possibility of greater restraint by the Soviet Union beyond its borders.

These are not negligible goals. Progress toward their realization will strengthen the security of the United States and promote a more peaceful and just world order. Seeking practical ways to advance these goals should be central to American statesmanship.

NOTES

1. See Walter W. Rostow, *The Diffusion of Power* (New York: Macmillan, 1972) pp. 177–181.

2. It is interesting and generally consistent with the analysis in this essay that Bernard Brodie, in one of the few relatively recent studies of arms control objectives, concludes that there is not much power behind the traditional arms control objectives, with the possible exception of that of saving money. "On the Objectives of Arms Control," *International Security,* 1:1 (Summer, 1976), pp. 17–36.

3. George Rathjens, "Changing Perspectives on Arms Control," *Daedalus,* (Summer, 1975), p. 203.

4. The principle architect of detente, Henry Kissinger, provides an extraordinarily valuable account in *Years of Upheaval* (Boston: Little, Brown & Co., 1982), pp. 228–301 and pp. 979–1031. A very full chronicle of how the detente relationship evolved and declined, and the mix of Soviet and American responsibilities, can be expected in Raymond L. Garthoff, *Detente and Confrontation: American-Soviet Relations from Nixon to Reagan* (anticipated in 1983, the Brookings Institution). Two excellent articles on the same subject are Strobe Talbott, "US-Soviet Relations: From Bad to Worse," *Foreign Affairs: America and the World, 1979,* 58:3 (1979), pp. 515–539; and Robert G. Kaiser, "US-Soviet Relations: Goodbye to Detente," *Foreign Affairs: America and the World, 1980,* 59:3 (1980), pp. 500–521.

5. William G. Hyland, "US-Soviet Relations: The Long Road Back," *Foreign Affairs: America and the World, 1981,* 60:3 (1981), p. 538.

6. Two good accounts of the CAT negotiations are available in: Barry M. Blechman et. al., "Pushing Arms," *Foreign Policy,* 46 (Spring, 1982), pp. 142–148; and Andrew J. Pierre, *The Global Politics of Arms Sales* (Princeton: Princeton University Press, 1982), pp. 285–290.

[7] For a detailed discussion of the position of non-aligned countries, see George H. Quester's chapter in this book.

8. For a broad discussion of the US-Soviet agenda for the next decade see the report of the UNA-USA national Policy Panel on US-Soviet Relations, *US-Soviet Relations: A Strategy for the 80s,* (New York: UNA-USA, 1981).

9. Dimitri K. Simes's article, "The Death of Detente?" *International Security,* 5:1 (Summer, 1980), not only chronicles detente but contains an extremely stimulating analysis of changes in Soviet policy, beneficial from the American standpoint, that took place in the course of detente, pp. 3–5 and pp. 8–14. The following is a list of some valuable contributions to the

public discussion of US strategy toward the Soviet Union, which represent a range of opinions, not all of which the author would endorse: Charles W. Maynes, "Old Errors in the New Cold War," *Foreign Policy,* 47 (Spring, 1982), pp. 86–104; Thompson R. Buchanan, "The Real Russia," *Foreign Policy,* 47 (Summer, 1982), pp. 26–45; Dimitri K. Simes, "Disciplining Soviet Power," *Foreign Policy,* 43 (Summer, 1981), pp. 33–52; Robert Legvold, "Containment Without Confrontation," *Foreign Policy,* 40 (Fall, 1980) pp. 74–98; Helmut Sonnenfeldt, "Russia, America and Detente," *Foreign Affairs,* 56:2 (January, 1978), pp. 275–294; Robert W. Tucker, "The Purposes of American Power," *Foreign Affairs,* 59:2 (Winter 1980–81), pp. 241–274; and Adam B. Ulam, "How to Restrain the Soviets," *Commentary,* 70:6 (December, 1980), pp. 38–41.

10. Jonathan Dean, "Promoting Change in Poland," *New York Times,* 20 March 1982.

11. Soviet Foreign Minister Andrei Gromyko's speech on 15 June 1982 at SSOD–II. See Document of the UNGA, A/S–12/PV.12. Also see a draft convention on the prohibition and destruction of chemical weapons in "Letter Dated 16 June 1982 from the Minister for Foreign Affairs of the Union of Soviet Socialist Republics to the Secretary-General of the UN," Document of the Ad Hoc Committee of SSOD–II (1982), A/S–12/AC.1/12.

12. Alan K. Henrikson, "The Emanation of Power," *International Security,* 6:1 (Summer, 1981), pp. 152–164.

13. For a detailed account of the Sverdlovsk incident, see Leslie H. Gelb, "Keeping an Eye on Russia," *New York Times Magazine,* 29 November 1981.

14. For a detailed analysis of Soviet motives and objectives in multilateral arms control, see Michael Nacht's chapter in this book.

TOWARD A STRATEGIC CONCEPTION OF MULTILATERAL ARMS CONTROL

W. SCOTT THOMPSON AND RICHARD E. BISSELL

Any approach to understanding multilateral arms control in the twentieth century, particularly in the American context, must be prefaced by a recognition of the ambivalence of foreign policymakers toward the concept. This uncertainty about its value is less a result of divisions of opinion among those in leadership positions than of a conflict between the practical orientation of governments and the idealistic orientation of much of public opinion. The first major modern arms control measures of a multilateral character, after all, were the series of Hague Conferences before World War I, which were held to satisfy the demands of internationally based non-governmental peace committees to stave off the impending era of mass warfare: a task at which those Conferences manifestly failed. Such is not to argue that governments have not on occasion embraced this public-spirited idealism, particularly in those democracies most responsive to the mood of their controlling electorates. As a result, multilateral arms control (MAC) has to be seen as the natural outcome of several different approaches to the endemic problem of arms buildups and technological advances in the science of war.

THE IDEALISTIC APPROACH

The most important source of support for MAC has been of an idealistic variety, and particularly so in the United States. The frustration of those concerned about continual expansion of defense budgets, arms inventories, and investment in new weapons technologies has led them to argue that bilateral and incremental arms control are simply Band-Aids on a major wound. It is argued that the governments of the world must be willing to undertake a political "leap of faith" if all the states are to agree upon substantial arms control or disarmament. In this view, despite whatever historical enmity may be preserved in the minds of statesmen, the mutual distrust of governments must be set aside in order to reduce even those defenses at the core of national survival. The onset of mass warfare in the late nineteenth and twentieth centuries was a major catalyst for this idealism, a conception of human affairs more traditionally associated with religiously based visions of "beating swords into plowshares."

For many American thinkers, this idealism was necessary to save the corrupt "Old World" of Western Europe from recurrent cycles of self-destructive wars, which threatened to involve the United States as well after 1914. The American peace movement after 1890 was thus the catalyst for the Hague Conferences, and it was American public pressure that led US administrations in the 1920s to undertake multilateral naval limitations and the Kellogg-Briand Pact approach to world peace. Likewise, after World War II, the US undertook a number of idealistic initiatives, such as the Baruch Plan for nuclear weapons and nuclear energy and the Open Skies proposal of Eisenhower.

Ironically, idealism has undermined support for the US-Soviet arms control efforts of the 1960s and 1970s, in arguing that these were inadequate, both in the number of participants and the scope of limitations or reductions. Idealism has been at the root of the current return to schemes of general disarmament, under consideration at the Committee on Disarmament (CD) in Geneva as well as at the United Nations Special Sessions on Disarmament (SSODs). It could well be said, in fact, that idealism must be stronger than ever, since there are now far more negotiating units to be included than in recent history (over 150 sovereign states), while the range of weapons technology (from the land mines of terrorists to the MIRVed ICBMs of the superpowers) is so vast. The expanding scope of the challenge, however, only seems to feed the appetite of idealism, with MAC identified as mankind's last best hope.

THE CYNICAL APPROACH

Another major approach to MAC is the cynical one. Those who see little hope for arms control, and no hope for multilateral approaches, have frequently proposed grand schemes simply for purposes of propaganda, either to satisfy domestic interest groups or to impress foreign audiences with their peaceful intent. In recent years, for instance, the Chinese delegates at the United Nations frequently have voted against or refused to participate in votes on disarmament resolutions, especially those proposed by the Soviet Union, in order to dramatize the Chinese view that the Soviets are engaged in propagandizing. With regard to the 1982 Special Session on Disarmament, for instance, the Albanian government expressed a similar view: "Albania, speaking before the vote, said it . . . would not take part in the voting on any of the other draft resolutions. The large number of resolutions adopted each year had absolutely no positive influence on the arms race. Certain resolutions were presented only for political and propaganda purposes."[1] Two categories of initiatives comprise the measures proposed by the cynical approach. One category of measures consists of meaningless proposals: e.g., to reduce all defense budgets by 50 percent. Such a proposal lacks meaning unless the base budget figures are known and accepted by all states, and unless the reductions can be verified by some impartial authority.

The other category of measures is propaganda initiatives that are unlikely to lead to serious negotiation. Several states have frequently proposed, for instance, the establishment of a "zone of peace" in the Indian Ocean, and indeed, a UN committee has met for a decade to explore the proposal. During the Carter Administration, officials attempted to establish a more concrete approach to such issues through bilateral US-Soviet talks on the Indian Ocean. With no progress, however, those talks also degenerated into quests for propaganda advantage.

The degree of cynicism in Soviet disarmament proposals, dating back to the revolution of 1917, has long been a matter of debate. In the 1930s, Maxim Litvinov was an untiring initiator of disarmament resolutions at the League of Nations, and with the opening of the United Nations in 1946, the Soviet Foreign Minister urged that disarmament be at the top of the agenda.[2] Yet in each case, the negotiation of verifiable, concrete agreements with the Soviet Union has been a difficult process of transposing rhetoric into binding legal documents.

THE TACTICAL APPROACH

Multilateral arms control has also functioned as a tactic in the foreign policies of governments, an approach of increasing importance as MAC has achieved some institutional history and as governments (particularly the US) have approached the issue with greater finesse. In one sense, the tactical approach is somewhere between idealism and cynicism on the spectrum; it is the object of good intentions but limited expectations of achieving improved national security. With the tactical approach, the focus is most frequently on technical issues rather than on political will or issues of good faith.

The object is to use such negotiations to improve a nation's position with regard to the weapons systems of adversaries, either directly or by limiting the military positions of potential adversaries. It has been argued by one participant, for example, that the 1921–22 naval limitations talks were a success because the American push for an agreement came "at a time when it was about to assume a controlling naval position."[3] The US was thus able to limit the expansion of the other navies, in particular categories of warships, at a time when the US itself wanted to cut back on its construction program.

There is much in the way of tactics that can be read into recent proposals for consideration at bodies such as the SSOD, especially in examining which states abstain or vote against the proposals. The proposal for establishment of a South Asia nuclear-weapon-free zone, sponsored by Pakistan, recorded three opposing votes: India, Bhutan, and Mauritius.[4] The proposal to initiate negotiations on the cessation of nuclear weapons production and on the gradual reduction of such stockpiles, proposed by the Soviet Union and its allies, recorded seventeen votes opposed (primarily the NATO allies).[5] Much the same lineup occurred on a proposal to prohibit the production, stockpiling, deployment, and use of neutron (enhanced radiation) weapons. On the other hand, in the case of a proposal to undertake a study on conventional disarmament, it was the Soviet Union and its allies that at first cast negative ballots in 1980 and then chose to abstain in 1981.[6] In such cases, clearly, the role of MAC forums is seen primarily as the mobilization of international opinion on issues being negotiated elsewhere, or for the eventual drafting of a treaty of prohibition or limitation of a particular weapon system.

THE STRATEGIC APPROACH

The last approach to MAC is a synthesis of long-term and short-term policies, and is suggestive of a "strategic approach" to such international negotiations. Such a strategy is needed as an antidote to the problems of the other approaches already described. Arms control cannot be achieved by leaps of faith; the issue of national survival, as a military question, is too important to be left to the vagaries of a world community in which there is no shared faith. Arms control cannot be abandoned to the cynics; it is too important to be put on the trash heap. Nor can multilateral arms control simply be a tactical issue focusing on particular micro-problems; the public constituency supporting MAC demands a greater legitimacy for the negotiations, and one that is more comprehensible to a broad audience. The strategic approach thus provides a broad basis for considering the MAC forums, as well as providing some priorities for making decisions on specific proposals.

MAC must be understood in the context of the global correlation of military forces. At a number of levels in that correlation of forces, the US has fallen behind its principal adversary, the Soviet Union. In terms of survivable ICBMs, in terms of European-based alliance conventional forces, in terms of overall military manpower, and a host of other measures, the US lags behind the Soviet Union.[7]

MAC must thus be one of several focuses for a US strategy during a period of relative military weakness. Given the wide range of subject matter open to consideration in most MAC forums, such as the SSOD of June–July 1982, the United States should be able to focus on those security sectors where the Soviet Union has maintained or sought superiority and thus accelerated the arms race:

space-based weapons systems, conventional forces, chemical and biological warfare, and as a matter of procedure, the Soviet reluctance to allow adequate verification and increased confidence-building measures. A strategic approach thus admits the need for MAC, endorses it as a useful approach over the long run, particularly in the context of an extended American inferiority in many aspects of the military balance, and allows for the US to approach current and future MAC forums with an intention of building a coalition for concrete, verifiable agreements. The strategic approach thus implies both a need for the US to take initiatives in MAC and a need for the US to take a strong rhetorical posture.

LIMITATIONS ON MAC EFFECTIVENESS

Two major problems emerge for forecasting a bright future for MAC: one "objective" and the other "subjective." The major problem is that which fuels the arms race phenomenon itself: the international arms slosh that has allowed the present buildup of weapons levels, the emergence of new technologies, and the diffusion of advanced weapons to all parts of the world. Such proliferation of military systems is more than a regrettable phenomenon, in terms of world peace. It is also a threat to the ability of military establishments like the US to maintain the power projection capability of the past. The experience of the British in the Falklands crisis, while not causing great costs, is an illustration of the liabilities associated with the arms excesses of recent decades. With these weapons systems and enlarged defense establishments throughout the world, the problem can be dealt with objectively only at the level of MAC. Yet the continuing arms slosh suggests that achieving results even in MAC forums will be arduous.

The subjective problem is the distrust of many governments (of particular importance, the American) towards the MAC mechanisms. Historically, the Soviet Union has been much more adept at making use of MAC in the context of cynical or tactical approaches. The bulk of the agenda of disarmament sessions, to the present day, remains dominated by initiatives of the non-aligned nations, with strong open or covert support from the Soviet Union. With the US at such a disadvantage historically, much of Washington considers the MAC forums asymmetrical; in addition, insofar as such forums are used for propaganda, the rest of the world finds them irrelevant. Many third world governments, and particularly those with nuclear or near-nuclear capability, have chosen unilateral military expansion over real diplomatic investment in the MAC process. After the first SSOD, for instance, a resolution to undertake a systematic study of all aspects of regional disarmament drew forty abstentions (the Soviet bloc plus many emerging third world military powers). The report was to be completed in time for submission to the second SSOD.[8] The general tenor of the third world toward such MAC exercises has been, and remains, that the first order of business should be nuclear weapons. Given the tactical position of the Soviet Union, a natural alliance has formed between the "east" and the "south."

The US thus approaches MAC negotiations with some disdain, and in some cases, concern. The posture chosen by American governments for most of the postwar period has been that of a tactical approach, attempting to find ways to attack Soviet political vulnerabilities, an approach that has yielded little success. During the Carter years, a wave of idealism swept up even the administration, as it was thought possible that the arrival of the Soviet Union at essential military parity with the US would yield more meaningful negotiating postures by the Soviet Union on both nuclear and conventional issues.

Thus, a number of issues of interest to MAC forums, such as arms reductions in the Indian Ocean, or limitations on arms transfers, were the objects of committed negotiations by the US, only to have them thwarted within the negotiating context by disagreements about fundamental purposes and processes, and poisoned in the strategic context by the Soviet invasion of Afghanistan and the subversion of Poland. In the first year of the Reagan Administration, therefore, there has been a reaction to the perceived idealism of the Carter Administration, a tendency to place MAC substantively lower on the priority list for attention. This antithesis to the Carter period is coming to an end, with the need to approach multilateral forums such as the second SSOD responsibly. It is possible, given the imperative to develop MAC policies, that a creative strategic synthesis could emerge.

THE FUTURE UTILITY OF MAC

From the perspective of American foreign policy, it would be easiest to dismiss MAC as a serious enterprise, to consign it to a propaganda function, and to use MAC forums to attack Soviet behavior on arms control issues as well as for military interventions around the world. That option is a real one, if only as a response in kind to the many countries that use United Nations platforms for public bickering. Such propaganda efforts tend to focus either on regional conflicts, as illustrated by speeches from the Middle Eastern countries, or on vapid generalities about the goodness of peace and the regrettable outbreaks of international violence.

It is both possible and desirable, however, to design a synthesis out of idealistic and realistic approaches that meets both the objective and subjective problems already described. The criteria of any serious approach by MAC should include not only a sharing of ideals, but also concrete initiatives that begin to meet the problem of international arms excesses, measures that could be taken seriously by the other countries involved in the MAC process.

A microanalytic approach to the status of MAC yields a number of encouraging signs. The principal vocal states that obstructed the MAC process in the past, France and the People's Republic of China, have changed their tone significantly, and in the preparatory resolutions submitted to the UN General Assembly in December 1981, the second SSOD Preparatory Committee found that only Albania entered pro forma, across-the-board objections to the MAC process. For the propagandistic, the first SSOD was amply satisfying, and for the remainder of the nations at the first SSOD, their idealistic goals may not have been met, but enough concrete issues were explored in debate to justify the second SSOD. The lack of progress on nuclear weapon issues has remained frustrating for the organizers of the SSODs, but issues of conventional disarmament and arms transfers were considered and kept under study. It could even be suggested that there is growing appreciation of the need for regional arms balances. The record is spotty here, but the report of the Study Group on Regional Disarmament (whose original mandate sparked forty abstentions, noted above) was accepted by the

General Assembly in December 1981 with no reservations.[9] The United Nations is thus being seen as a valid institution in which to consider MAC issues. Finally, the timing of the second SSOD was important, just as the United States and the Soviet Union undertook new arms reduction talks. The credibility of the US at the START would have been damaged by treating the second SSOD as a frivolous exercise.

A macroanalytic approach to MAC negotiations, however, is of even greater importance for establishing their future value. The fact that arms control and the negotiating process are a function of the strategic balance cannot be avoided. As a result, the American posture cannot be a static one: as the strategic balance is dynamic, so the American use of MAC would need to be dynamic. The period that the US has entered, that of increased tensions with the Soviet Union, will above all be a time of political and psychological testing. The US will not be able to redress the strategic balance with the Soviet Union unless it is able to mobilize both domestic opinion behind American foreign policy as well as foreign opinion against aggressive actions by the Soviet Union. It needs to be recalled here that the principal traditional sources of support for MAC have been those idealistic sectors of public opinion that work for complete disarmament. To the extent that opinion supports the multilateral approach as much as the content of MAC initiatives, it is important for the US government to remain actively involved in MAC forums, with the intention of redressing the Soviet strategic advantage. The US has now assumed an unaccustomed role, that of the weaker party militarily, and so long as this period lasts, the traditional tools of the weaker parties need to be utilized, such as multilateral forums and the limitations imposed by existing legal conventions on military questions.[10]

A number of multilateral forums can be utilized for implementation of a MAC strategy. The CD meetings in Geneva, for example, have been intermittently preoccupied with the problems of chemical weapons and verification, especially in the context of a comprehensive test ban (CTB). That the CD membership is more limited than the General Assembly of the UN is a positive factor, since all of the principal military powers are represented at the CD.

The SSOD process may have somewhat of a weakening effect on the CD, as many of the UN members not represented at the CD would like to see more issues considered at a universal forum such as the General Assembly, and to see the work of the CD more closely tied to the UN and the CD membership expanded.[11]

Other types of MAC forums have been established as a result of agreements reached on specific weapons or in the context of specific regions. In the case of the Non-Proliferation Treaty, for instance, the International Atomic Energy Agency has been given a major mandate to conduct safeguard maintenance against the transfer of weapons-grade uranium from civilian programs to military endeavors. In the case of the Biological Weapons Convention (1972), a more limited forum was created, in the shape of a review conference composed of the (now more than eighty) signatories to the Convention, which meets by treaty requirement at least every five years. Obviously, more limited types of consultative bodies are created when the list of signatories is inherently limited, as in the cases of the CSCE, the MBFR talks, the Treaty of Tlateloco or the Antarctic Treaty.

The utility of MAC forums, and the related agreements, may lie in restraining Soviet attempts to achieve military superiority. Such a possibility lies at the root of concern, both in the US and abroad, that the Soviet Union is successfully developing an anti-satellite capability (signs of such research were evident as early as the mid-1970s), in spite of the intent and spirit of the 1967 Outer Space Treaty. Because the Soviet development of such ASAT weaponry results in the de facto militarization of space, strong and persuasive voices are being raised in the western arms control community for an abandonment of efforts to negotiate restraints on that particular technology, and for the US to proceed with its own ASAT program. In this particular case, such a move regrettably implies the militarization of space; more generally and more importantly, it illustrates an evident weakness of MAC approaches to issues at the frontier of military technology, particularly those that can be concealed within the research and development programs of the "civilian" sector. It could easily be argued here, for technical reasons, that there is little utility in pursuing the issue in a multilateral forum.

MAC: A STRATEGIC FORUM FROM
AMERICAN WEAKNESS?

The US faces a number of dilemmas in responding to initiatives at MAC forums. It is evident that a certain number of issues (particularly conventional arms) are properly addressed in a multilateral forum, and that a number of such forums already exist. At the same time, major liabilities are attached to any American efforts to use MAC forums, especially owing to the historical US position, the bias in domestic American consideration of arms control issues towards disarmament rather than verifiable arms control, and the unrealistic manner in which most MAC forums attempt to frame answers to problems of disarmament and arms control.

The US position at past multilateral forums is not conducive to its present need to define a positive strategy. The perceptions of other governments, not entirely erroneous, are that the US largely disdained MAC because it existed primarily as a propaganda forum for the Soviet Union, and that the US entered substantive discussions only as a tactical tool. As a result, most countries tend to doubt American "sincerity" in approaching multilateral forums at the present time. It is a problem not only by virtue of past American views, but also because of a general distrust of the major military powers on the part of lesser powers.

The problem is not insurmountable, however, if only for the reason that the US need not convince all 157 governments represented in the UN General Assembly. In any MAC forum, the number of key states is relatively limited to approximately the number of states in the Committee on Disarmament. The number of important states is limited in terms of achieving measurable progress on reduction of conventional arms, even in various regional contexts. And from the longer-term US perspective, the value of MAC diplomacy is most importantly measured against progress in righting the asymmetrical Soviet-American military balance. As the number of states anxious about the Soviet military buildup has increased, so has the willingness to accept sincere American positions in favor of arms limitations.

The third world is going through a potential transformation in its view of superpower responsibility for the level of arms inventories in the world today. The focus in disarmament discussions can no longer be dominated by the coalition between the non-aligned movement and the Soviet Union, which cast the US nuclear forces as the villain; instead, it is the inordinate Soviet defense spending and aggressive behavior that is presently under increasing examination. Such is the result of Soviet behavior in recent years, and the source of a new coalition for US policies towards MAC forums in coming years. Concretely, such a coalition will focus, for example, on questions of transparency in defense spending, a proposal suggested by President Reagan at the SSOD–II.

The US is also at a disadvantage in MAC forums as a result of the open discussion of issues undertaken in this country. For all the evident virtues associated with a free press and public participation in matters of great national security, the potential manipulation of the press and public opinion by foreign adversaries is a constant danger in the utilization of MAC forums. As discussion and negotiation of such issues is usually protracted over a period of years, the possibilities of such manipulation can grievously undermine the position of the US government.

Within the MAC forums, there exists a temptation to undertake a sweeping approach to arms control issues. The time required for negotiating among multiple parties such as in MAC forums tends to afflict the proceedings and result in blanket bans of particular technologies, or imposition of gross limitations abundant with escape loopholes. In the former category, for instance, are the Hague Declarations and Conventions on asphyxiation gases (1899), expanding bullets (1899), the use of balloons (1907), and the attempt of the 1932 Disarmament Conference to limit the use of aircraft. The last ban on the use of aircraft failed not because the parties were unwilling to camouflage various gaps in the proposed Convention, but simply because the Germans elected Adolf Hitler to the Chancellorship before the agreement was signed.[12] Since the negotiators of the ban on aircraft could find no plausible means of preventing the development of civilian air corps with military potential, they instead came up with a complex formula including the number of aircraft, total horsepower of the motors, and the wing area, to be included in the 1932 Draft Convention on Disarmament.

The problem with general limitations negotiated in MAC forums is that various classes of weapons systems are favored by different powers, and as a result, asymmetries readily develop unless proscribed by a treaty. After the 1921–22 naval limitation treaties, for instance, most classes of warships other than cruisers and battleships were not limited except by total tonnage. As a result, the Japanese developed an enormous fleet of small frigates. The French, on the other hand, undertook plans for an expanding submarine fleet: quite legally under the Washington Treaties, the French had plans in 1927 for 47,000 tons of submarines, even though the US planned only 2,000 tons of submarine construction, and the British 12,000 tons.[13] The great challenge in MAC forums, then, is to inject into a highly unwieldy negotiating body the capability to come up with meaningful diplomatic/legal results capable of influencing the military plans of a superpower with the capacity of the Soviet Union.

A major remaining problem with MAC forums is that they are unlikely to be able to deal with the issues of greatest importance to US security. The Soviet Union has not achieved its present military posture by taking positions that are politically popular, and it is unlikely to retreat from an advantageous correlation of military forces with great haste. But such a problem illustrates, as well as anything could, the extent to which MAC must be seen in a strategic, long-term context, rather than simply as a means by which to achieve tactical ends.

There are, after all, within the UN and other international arms control organizations, a number of positive developments that could yield great advantage in MAC initiatives. At the political level, the Soviet Union has been in substantial retreat since its invasion of Afghanistan and its threatened use of force against democratizing forces in Poland. The extent to which the Soviet Union overplayed its hand in both cases has entailed significant political costs, which could be increased significantly if it becomes more widely recognized that both cases flow from the evolution of unbridled Soviet *military* might. That might has to be leashed, as many governments recognize, and a multilateral forum is likely to be the best locale for doing so.

The present weakness of the US vis-à-vis the Soviet Union in a wide range of military categories makes MAC forums particularly useful since, whatever the outcome, it is more likely to improve the American strategic position than that of the Soviet Union. There has been no long-range consideration in recent years of MAC possibilities that would present distinct disadvantages for the Soviets. Any reconsideration of the Montreux Convention to tighten naval access to the Black Sea, for instance, would inevitably result in discomfort for the Soviets as they consider access to the Mediterranean. A meaningful examination of defense expenditures would provoke a close look at what the Soviet Union inadequately identifies as the defense budget, and attempt—in the glare of the world's attention—to delineate exactly what constitutes Soviet defense expenditures.

Above all, one has to ask what other avenues exist that might provide for some reduction of Soviet capabilities. In the strategic balance between the Soviet Union and the US, a limitation on Soviet capabilities is not only beneficial for global peace and security; it helps to redress the imbalances that presently exist on a bilateral basis. Since the US will have great difficulty in obtaining anything more than proportionate reductions (as opposed to restoration of parity) as a result of bilateral discussions (in START, MBFR, or elsewhere), the US would do well to rely upon the mobilization of official opinion in MAC forums to help restore the American position.

THE MAC EXPERIENCE: SECOND SSOD

The utility of MAC should not be considered simply in the abstract, however, since the US had a major opportunity in the summer of 1982 to test a new approach to MAC: the second SSOD held in New York in June–July 1982. This meeting, while allowing only five weeks for consideration of a wide range of issues, symbolized an interest and commitment by the majority of UN members towards more aggressive handling of disarmament issues, rather than simply leaving them to the great powers or to the elite CD group in Geneva. Faced with this opportunity, how did the US respond?

That President Reagan attended SSOD–II—in contrast to President Carter, who sent his Vice President to the first SSOD in 1978—

gave a dramatic fillip to the US effort at the session. Reagan had, of course, challenged Soviet leader Brezhnev to meet with him in New York at the time of the session, but the Soviets instead delivered their traditional representative at such gatherings, Foreign Minister Gromyko. As a result, the US was in a better position than the USSR to impress its views upon the session, and upon the media and public opinion, which followed the session with unprecedented interest.

The US unveiled three initiatives at the session, which were designed in the context of US strategic interests and with a view to Soviet vulnerabilities. The first initiative called for a conference on military expenditures to build on UN work—obstructed in the past by the Soviets—on developing a common system for accounting and reporting. Underscoring that there is conclusive evidence that the Soviet government has provided toxins for use in Laos and Kampuchea and is itself using chemical weapons against freedom fighters in Afghanistan, President Reagan in a second initiative called for the USSR, Laos and Vietnam "to grant full and free access to their countries or to territories they control so that UN experts can conduct an effective, independent investigation to verify cessation of these horrors." [14] As a third initiative, the US presented a package of proposals for incorporation in UN public information activities in the disarmament field (the UN "World Disarmament Campaign"). These proposals called for a freer and fuller flow of information and views on disarmament and related matters throughout the world. These proposals took special note of President Reagan's offer to President Brezhnev to address the American people on television in exchange for the chance to speak to the Soviet people on Soviet television, as well as of President Reagan's call for Soviet and American journalists to exchange views on major events on each others' television.

In addition to presenting these initiatives, the US vigorously advanced its views in the various SSOD working groups. It was joined in such efforts by its allies, which put on the table a host of their own initiatives that caused the Soviets discomfort, especially in the area of verification mechanisms.

Widely perceived as a casualty of the unpropitious international climate, the second SSOD itself ended with scarcely any concrete accomplishments.[15] Nevertheless, the energetic efforts of the US and its allies substantially offset Soviet diplomacy at the session, which was highlighted by the Soviets' "no-first-use" of nuclear weapons pledge. Indeed, despite their seemingly attractive initiatives, the Soviets were considerably more isolated and defensive at the session than has been the norm in the past. Thus, in contrast to their self-portrayal as the "natural ally" of the non-aligned countries, the Soviets seldom were able to make common cause with the third world and indeed frequently confronted non-aligned pressure. This relative Soviet isolation and defensiveness can be attributed not only to Western diplomacy but also to growing non-aligned sophistication and skepticism vis-à-vis the USSR. As noted above, this skepticism stems from awareness of the Soviet misdeeds in the international arena (e.g., Afghanistan and Kampuchea). If the US and its allies continue to take a vigorous strategic approach in MAC, opportunities to exploit these favorable trends should grow.

In effect, taking MAC seriously means that the US has to reconsider its view of the United Nations. That organization, which serves as the umbrella for this current MAC endeavor, clearly has a very disappointing history in achieving arms control. At the same time, if there is scope for a renovated American approach to multilateral arms control, it would presumably be propitious as well to reconsider forums previously committed to the diplomatic wastebasket. If the US is now in the business of constructing new coalitions to meet a present and persistent danger, no forum should be arbitrarily ignored. The potential for new coalitions is greatest in the universal organization of the UN. The implementation of a new strategic approach to the UN will not be done overnight; it must begin with a single step, and the second SSOD proved to be an appropriate opportunity to take a new direction. In that way, multilateral arms control might be returned to a constructive role in an American strategy for the 1980s.

NOTES

1. *UN Monthly Chronicle,* (March, 1982), p. 38.

2. For a view that the Soviet proposals should be taken seriously, see Allen W. Dulles, "Disarmament in the Atomic Age," *Foreign Affairs,* 25 (January, 1947), pp. 204–216.

3. Allen W. Dulles, "Some Misconceptions about Disarmament," *Foreign Affairs*, 5 (April, 1927), pp. 413–424.

4. *UN Monthly Chronicle,* op. cit., p. 41.

5. Ibid., p. 43.

6. Ibid., p. 48.

7. See, for example, the writings of the Committee on the Present Danger and W. Scott Thompson, ed., *National Security in the 1980s: From Weakness to Strength* (San Francisco: Institute for Contemporary Studies, 1980).

8. Stockholm International Peace Research Institute, *World Armaments and Disarmament* (Stockholm, 1979), p. 568.

9. *UN Monthly Chronicle* (March, 1982), p. 49.

10. These conventions range from chemical weapon bans to CSCE-related restrictions on military activities.

11. Stockholm International Peace Research Institute, *Arms Control: A Survey and Appraisal of Multilateral Agreements* (New York: Crane Russak, 1978), pp. 46–47.

12. See Edward P. Warner, "Can Aircraft Be Limited?" *Foreign Affairs,* 10 (April, 1932), pp. 431–443. Warner comments on the impetus of such a Convention—and thus foreshadows much of the debate on nuclear weapons today—by saying: "Some military men and a vast number of civilians have come to take it for granted that the next war will be fought almost exclusively in the air, and that it will be ended within a few hours or a few days by the destruction of all the great populous centers in the territory of the less-prepared of the combatants" (p. 431).

13. Allen W. Dulles, "Some Misconceptions about Disarmament," *Foreign Affairs,* 5 (April, 1927), p. 415.

14. US President Ronald Reagan's speech on 17 June, 1982 at SSOD–II. See Document of the UNGA, A/S–12/PV. 16. The UN has been investigating allegations of chemical weapons use in Asia since the beginning of 1981, but this investigation has been inconclusive. Among the reasons for this is that the investigators have been barred by the Afghan, Laotian and Vietnamese governments from conducting on-site visits. Another factor undoubtedly is the key post held by Under Secretary-General V. Ustinov, to whom the UN disarmament staff reports.

15. One exception related to the "World Disarmament Campaign," with respect to which agreement was reached on a text calling for objectivity, universal participation, and discussion and debate in all countries on all points of view related to disarmament issues. Strong Western efforts, in association with the non-aligned, succeeded in overcoming considerable Soviet resistance to elements of this text.

UN DISARMAMENT EFFORTS: IS THERE LIFE AFTER THE SECOND UN SPECIAL SESSION ON DISARMAMENT?

CHARLES WILLIAM MAYNES

The first question any American writing on disarmament in the wake of the remarkably unsuccessful Second UN Special Session on Disarmament (SSOD–II) in June–July 1982 has to answer is: why should the United States pay any attention whatsoever to what takes place in the UN in the field of arms control and disarmament? The numbers are wrong, the forum is wrong, and the issues are wrong. Thus, it is frequently argued that,

- Arms Control agreements cannot be negotiated, perhaps not even rationally discussed, in bodies with 150 plus members.
- Arms control is too important an issue to be entrusted to a body that the US cannot adequately control.
- Finally, the UN avoids a number of issues of concern to the US, preeminently conventional arms flows into the third world.

The Special Session of the UN General Assembly on Disarmament in retrospect seemed designed to prove the skeptics' case. In contrast to the first Session, member states could not reach a consensus on a final document, US-Soviet relations were probably set back by some of the hot rhetoric of the session, and the press devoted so little attention to the UN Session that its occurrence did not serve the public education function many had foreseen.

There are, however, at least four reasons for taking the UN seriously in the field of arms control and disarmament.

- The relationship between power and rhetoric in the UN in the arms control field may be in the process of a very important change.

• The UN continues to play a significant but misunderstood role in the preservation of the non-proliferation regime.

• The UN can play a critical role in agenda setting that favorably or adversely affects US interests in non-UN forums.

• Finally, the nature of the approach that the US takes toward the public diplomacy of arms control can have an important effect—positive or negative—on the preservation of the fragile popular US consensus regarding the administration's defense effort, especially in light of the mass movement for nuclear disarmament.

This paper will examine each of these points in more detail.

RELATIONSHIP BETWEEN RHETORIC AND POWER

For most of the UN's history the story of arms control discussions has been one of efforts by the majority of members to bring pressure on the superpowers to disarm. The reasons behind these efforts, however, are not well understood. Some view third world interest in disarmament as simply a question of economics. Thus in a study prepared for the Aspen Institute prior to SSOD–I, Lincoln Bloomfield and Harlan Cleveland made the following assertion: "We can thus advance as an axiom that the dominant interest of the large majority of states participating in the SSOD process lies not primarily in strategic or, *a fortiori,* conventional arms control, but in economic and social development in the poor countries."[1]

No doubt a desire to channel hoped-for savings from disarmament into development was a powerful motivation of third world countries at both Special Sessions and remains a powerful motivation today. Indeed it is a motivation not unique to developing countries. President Eisenhower was the first postwar head of state to employ successfully the rhetorical device of citing the number of schoolhouses or hospitals that a bomber or battleship represented. So Bloomfield and Cleveland are on solid ground in mentioning the motive of development in third world approaches to disarmament.

Nevertheless, there seems to be a deeper motivation at work. In the long run, all non-nuclear UN members have a vested interest in trying to reduce the disparity of power that exists between themselves and the superpowers. Since that disparity rests on the uniquely powerful nuclear status of these superpowers, it should not be surprising that other UN members try to focus UN arms control discussions on the sins and omissions of the superpowers and have paid particular attention to the issue of nuclear arms. Nor should it be surprising that the determination of the Soviet Union or the United States to resist efforts of other UN members to have a significant influence through UN decisions on their bilateral arms control negotiations has never enjoyed widespread support even among non-aligned countries otherwise favorably disposed to one or both of the superpowers. In a sovereign state system the pressure from the majority will always be to focus on those factors that are principally responsible for any significant degree of inequality among states. Hence the non-aligned reaction to efforts to talk about non-nuclear issues: "The super-armed are trying to disarm those already disarmed."

The Soviet Union has been much more successful than the United States in dealing with this unrelenting pressure for equality. A regular feature of every General Assembly is a specious Soviet initiative designed to exploit third world concern about the inordinate power of the United States and the Soviet Union compared to the rest of the UN membership. Hence, the Soviets have put forth proposals barring first use of nuclear weapons (most recently at the second Special Session), an end to all foreign bases and arbitrary cuts in defense budgets. A perennial US task at the General Assembly has been to explain to the rest of the membership why the United States cannot accept the most recent Soviet initiative. The Soviets feel comfortable making such proposals because they know the US will prevent, at a political cost to itself, their adoption in any form that can have real effect.

The UN may, however, be in the process of a significant change in the way it deals with disarmament questions. The reason is that the relationship between power and rhetoric in the field of arms control may be shifting in unanticipated ways. The shift in power is obvious. In 1950 the United States alone accounted for approximately 50 percent of the world's military spending. If the Soviet Union's military spending were added to that figure, the problem of the world's armaments could be seen as largely an American-

Soviet problem, even without taking into account the problem of nuclear weapons. By the mid-1970s, by contrast, the US share had dropped to 25 percent. Assuming that the Soviet military budget is, at least in absolute terms, roughly the size of the American budget, then the US and the Soviet Union represent only half of the problem whereas three decades ago they represented practically all of it.

One would expect such a significant change in the real world to begin to alter the character of UN debates and there is some evidence that such an alteration is taking place. When India, for example, speaks out on the issue of superpower naval presence in the Indian Ocean, it is not only adopting a moral position on the issue but it is also trying to protect its own military power by pressing for a solution that will leave it dominant in the region.

Nor is this an isolated example. Pakistan raises the issue of nuclear-free zones in South Asia more to curb India's power than to clip the wings of the superpowers. Africans raise the issue of a nuclear-free zone in Africa less to embarrass the superpowers than to attempt to limit the options of South Africa. Egypt presses a nuclear-free zone in the Middle East—Israel belatedly expresses interest in the same issue—because of local rivalries.

A change of approach in the area of conventional arms has been slower to develop because their acquisition is the easiest step a third world nation can take to reduce the disparity in power between the weak and the strong. Conventional arms not only provide protection against domestic opponents or regional enemies, but they also make a replay of the colonial era more difficult.

There is, in addition, a doctrinal reason why the UN has been slow to deal with the issue of conventional arms: the founders of the UN, unlike the founders of the League of Nations, were not convinced that the acquisition of arms per se was the cause of war. Quite the contrary, they believed that if Germany's neighbors had armed adequately in the mid-1930s, World War II might never have taken place. For this reason, whereas the League's articles elaborate a disarmament program, the UN Charter envisages collective security as the proper response to aggression.

Nevertheless, realities are now changing so fast in the conventional arms area that a shift in Third World attitudes in the UN on this subject would seem in order. According to the most recent figures from the US Arms Control and Disarmament Agency (ACDA), between 1970 and 1979 the total arms imports of the developing countries as a group increased more than four-fold, from $4.1 to $19.2 billion. If one allows for inflation, the third world's arms imports more than doubled during this period. In 1979, the developing countries were the recipients of 80 percent of global arms transfers. It remains true that the principal culprits in the supply of conventional arms to the third world are the members of NATO and the Warsaw Pact, which account for 91 percent of international arms exports. Nonetheless, arms exports by third world countries increased substantially in the 1970s, rising from $230 million in 1970 to $1.3 billion in 1979.[2]

In short, both the volumes being exported and the emerging new sources of supply are creating new concerns, which explain the relative success achieved at SSOD–I in the conventional arms field. Paragraph 22 of the final document of the 1978 Special Session on Disarmament may contain too many caveats for those who would like to see the conventional arms issue taken more seriously, but it does mark a multilateral departure. For the first time UN members were stating that in addition to continued efforts to reduce nuclear arsenals, "there should also be negotiations on the limitations of international transfer of conventional weapons."[3]

Nor was this departure an accident. It obviously did reflect the insistence of countries like the US that the Special Session would be a mockery if it failed to deal with the problem of conventional weapons transfers. But what is perhaps more important is that all UN members were willing in the final analysis to respond positively to this insistence. In brief, the explanation is not that UN members have suddenly acquired a larger view of world order; rather they are experiencing an emerging awareness that new forces are at work that will have a significant impact on their security. Their behavior at the first Special Session was at least a first step in demonstrating such an awareness formally.

One should understand, however, that multilateral arms control negotiations, like bilateral arms control negotiations, involve bargaining and compromise. Little has happened since SSOD–I to build on the consensus reached. The collapse of SALT II and the end of further negotiations on a comprehensive nuclear test ban (CTB) deprived the superpowers of the leverage necessary to press other UN members to begin more serious work on the issue of conventional arms control.

PRESERVATION OF THE NON-PROLIFERATION REGIME

The Non-Proliferation Treaty (NPT) is unique in that without excessive duress a majority of the signatories defied the fundamental rules of the sovereign state system and accepted a legal form of discriminatory status (since under the treaty a few nuclear states are treated more favorably than non-nuclear states). But those now tolerating discriminatory status are increasingly uneasy over its existence, for they feel that the basic bargain that persuaded them to sign the NPT is being violated. That bargain involved the willingness of the non-nuclear powers to accept a subordinate military status in return for promises from the nuclear powers that the latter would make a good faith effort to control and reverse vertical proliferation of nuclear weapons and that they would provide non-nuclear states with the fruits of peaceful nuclear technology. For a variety of reasons the last promise has been difficult to fulfill, but in any event it is the first promise that is the more important.

It is essential to understand why. It is not that potential nuclear states like Pakistan are able to cite superpower failure to live up to the NPT as the reason why they must go nuclear. Nothing so mechanical is involved. Rather, non-performance by the superpowers creates an atmosphere of acquiescence within the international community towards the new proliferators. One way to view both SSOD–I and SSOD–II, and for that matter all UN disarmament debates, is an additional review commission on the efforts of the superpowers to live up to their NPT commitment to reduce their nuclear arsenals. At SSOD–I the Soviet Union and the United States made a major effort to persuade other member states to accept the SALT process, which until SALT II did not involve actual reductions, as a significant step towards fulfillment of their NPT obligation. The United States and the Soviet Union judged SSOD–I favorably in large measure because they succeeded in their mutual objective of gaining acceptance of the SALT process as evidence of NPT treaty fulfillment.

THE UN AS AGENDA-SETTER

One vital function of the UN has always been that of agenda-setter. Even in areas where the UN itself is barred from playing a direct role, it can influence the activities of non-UN diplomacy. The best examples lie in the economic area. UN debates helped to legitimize the concept of GSP (generalized system of preferences) for developing countries. Initially, the reaction of industrialized countries was very hostile. By the end of the 1960s the developing countries had won the philosophical battle and one developed country after another began to adopt GSP through unilateral decisions.

Perhaps the most spectacular impact of UN debates on non-UN diplomacy lies in the area of national resources. Over the years the developing countries have managed to establish the legitimacy of the concept of national sovereignty over natural resources. The United States, almost alone among UN members, refused to accept this concept because as formulated in UN debates it never provided sufficient recognition of the right to prompt and adequate compensation for expropriated firms. The US, however, has been increasingly in a minority. By the time OPEC countries moved to raise sharply the price of oil, a climate of acquiescence had developed that was of enormous assistance to the OPEC countries in defending their decision politically.

A similar example of agenda-setting is now taking place in UN forums with respect to nuclear issues. Many US government officials, both in this and in earlier administrations, view a comprehensive test ban treaty (CTB) as an important but secondary issue. Within the UN context, however, the CTB is gradually acquiring the kind of symbolic importance enjoyed by an issue like national sovereignty over natural resources. In the disarmament field it is becoming the litmus test of superpower sincerity in carrying out the obligations they incurred by sponsoring and signing the NPT.

It would be foolhardy to argue that the United States need not be concerned with the issue of agenda-setting. To cite one prominent member of this administration on the point, Paul Nitze has argued publicly that next to the hardware decisions necessary to preserve US security, the single greatest task the US faces is to gain political support from non-nuclear states for US defense and arms control policies. Neglecting UN disarmament issues runs the risk of placing the United States on the political defensive inside and outside the UN for the remaining years of this administration.

Unfortunately, it does not require a UN success for the agenda-setting process to take place. A UN failure such as the SSOD–II also influences the way non-nuclear states address arms control issues. Much depends on the perceived causes of failure. If non-nuclear states begin, for example, to view the futility of UN debates on arms control as final proof that the superpowers are not taking their NPT obligations seriously, again a climate of acquiescence can develop toward the next generation of nuclear proliferators, making their political task of going nuclear much less painful. Such a development cannot be in the interest of any US administration, for as President Reagan noted in his presentation to the SSOD–II, "strengthening the non-proliferation framework . . . is essential to international security."[4]

DEFENSE POLICY AND PUBLIC OPINION

A final consideration that is becoming more and more urgent is the role that positive public diplomacy now plays in maintaining the support of the fragile consensus within the West for an adequate defense policy. Currently, a crisis is developing with respect to that consensus. Hundreds of thousands of Europeans have marched in the streets to protest the nuclear policies of NATO; within the United States a related movement against nuclear weapons has developed. One-half million people demonstrated in New York City at the opening of the SSOD–II. Many pollsters believe the nuclear freeze movement will play a key role in the 1982 and 1984 US elections. When Cardinal Cooke, the most patriotic of church leaders, can defend US nuclear doctrine only if the US government is making a sincere effort at arms control, the link between a positive public diplomacy and a stable defense consensus should be clear to all but those unwilling to be instructed by reality.

The reasons behind the current disarray over NATO's nuclear

policy deserve more attention than they have received. Contrary to the opinion expressed in various editorials, the problem is not that top US officials have been foolish enough to admit in public what everyone has always conceded in private about the nature of NATO nuclear doctrine in Western Europe. Something much more profound is taking place.

In effect, a growing number of people in Europe and the United States are concluding that Western leaders, and in particular the leaders of the United States, have violated a basic bargain struck when NATO first began to organize its defense. The elements of that bargain were that the attentive public on both sides of the Atlantic would agree to permit a handful of government strategists to devise a nuclear strategy to defend the West and would not question the logic of that strategy, but in return that attentive public asked those same strategists to make a genuine effort to control the nuclear genie through arms control negotiations with the Soviets. The attentive public did not insist on rapid progress in return for its silence and acquiesence. But, for the preservation of the general peace of mind of the attentive public, it was critically important that there be a general feeling among the larger public that the overall direction of events was positive even if slow.

It is in this context that one needs to understand the political impact of the failure to ratify SALT II, of the return to Cold War rhetoric even before Afghanistan and Poland, and of the more public discussion of the possibility of nuclear war, limited or total. The effect was to close off previously open avenues of hope, to cause the public to conclude that an earlier implicit bargain had been broken, and to demand a voice for the first time in the determination of nuclear doctrine. In this sense what we are witnessing is a democratization of a doctrinal debate that up to this point has been the preserve of a handful of specialists.

The Reagan Administration belatedly recognized the strength of the forces it had helped to unleash. As a political response, the President's proposals for a zero option for intermediate-range missiles in Europe and for deep cuts in strategic arms were successful. They slowed the momentum of the peace movement on both sides of the Atlantic. But the success is likely to be temporary without repeated demonstrations that the US government is according a high priority to arms control negotiations with the Soviets.

In this regard, the UN system offers any administration repeated opportunities to reassure the American people. High visibility UN forums, such as the Special Session, can be used as positive opportunities for political theater as well as occasions for serious discussion.

The posture the US adopts in the UN or in similar settings can influence the currently volatile and even dangerous public perceptions of US intentions. Adopting the negative posture urged by many, who ignore or are ignorant of the domestic politics of arms control within NATO, could fatally weaken the fragile defense consensus within the West and inside the United States.

If readers accept the argument that the United States therefore cannot afford not to take UN disarmament efforts seriously, what are the options among which the United States can realistically select? They include the following: superpower solidarity, Cold War confrontation, allied alignment, or sympathetic bystander.

SUPERPOWER SOLIDARITY

As most observers recall, the UN founding fathers assumed that the World War II alliances would last into the postwar era and they structured the UN with the veto system in the Security Council to reflect that assumption. The founding fathers turned out to be spectacularly wrong in their assessment of US-Soviet relations. Nonetheless, their central insight was correct. The UN does work best when there is, if not comity between the superpowers, at least a degree of cooperation.

The first SSOD was judged a success by some and not a failure by the rest primarily because there was sufficient US-Soviet cooperation during the session to manage the process. Neither side pressed issues designed primarily to embarrass the other. For example, the Soviet Union did not insist on a vote on the neutron bomb issue. Each superpower behind the scenes also worked to rein in countries that could have destroyed the session by forcing contentious issues to a vote when the majority of members were determined to achieve an agreement by consensus.

The possibility of this degree of cooperation today is obviously much less than it was in 1978. Indeed the failings of SSOD–II in 1982 can largely be traced to the lack of Soviet-American cooperation. The hard-line opening speeches by Foreign Minister Gromyko and President Reagan set the tough tone for the rest of the session.

The first SSOD was difficult enough from the standpoint of containing US-Soviet competition. The NATO members chose precisely the time of the SSOD–I to meet in Washington to establish the three percent real growth defense budget target. President Carter used the occasion to denounce the Soviet Union for its aggressive activities in the third world. Finally, primarily for domestic reasons related to President Carter's eroding popularity, the opening US presentation at the SSOD by Vice President Mondale struck many as spectacularly inappropriate in the themes it raised and the hard-line approach it took. Nevertheless, the Soviets did not rise to the bait, for the two nations had a lot more to protect in 1978 than they seem to have today. A SALT agreement was under active negotiation, considerable progress had been made in negotiating a comprehensive test ban treaty, and the conventional arms transfer talks had gone much better than predicted. Finally, even though US-Soviet relations were entering into much choppier waters, the relationship between the two countries—at least in the UN framework—remained relatively sound.

The situation is much different today. SALT II will not be ratified. It is not clear whether the new arms control negotiations under way—START, MBFR and INF—are serious in intent. The style of the relationship is even more strained than it was during the last days of the Carter Administration.

One conclusion, therefore, might be to rule out the option of superpower solidarity in the near future. There is at least a remote possibility, however, that this may be a premature assessment. The Soviets, like ourselves, must weigh short-run gains against long-run interests. In the short run, both superpowers will be sorely tempted to try to score political gains. The US tried to use SSOD–II to rally the support of friendly countries against apparent Soviet use of chemical warfare in Afghanistan, continued Soviet occupation of Afghanistan and military support of Vietnamese aggression, and Soviet reluctance to allow intrusive inspection measures. The Soviet Union, on the other hand, attempted to rally international support against US strategic doctrine, in particular its unwillingness to renounce the first use of nuclear weapons, and tried to score political points against the US for its support of Israel, even though Israel invaded Lebanon against US wishes.

For a variety of reasons, however, including the fact that the Soviets have been working this vineyard longer than the US, the Soviet Union may have gained more support for its positions than did the US. But the US did succeed in embarrassing the Soviets over Afghanistan and on the issue of chemical warfare. So the temptation will continue to be strong for both sides to seek such short-run gains.

An alternative approach would be to go to the Soviets and state that notwithstanding escalating differences on a variety of short-run political issues, the two sides continue to have a long-run interest in the preservation of the non-proliferation regime and that therefore the US would be willing to explore whether it is possible for the two sides to cooperate on issues of common interest in multilateral forums. The likelihood is that the Soviets would desire to pursue short-run objectives, but in that event the US would at least be able to point out in future US-Soviet discussions that the Soviets made the decision to reject a policy of limited cooperation with the United States.

COLD WAR CONFRONTATION

The benefits of the Cold War confrontation approach are largely domestic. Few allies and even fewer friends will join the US in this approach. Their support depends on the degree that the US avoids demagogy and concentrates on pressing the Soviets hard with reasonable proposals in areas where they are sensitive or vulnerable. An outstanding example may be the issue of chemical warfare. Apparently, the US has evidence of earlier Soviet involvement in the use of chemical warfare in Yemen during the Egyptian ''police operation'' there. The US continues to collect evidence of Soviet activities in Southeast Asia and in Afghanistan. The evidence is beginning to persuade even those originally quite skeptical.

There are other areas where the Soviets may be sensitive or vulnerable. One may be the area of confidence-building measures designed to reduce the likelihood of surprise or accidental attack. The

Soviets have reportedly been reluctant to agree to be forthcoming on the subject of advance notice of military maneuvers. Another area of vulnerability may be the issue of defense spending. Soviet proposals regarding reductions of military budgets have been transformed into a potentially embarrassing discussion of the problems of transparency. At SSOD–II President Reagan raised these issues, albeit in a speech so hard-line that the tone may have denied the US potential support. Whatever the approach adopted in the past, the US should persistently pursue these themes, perhaps in a less combative tone.

At the same time it is necessary to recognize that two can play this game and for a variety of reasons, if the US does not calibrate its approach very carefully, it is probably more vulnerable than the Soviet Union. US positions on such questions as the proper international response to Israel's invasion of Lebanon or South Africa's aggressive actions against neighboring states create powerful targets of opportunity for the Soviet Union. The neutron bomb issue is ideal for demagogic debate. In sum, while the US in a full-court Cold War approach could bruise the Soviet Union, the US itself would not go unwounded.

ALLIED ALIGNMENT

The US can try to forge a NATO common front. This approach has many advantages. Each NATO member enjoys separate strengths in the UN context, e.g., the French ties to Francophone states and Canada's reputation as a reasonably honest broker. The example of allied cooperation also has certain diplomatic and domestic advantages, and the need to develop a common position can place useful pressure on the Washington bureaucracy to plan ahead. Without this pressure, the traditional pattern is likely to repeat itself: the tendency will be to contend that the whole problem of UN disarmament efforts can go away if only the US stops paying attention to it; then when that prediction proves unfounded, the US, under pressure, will agree to last-minute positions before each international event. These leave great bureaucratic bitterness because their adoption has been so unexpected.

There are, however, disadvantages in working with the allies.

They will be more anxious than the US to appear reasonable before the rest of the UN members. Like any coalition, the western alliance tends to be driven by either its most liberal or conservative members. At the first SSOD, US-French relations became very strained because of the far-reaching positions on disarmament that France under Giscard d'Estaing was advancing.[5] At SSOD–II US allies were fairly supportive of US positions but Canada's strong support for a strategy of suffocation—a Comprehensive Test Ban, a halt to the flight-testing of all new strategic delivery vehicles, and a cessation of the production of fissionable material for weapons purposes—suggests that US allies, in any effort at cooperation, will press positions more advanced than those most US administrations will find easy to accept. Finally, US leverage over European positions may be greater if the US stands apart from any common Western European effort than if it participates. At a minimum, provided the US stands apart, Europeans cannot feel betrayed if the US fails to support European initiatives.

SYMPATHETIC BYSTANDER

The position of sympathetic bystander represents a decision to practice damage limitation. As a sympathetic bystander, the US would recognize that a hostile attitude would be self-defeating, but it would also recognize that it suffers from special limitations in trying to play a more active role. In UN forums the US could limit its public participation to a positive rhetorical speech by a prominent administration figure and in private it would work with like-minded states to limit the damage. This is a variant of the options of Superpower Solidarity or Allied Cooperation, but with this difference: the US would harbor few illusions about the possibility of anything positive emerging from UN deliberations.

CONCLUSIONS AND RECOMMENDATIONS

All of the options have serious disadvantages. The UN remains a forum for third world pressure on the superpowers, and in the current context particularly on the United States, to quicken the pace of the arms control process. The mood in the US and USSR is not right for more than very limited superpower solidarity, and the alliance is not ready for a common alignment on some of the issues that will be raised on a regular basis, yet the stakes are too high for the United States to stand by as a passive but sympathetic bystander. At the same time, the US might lose any effort to engage in Cold War confrontation. The result is that the US needs something more than a position of passivity and something less than a policy of active engagement. In other words, the US must set a few limited goals and actively pursue them.

NON-PROLIFERATION

The centerpiece of the US posture should be an effort to shore up the non-proliferation regime. Here the Reagan Administration has a possible advantage in its preference for START, which, whatever its complications in terms of negotiations with the Soviets, does have this great political benefit with the non-nuclear states: it seems much more consistent with the terms of the NPT than SALT. In this connection, it is worth noting that while many key third world delegates were unenthusiastic about SALT I, they were attracted to the Carter Administration's deep-cuts proposal of March 1977. With a less confrontational presentation, the President might have received a better UN reaction to the mention of START in his SSOD—II speech. However this may be, given third world enthusiasm for a deep-cuts approach, the US should continue to stress the extent to which START can be a radical departure in the arms race, designed to deal with the problems of vertical proliferation and superpower compliance with the provisions of the NPT.

The CTB has become the key symbolic test of the willingness of the superpowers to live up to their NPT obligations. Unfortunately the Reagan Administration has been hesitant to move forward on this issue. In July 1982 the Administration reportedly decided to postpone a resumption of the trilateral negotiations with the United Kingdom and Soviet Union pending a review of the verification possibilities, especially relating to low-yield explosions. Similarly, the Administration has decided not to seek Senate ratification of the Threshold Test Ban Treaty negotiated by President Nixon and of the Treaty on Peaceful Nuclear Explosions negotiated by President

Ford pending a review of their verification provisions. Though these two treaties were not popular with the developing countries, their ratification would be a step forward given the current frigid political climate. Once the current review is completed, the Reagan Administration could also announce the formation of a study group under orders to determine the extent to which a lower threshold could be quickly and safely negotiated. These modest steps would help regain some of the US credibility lost on this issue by the Carter and Reagan Administrations.

Finally, the Administration could look more creatively at the issue of negative security assurances, despite its opposition to a blanket no-first-use pledge. It could confirm the pledge of the Carter Administration at SSOD–I that it is the policy of the United States that it "will not use nuclear weapons against any non-nuclear-weapons state party to the NPT or any comparable internationally binding commitment not to acquire nuclear explosive devices, except in the case of an attack on the United States, its territories or armed forces, or its allies, by such a state allied to a nuclear-weapons state or associated with a nuclear-weapons state in carrying out or sustaining the attack."[6] There is, in fact, an opportunity here to make a modest step forward. At SSOD–I France alone among the nuclear powers refused to make a statement on negative security guarantees. That refusal blocked the possibility of giving the statements made at the session greater legal force by enshrining them in a Security Council resolution which noted with approval the pledges by the major nuclear powers.

At SSOD–II French Foreign Minister Claude Cheysson made the following statement, which opens the door to such negotiations within the Security Council:

[France] states that it will not use nuclear arms against a State that does not have them and that has pledged not to seek them, except if an act of aggression is carried out in association or alliance with a nuclear weapon State against France or against a State with which France has a security commitment. In thus moving closer to the kind of guarantee already made by others France hopes to facilitate the drafting of a Security Council resolution on this issue.[7]

No doubt the negotiations would be difficult because the Soviets might seek endorsement by others of its broader and less conditional pledge made in a unilateral statement at SSOD–II.[8] The US could determine through private soundings whether, in the interest of a modest step to shore up the NPT regime, the Soviet would eschew such a tactic.

Another possible initiative to shore up the non-proliferation regime would be a safeguard tax on nuclear exports, provided that the proceeds are used to develop a more adequate safeguards system under the IAEA. The Soviets have long urged that the US work with the USSR in strengthening the IAEA, yet the developing countries have objected to increases in the safeguard budget at the expense of other IAEA programs. A tax as suggested might resolve these conflicting pressures.

CONVENTIONAL ARMS

Notwithstanding the traditional UN preference for collective security rather than disarmament, a point already discussed, it is a scandal that the United Nations remains unable to publish even the statistical information offered by the League of Nations in the field of arms transfers. Since it seems unlikely that an effort to persuade the UN members to follow the League's lead in this field will succeed even today, the US could announce that henceforth it will provide this information to the membership in the form of an annual report to the Secretary General, which the United States will request be distributed to all members as a document of the Council.

VERIFICATION

At the first SSOD the French floated a proposal to create an International Satellite Monitoring Agency. The United States was unremittingly hostile for reasons that were never clear; concern appeared to center on a fear that if a rival center of information about arms control verification were to be created, experts at that center might challenge future American assertions that certain events constituting violation of a treaty had taken place.

The concern is not trivial because interpretation of satellite data is a difficult art. Nonetheless, the US ought to take a broader view of this issue. Other states will enter the space age. It may then be in US interests to minimize the number of states claiming to have the capacity to monitor military movements or at least to have a center that meets certain standards sufficient to maintain its credibility.

The Reagan Administration has argued that there must be a much greater degree of transparency if future arms control agreements are to be concluded. The President's SSOD–II speech underscored this point. Consistent with the US insistence on openness should be another look at the French proposal. On the face of it, the proposal is one that should alarm the Soviets more than Americans.

PRESIDENTIAL INVOLVEMENT

The Reagan Administration, in having the President address SSOD–II, did not make the mistake of the Carter Administration. The President recognized that it was a unique occasion for him to talk to the American people as well as to the outside world.

But presidential involvement should not require an SSOD. The democratization of the arms control dialogue, already discussed, will require presidential involvement on a more regular basis if this administration, or any future administration, wants to maintain some control over the direction in which public opinion moves on key arms control issues. With this point in mind, the administration could explore the following possibilities: an annual presentation by the president himself of the US view of the state of the world to a meeting of the UN Security Council to which heads of state would be invited; an annual address to the UN General Assembly; presentations of the initial US position at the beginning of major arms control negotiations. The point in each case would be to demonstrate at the highest level that the US is a serious partner in the arms control process.

It is easy to be cynical about arms control in any forum within one's own government, in bilateral channels, or in multilateral forums. The issues are intractable, the fears genuine, the conflict of interests severe, and the process endless. At the same time, there is one important reason why all governments, and particularly the

US government, must keep trying to make progress even under the most adverse circumstances. A world of many nuclear powers would not only radically reduce the power position of the United States itself, but it would also be a highly unstable world. The existing non-proliferation regime, President Reagan correctly stated at the SSOD–II, serves the interests of the international community. It is vital that the US seize every opportunity to protect and strengthen that regime. The US approach to multilateral arms control can be an important determinant in whether that regime continues to endure or collapses.

NOTES

1. Lincoln P. Bloomfield and Harlan Cleveland, *Disarmament and the United Nations: Strategy for the US*, Policy Paper, Aspen Institute for Humanistic Studies, Program in International Affairs, 1978, p. 12.

2. US Arms Control and Disarmament Agency, *World Military Expenditures and Arms Transfers: 1970–1979* (Washington, D.C.: US GPO, March, 1982), pp. 85 and 88. For wide-ranging discussions of conventional arms limitations, see Edward C. Luck's chapter in this volume and the Report of the UNA-USA National Policy Panel on Conventional Arms Control, *Controlling the Conventional Arms Race* (New York: UNA-USA, 1976).

3. UN Department of Public Information, "Final Document: Special Session of the General Assembly on Disarmament," (New York: UN, 1981), para. 22, p. 7.

4. US President Ronald Reagan's speech on 17 June 1982 at SSOD–II. See Document of the UNGA, A/S–12/PV. 16.

5. Some of the prominent proposals from France at SSOD-I in 1978 related to: 1. establishment of an International Satellite Monitoring Agency; 2. establishment of an International Institute for Research on Disarmament; and 3. establishment of an International Disarmament Fund for Development.

6. Former US Secretary of State Cyrus Vance's statement, 12 June 1978. Also see Document of the Ad Hoc Committee of SSOD–I (1978), A/S–10/AC.1/30, p. 1.

7. French Foreign Minister Claude Cheysson's speech on 11 June 1982 at SSOD–II. See Document of the UNGA, A/S–12/PV. 9, p. 69.

8. Soviet Foreign Minister Andrei Gromyko's speech on 15 June 1982 at SSOD-II. See Document of the UNGA, A/S–12/PV. 12.

II. THE INTERNATIONAL POLITICAL CONTEXT

This section describes and analyzes the international political context, which largely defines what can and cannot be accomplished through multilateralism. It could plausibly be argued that East-West control progress has been determined more by political conditions than technical or military factors. In the multilateral arena, however, there is no doubt that arms control has predominately been a political enterprise, with technical issues usually relegated to secondary consideration. If the strategies outlined in Section I are to succeed, they must be tailored to meet, and if possible to shape, the international political context.

Multilateral politics are extraordinarily complex, since they meld East-West, North-South, regional, and intra-alliance relationships. The three chapters that follow do not attempt to address the policies of all relevant actors and further research is needed on the positions of individual countries, such as China, which have participated actively in global debates since 1979. They do analyze, however, the three fundamental groups with which US policies must interact: allies in Western Europe and Japan, the Soviet Union (its allies form the only consistent voting bloc in global forums), and the nonaligned states.

In the first chapter, Gregory F. Treverton assesses the reasons for continuing differences in perspectives between the US and its closest allies in Western Europe and Japan. Addressing the continuum of negotiations ranging from regional to functional to global forums, he concludes that the degree of allied unity or diversity varies according to the nature of the subject and the forum. Michael Nacht finds little reason for optimism based on his analysis of Soviet motivations and objectives in multilateral arms control. While Soviet diplomatic methods have matured and there have been a number of constructive multilateral agreements, prospects in the foreseeable future are uncertain despite the change of leadership in Moscow. In his chapter on non-aligned attitudes, George Quester demonstrates that it is impossible to generalize about non-aligned policies and interests, which vary from one subgroup to another. He emphasizes the tactical nature of non-aligned rhetoric on disarmament, which should be differentiated from the hard-headed and sophisticated security and political objectives that underlie the rhetoric.

MANAGING THE ALLIANCE POLITICS OF MULTILATERAL ARMS CONTROL

GREGORY F. TREVERTON

Makers of US foreign and security policy rarely have seen multilateral approaches to arms control as central to national security interests. Thus they have not been major issues in dealings with Western Europe or Japan. For their part, American allies have laid somewhat more emphasis on the political, if not the security, aspects of multilateral arms control. This chapter looks both at the broad global forums, such as those under UN auspices, and at the more restricted multilateral gatherings, such as the Mutual and Balanced Force Reduction (MBFR) talks in Vienna or the military aspects of the Conference on Security and Cooperation in Europe (CSCE) which have, from time to time at least, been more central to American foreign policy and to US relations with allies. The analysis is necessarily speculative and conceptual; the more restricted multilateral discussions are few in number, and while the record of the global forums is huge, it is not easy to interpret the interests that lie behind the rhetoric.

WHY MULTILATERAL NEGOTIATIONS?

Analytically, the size of arms control negotiations ought to turn on (a) how many nations must take action to produce an outcome, and (b) how many nations (or, conceivably, non-state actors) have a stake in that outcome. Logically, all (a) states will also be (b) states, but the converse is not true. Many states that regard themselves as having a stake in the outcome may be neither necessary to produce it nor even much able to affect its shape; indeed, most members of the United Nations are in that category. That raises the obvious tension between restricting negotiations to the (a) states, or even a subset thereof, thus making the actual process of negotiations easier and the chances of success higher, on the one hand; and, on the other, expanding negotiations in recognition of mankind's wider stakes in the venture.

As a result, negotiations range across a continuum. The different levels of discussion are a function both of the number of participants and, clearly related to size, the purpose of the discussion. At one end of the continuum are the universal gatherings, generally in or around the UN, such as the Special Sessions on Disarmament (SSOD). These serve as expressions of general sentiment, as ways of establishing a political agenda, and of exerting moral and political pressure. Seldom is there any expectation that they will themselves produce results affecting military preparations, forces or deployments of any nation, although they do occasionally bless such results negotiated elsewhere.

A middle level of forum would comprise, among others, the International Fuel Cycle Evaluation (INFCE) of the late 1970s, the Committee on Disarmament (CD) and the military aspects of CSCE. Obviously, discussions at this level vary considerably, performing different functions in different mixes. But one strong thread running through them is analyzing specific issues. That was explicitly the purpose of INFCE; it is also a central task of the CD through its working groups on chemical weapons, CTB verification and radiological weapons. As would be expected, these middle negotiations also perform some functions that move along the continuum in both directions, fulfilling an agenda-setting purpose in one direction and aiming for limited agreements with operational consequences in the other.

At the other end of the continuum are negotiations restricted to only those states whose military forces or efforts would be directly affected by the negotiating outcome. Such an outcome is the explicit purpose; here the prototype is SALT or START, but the category also includes restricted multilateral negotiations like MBFR. Note that, quite apart from larger human concerns, the outcomes even of very restricted negotiations can have strong indirect effects on the military deployments of non-participating states. For example, the Anti-Ballistic Missile (ABM) treaty signed by the United

States and the Soviet Union in 1972 had the fortuitous side effect for Britain, France and China of guaranteeing that their small nuclear forces would be able to penetrate to Soviet cities.

The current Geneva talks between the United States and the Soviet Union over long-range theater or intermediate nuclear forces (LRTNF or INF) are an even starker case in point. Only the United States and the Soviet Union are at the table, but the Western interests represented by the US also comprise nuclear forces held by West European NATO members under "dual-key" arrangements, forces that are likely to be explicitly on the table in Geneva, as well as British and French independent nuclear forces, which will be indirectly a subject of the negotiations. There are also the broader concerns of both East and West Europeans who share a neighborhood with the nuclear forces being discussed.

From the perspective of relations between the US and its allies, the different levels of negotiations have different implications. Given the circumstances of the universal negotiations, all participants, including the United States and its allies, have considerable incentive to indulge in grand statements of grand objectives. Little is at stake save rhetoric. That fact, however, suggests two rather different prospects for unity among the allies. Most of the time the US and its allies should not have much difficulty making common front. Since concrete interests are seldom at stake, inter-allied unity should be perceived by all the allies to be more important than anything else, even if unity is itself not all that important. When unity should matter more—for example, when proposals in universal gatherings run against, even in rhetoric, elements of NATO doctrine—it should be easier to achieve.

At the margins, however, American allies will be tempted by what economists call "free riding." If only rhetoric is at stake and if the United States can be counted upon, as the major partner in the alliance, to protect any concrete stakes that are at play, they will have incentive and opportunity to break ranks with the United States, taking more "progressive" positions for the benefit of third world galleries or domestic constituencies. In other manifestations, "free riding" suggests why it is rational, if frustrating for Americans, for European NATO members to spend lower portions of their GNP on defense than does the United States.[1] The smaller they are, the more they know that any increase in their defense spending will only marginally increase the amount of collective defense they enjoy through the Alliance; for decreases, the logic is the same in reverse, hence the incentive to spend less. More apt for the purposes of this analysis, free riding suggests why it is both cheap and tempting for the Europeans to take positions more supportive of the Palestine Liberation Organization (PLO) than can the United States; they may reap gains in the Arab world for doing so, and they can in any case be sure that basic Israeli security, an interest they share, will be safeguarded by the United States.

Three additional comments on the logic of free riding are important. First, the smaller the ally, the greater the temptation to free riding, again recognizing that any temptation in that direction will be small. Why that is so is suggested by an extension of the defense spending example: the smaller the ally, the less significant a break in alliance unity a deviation by it is; thus it can enjoy whatever domestic or international gain its different position gives it, with only marginal cost to alliance unity. Second is the obverse commentary: only in bizarre circumstances can the United States free ride. From the perspective of the alliance it is so large that it must calculate that it will bear the consequences of its action. If it seeks to jump "ahead" of its allies, that will become the position of the alliance, for good or ill. (Perversely, free riding only arises for the US in the unusual circumstance that it and the Soviet Union share a security interest—such as maintaining a duopoly in satellite verification. Then the United States might, analytically, be tempted to support proposals for an international satellite agency if it could be sure the Soviet Union would oppose them.)

Finally, free riding is an analytic construct. It suggests how states may have their cake and eat it too. It does not settle the issue of why they act as they do. In particular, to talk of free riding by US allies in multilateral arms control is not necessarily to demean their motives. It may be, for example, that domestic political concerns are important in shaping particular approaches by the allies; in that case, free riding only suggests why it may be easier for those considerations to influence policy by comparison to more general national security concerns. More important, it may be that what can be interpreted in this analysis—and frequently strikes Americans—

as free riding is not that at all. It may be simply a different opinion; Europeans or Japanese may hold their view not because the United States does not and cannot—the logic of free riding—but simply because they believe it is right and wish the United States shared that view. When the United States is isolated from its allies, it may be because it has chosen an extreme position, not because they are free riding.

The incentives in more restricted multilateral negotiations should be rather different. To the extent that the military forces of American allies are on the table and to the extent that outcomes will affect those forces or important political interests attached to them, the allies will have an incentive to take positions that reflect real, not just rhetorical, interests. That the West Germans have been so reluctant in MBFR to assent to any arrangement that would appear to constitute a "special" zone on German soil is hardly an accident; real interests are at play.

As a general matter, we would expect Western Europeans or Japanese to differ from the United States in multilateral negotiations the more: (a) real and different their interests are from those of the United States; and (b) the negotiations will affect those interests. Those conditions state no more than the obvious. These truisms are, however, more complicated than they seem because interests at play in negotiations differ in both *kind* and *intensity*. Political interests are involved as well as narrower military concerns; indeed, universal negotiations may touch only general political interests— in being seen to hold particular principles or to be sympathetic to "third world" concerns—and those interests are in most cases weak, even if the subjects being discussed in those arenas are critical. By contrast, the West German concern about a special security zone on German territory invokes both important military and political interests. Americans and their allies may differ over what sort of interests are involved. That is true even in negotiations as important as those on intermediate nuclear forces (INF), a point developed below.

Finally, the type of negotiation will affect how differences among the allies play out, how visible they are, and what are their consequences. In universal forums, positions taken by allies that differ from those of the United States will be relatively visible—votes recorded and speeches given—but not too important. Even if the allies could be fairly described as free riding, that would not be too expensive for the United States. The votes and speeches are soon forgotten, and (especially given the general American disdain for the UN and its kin) the principal cost may be a small accretion to the public perception that the allies are unreliable. By contrast, European-American differences during SALT II, a negotiation that was crucial to both sides of the Atlantic even if only the US negotiated, led to intense consultations and no little transatlantic acrimony, much of it spilling into print.

In yet a third case, MBFR, maintaining NATO unity is itself a crucial goal of the negotiations; it could hardly be otherwise in negotiations conducted between alliances. For all the participating Western powers the imperative of unity outweighs desires for substantive movement, a calculation embodied in the principle of consensus: hence differences of view lead to immobilism.

In still another case, the European-American discussions of restraining arms transfers conducted during the Carter Administration—a variant of the middle-level forum, one conducted largely among the Western powers—differences of view led to both acrimony and immobilism. That experience is suggestive, analytically, of the middle-level forums dominated by analysis of specific issues. US allies may be less reluctant to articulate different positions in these forums, for three reasons: they often touch economic stakes, where differences of interest are regarded as more normal and less dangerous; it may be easier to articulate differences in discussions labelled "technical;" and there may be no "East" to serve as an incentive for Western unity.

So much for analytics. Does recent experience suggest that its insights may not be too far from the mark? The next section surveys, in a conjectural way, the evidence from more restricted multilateral negotiations; the following section looks at universal forums.

MORE RESTRICTED MULTILATERAL TALKS

MBFR. The Mutual and Balanced Force Reduction Talks (MBFR) are the most explicitly multilateral of the negotiations aiming at a specific agreement. From the perspective of the United States and its European allies, the original purpose of the negotiations was overtly political: to defuse pressure in the American Congress for reductions in American forces stationed in Europe. At the same time, the issues that have been the subject of negotiation are substantively important force deployments on the central front. The negotiations comprise a number of interesting features.[2] They are explicitly bloc-to-bloc talks, thus requiring the United States and its allies to come to a common negotiating position on every issue. Given NATO's practice of decision by consensus, that makes for ponderous decision making. The form of the negotiations has meant, however, that they are as much about maintaining Western unity as anything else. That largely procedural goal outranks substance, and the record of sustaining that unity through nearly a decade of negotiations is impressive.

Differences have also been muted because as time has worn on, few people, in the West or elsewhere in the world, have known or cared much about MBFR. The differences that have appeared within the Western group have been rather straightforward reflections of different political and military stakes. Early on, while agreeing to the primary need to prevent American troop withdrawals from Europe, the Europeans were anxious that any actual program of reductions also include them.[3] Throughout, the Germans have been sensitive to the creation of any special zone on German territory, a worry that has inhibited Western approaches even on seemingly innocent issues, like confidence-building measures (CBMs). As MBFR has waxed and waned, the flank countries excluded from the negotiations have expressed contradictory concerns: that the process of negotiations on the central front would attract attention—and more defense spending—there and that any negotiated stabilization on the central front might lead to an increase in competition on the flanks.[4]

Interestingly, the difference in perspective—technical versus political—that so often divides European and American perspectives on arms control has not been a central feature of MBFR. The reason is the role of the Federal Republic. To be sure, Chancellor Schmidt often talked of the political need for movement in the talks, but beneath this rhetoric the Germans have been more cautious than the Americans, for a number of reasons. Most obvious, the military interests of the Federal Republic are real. Incaution would open the government to opposition taunts that it was playing politics with German security. Because conventional forces are less emotive than nuclear ones (even if more expensive), there has been less political pressure in Germany to reduce them.

CSCE. The experience of MBFR's kin, the military aspects of the Conference on Security and Cooperation in Europe (CSCE), has been similar. The military aspects have been second-order business, and the size of the negotiations—along with the principle of consensus—has made it unlikely that results would much affect actual military practices.[5] Those factors, plus the processes of consultation (first the Europeans within the EEC, and then NATO-wide consultations including France and the North Americans within NATO), have made for considerable unity. Differences in emphasis have been predictable: the Italians and others on the flanks were, for example, more tempted by proposals to extend CBMs to the flanks.

At the same time, there have been hints of both free riding and of the greater, or different, European interest in the political factors at play. For example, eager to establish their credentials as once again interested in arms control, the French pushed for a European Disarmament Conference, to be spun out of the CSCE. They were free riding to the extent that the United States (and other NATO states) could be counted on to oppose the idea or make sure that it took a form congenial to Western interests. (The West Germans were tempted by the idea for the same reason that they liked CSCE CBMs: it would include Soviet territory in Europe, lessening the asymmetry of MBFR, which included all of Germany and none of the Soviet Union.) There has also been evidence of European political interests somewhat at variance from American: the Europeans not only have urged less confrontation with the Soviet Union over human rights, but also have shown greater interest in movement on the military aspects as well.

INF. It is paradoxical to include in this chapter what is in form a bilateral Soviet-American negotiation. But the Intermediate Nuclear Forces (INF) talks are in fact, if not in form, multilateral from the perspective of the United States and its allies. They are also serious business, and thus a test of transatlantic cohesion when outcomes really matter.[6] To exclude them would be to narrow our vision of "multilateral" negotiations.

The Geneva talks represent an innovation in processes of interallied consultation. America's allies are not at the table, but their interests—and some of their forces—are, directly or indirectly. NATO's Special Consultative Group (SCG) reflects that state of affairs: it operates not on the basis of consensus, as in the case of MBFR, but rather on the principle of American "leadership."[7] As a practical matter, the Europeans have what amounts to a veto over American negotiating positions, at least if they are themselves united. Thus far the process has worked reasonably well. Europeans have influence to match their interests but are spared the formal responsibilities that would make for difficult choices given their own internal policies; they can prod their ally first, then carp later. Whether the process eventually will come to accentuate differences across the Atlantic remains to be seen.

The most important transatlantic difference at play runs to the conception of the negotiations, a difference that is as frequently observed as it is infrequently analyzed. For Americans, the negotiations are primarily technical; hence outcomes must be justified in terms of their effects on military balances. Europeans are hardly ignorant of the military aspects; after all, those Soviet SS-20s are meant for *them*. But for them the face of the issue is preeminently political, in two senses.[8] Most pressing is the need to manage their domestic politics surrounding the prospect of actually deploying the American cruise and Pershing II missiles in Europe. That makes a serious effort in the INF talks imperative for the Federal Republic but important even for Britain.

More generally, Europeans, particularly Germans, are bound to see the negotiations as preeminently political in another sense. The precise configurations of weapons that result from negotiations will be less important than what the process signals about political intentions, both East and West. Hence the willingness of the Carter Administration to constrain cruise missiles in the SALT II protocol disturbed Europeans because it suggested that the United States was prepared to separate Europe's security from its own, even if it could be shown that those constraints would have had little or no practical effect. NATO could not have deployed cruise missiles before the end of the protocol in any case, so no weapons deployments or plans actually would have been changed. Similarly, the process of the INF negotiations will be seen by Europeans as important, and they will be less worried than Americans (though not unconcerned) about the initial imbalance in the Soviet favor, the difficulties of counting and verification, and so on.

That raises the prospect of serious transatlantic strain in the INF talks. What Americans see as a fig leaf to cover the deployment of the 572 new missiles, Europeans probably come closer to regarding finally as a means of avoiding those deployments. At a minimum, Europeans will be tempted to take seriously, or even to agree to, Soviet negotiating offers that will be unappealing to Americans in technical terms. Suppose, for example, that in a year the Soviets offered to reduce their SS-20s by 20 percent if NATO did not deploy any of the 572 missiles. That would leave the Soviet Union with about the 250 SS-20s that many Western analysts estimated was the original target for the program, and NATO would have no new missiles. Europeans might be tempted by such a deal; Americans would not. The prospects for serious strain across the Atlantic, rooted in differing conceptions of the negotiations, are real and serious.

INF offers an interesting test of Japanese interests in arms control. So far the Japanese have been virtually silent on the INF score, at least in public. Yet their recent emphasis on the growing SS-20 and other nuclear threats to them suggests that they would be discomforted by any NATO approach that focused exclusively on Soviet missiles within range of Europe, especially if that seemed to provide an incentive for the Soviets to move missiles eastward.

In his speech to the 1982 SSOD, Japanese Prime Minister Zenko Suzuki expressed that concern directly, urging that "the Soviet Union abolish all ground-launched intermediate-range nuclear missiles *throughout its territory* and that the United States, in response, not deploy its planned new missiles in Europe, thereby greatly enhancing the security not only of Europe but also of Asia. . . ."[9]

NON-PROLIFERATION AND ARMS TRANSFERS

The inclusion of non-proliferation and arms transfers is also paradoxical. In form they are universal: more than 100 states are adherents to the Non-Proliferation Treaty (NPT), and at least as many nations have an interest in international arms transfers. In fact, again, much of the real action takes place in more restricted groupings. Moreover, in both cases much of the negotiation has been explicitly *among* the United States and its allies, rather than between them and the East.

That has made for differences of view related closely to obvious interests. In the larger, more universal forums at which non-proliferation and arms transfers have been discussed, those differences have been muted somewhat. But even there the differences have been apparent: France refused to sign the NPT, Britain qualified as a nuclear-weapons state, and for the Federal Republic the decision, not easy, ratified a course the country intended to take in any event.

Differences of view have been more specific, and probably sharper, when the issues have been taken up in smaller discussions among the United States and its allies. Those discussions have been more operational, and hence have raised the prospect of taking actions affecting real interests. Moreover, it does appear that American allies may be less reluctant to differ with the United States in more restricted discussions, away from the glare of international publicity and lacking the presence of "the East" as a rallying point for Western unity.

When the Carter Administration sought the agreement of its allies in restraining arms transfers, they saw the issue explicitly in economic terms. Britain and France, in particular, remain relatively more dependent on arms exports than does the United States. While their arms exports have constituted smaller fractions of total exports than has been the case for the United States, they are much more needful of exports to support longer production runs than domestic needs would justify. Those longer runs in turn are necessary to lower unit costs and to sustain research and development establishments.[10] To those two countries in particular, the Carter Administration's commitments to reduce its own sales and to buy more European weaponry were unconvincing. They countered that they were unwilling to talk about restraint until the Soviet Union, the world's second-largest exporter, was brought into the discussions. The American effort to do so foundered because Soviet notions of how to proceed were different, because Moscow sought to turn the discussions to American arms sales to key third world allies, and because the American administration itself was divided over the utility of the enterprise.

Arms transfers was a "West-West" discussion because the Soviet Union could not be brought in; much of the non-proliferation discussion has been West-West because the Soviet Union has been generally on the side of the non-proliferation angels. The Western nations (plus the Soviet Union) were able to agree on guidelines for nuclear exports in the forum of the London Suppliers' Group, but they have found it more difficult to move beyond those guidelines. When the Carter Administration moved, early in its tenure, to persuade the Federal Republic not to transfer to Brazil sensitive nuclear facilities (for enrichment and, especially, for reprocessing) under the nuclear agreement between the two, Bonn refused. It argued that nothing on the London Group list of proscribed items would be transferred, and that safeguards would be adequate. The Germans also tended to see the American initiative in economic terms: having failed to sell Brazil American nuclear reactors, the US was trying to wreck a good deal that West Germany had made.[11]

A similar European perception also ran through the International Fuel Cycle Evaluation (INFCE), another Carter initiative that came to an end in 1980. The initial thrust of the American approach was that breeder reactors were unnecessary in light of realistic projections of demand for nuclear power and were, to boot, dangerous in proliferation terms because of the weapons-grade plutonium they produce. To Europeans, France in particular, however, that looked like an attempt to depreciate a technology in which Europe led America.[12] It was also deeply rankling to the Japanese, for whom the injury seemed thrice compounded: the Carter policy appeared to ignore the needs of energy-poor Japan; it seemed unjustified in light of Japan's exemplary non-proliferation record; and it seemed to discriminate against Japan even by comparison to US agreements with Euratom.[13]

MORE UNIVERSAL FORUMS

Direct evidence bearing on the extent of transatlantic differences in the more universal arms control forums is hard to read. Many of these forums, like the UN Special Session, are not negotiations at all. The rhetoric is general and hortatory, more likely to blur than to reveal the hard edges of national interest, and the temptation to play to the gallery is particularly strong.

With these qualifications, the results of the second Special Session in 1982 were fairly predictable. By comparison to the first SSOD in 1978, American allies, including Japan, were less venturesome in making new proposals and more explicit about the growing Soviet military arsenal.[14] The broad outlines of their comments were fully consistent with American policy: strong support for President Reagan's initiatives in the INF and START negotiations, commitment to non-proliferation, reiteration of the importance of verifying any arms control agreements, and indication of the importance of conventional, as well as nuclear, arms control, including restraints on arms transfers.

The most noteworthy issue from the session was no-first-use (NFU) of nuclear weapons. The Soviet Union, which, in the past, has often urged a joint agreement with the US on NFU of nuclear weapons, declared at SSOD–II in June that it would not be the first to use nuclear weapons and called upon other nuclear-weapons states to accept a similar obligation.[15] This came in light of the suggestion by former American officials that NATO contemplate abandoning its own first use doctrine.[16] However, the possibility of first use remained official NATO doctrine, reinforced by understandable European caution about any change in nuclear arrangements. Moreover, the American administration was strongly opposed to dropping the first-use doctrine. For those reasons, it was predictable that the Europeans would not be tempted by the Soviet NFU proposal. Nor was Japan, given the implicit response to the Soviet nuclear threat that is inherent in the US-Japan defense treaty. Instead, several of the allies (France, Denmark) stressed the importance of regional arrangements, including nuclear-free zones agreed by local states. Others (Japan, Belgium) made general arguments about the need for "negative security guarantees:" guarantees to states that have renounced nuclear weapons that such weapons will not be used against them. Chancellor Schmidt of the Federal Republic sought to broaden the issue by noting that the UN Charter bans *any* use of force.

The NFU issue at the 1982 SSOD was an interesting contrast to the first Special Session in 1978. In preparing initiatives a year before that session, it was the United States that sought to frame an NFU pledge. The rub, of course, was NATO doctrine, and there were other uncomfortable cases, such as Israel, in which the US would find it difficult to rule out such a use. European NATO members and Japan (and Israel) could thus press those concerns on Washington, as the sustainer of the alliance, and be sure they would be heard. The resulting American statement was convoluted, sounding more like a promise of some first use than of none.[17] American allies could be confident that real interests they shared with the United States would be protected, even if the result was an initiative robbed of much of whatever political effect it might have had. Interestingly, at the 1982 Session France also sought to make an NFU pledge. Given its membership in NATO (even though it does not participate in the military command) and its other commitments, it confronted many of the same problems as had Washington five years earlier, and it ended with a pledge about as qualified.[18]

Most of the other differences between the US and its allies during the second SSOD reflected particular circumstances or interests, again predictable. In his speech, French Foreign Minister Claude Cheysson was at pains to explain why France cannot now take part in either the INF or the START talks, while Danish Prime Minister Anker Jorgensen outlined the special character of the existing "nuclear-free zone" in Denmark and Norway. Prime Minister Margaret Thatcher of Britain, in the concluding stages of a war in the Falklands, was perhaps more straightforward than President Reagan about the limitations of arms control and the fallacy of the proposition that weapons themselves are the cause of war.

There was more allied unity and less free riding at the second Special Session in 1982 than at the first in 1978. At the first session, for example, French President Giscard d'Estaing suggested an international agency for satellite verification.[19] That was widely scorned in Washington as an effort to break into what was still largely a Soviet-American duopoly of satellite reconnaissance. To the extent those American concerns were on the mark, the proposal was a straightforward attempt to reap a technological benefit. It was free riding to the extent that France counted on the United States (and probably the Soviet Union as well) to oppose the initiative—thus making France look all the better in the eyes of the third world—or to water it down to protect security interests that, after all, France shared. By the 1982 Session the French idea had entered the mainstream of the UN discussion, and at least three allies (Japan, Italy, and Belgium) supported it in one form or another.

A more extreme illustration of free riding from the 1978 SSOD was Canada. Prime Minister Trudeau called for the "suffocation" of the arms race through bans on nuclear tests, flight tests of strategic missiles, production of fissile material, and reductions in spending on new strategic weapons. At the same time he pledged that Canada would relinquish its nuclear role in NATO, thus becoming a non-nuclear state.[20] Both sets of actions were "free riding," but the latter was a particularly stark form, more than symbolism and thus especially disturbing. Obviously American nuclear guarantees to allies are not divisible, all the less so when the ally is an adjacent state, so allies will be tempted to have their cake and eat it, too: sustaining their nuclear protection but not sullying their hands with a role in its provision, the essence of free riding. Mr. Trudeau's speech to the 1982 Session was, however, more moderate in tone. He did not disclaim the "suffocation" program but argued that it was never meant to be applied unilaterally, nor was it inconsistent with the stabilization approach of the INF or START talks. His change in tone presumably reflected some combination of his sense of the changed East-West climate, a perception of Canada's isolation within the Alliance on those issues and worries about his relations with the Reagan Administration.

As additional evidence from universal forums, a quick survey of recorded General Assembly votes on arms control issues provides additional examples of free riding but also gives indications of circumstances in which differences between the United States and its allies are more likely.[21] As expected, most of the time the United States and most of its allies vote the same way. Also as predicted, in a small but significant number of cases, the United States stands nearly alone in its vote. These include votes on: a cessation of nuclear tests (against, with Britain); forbidding nuclear and related cooperation with South Africa (against, with France, Israel, and

Britain); condemning the Israeli attack on the Iraqi reactor (against, with Israel); refraining from producing chemical weapons pending negotiated results (against, alone); and condemning the Israeli raid and calling upon Israel to renounce nuclear weapons (against, with Israel). This pattern is noteworthy in several respects. First, most of the cases involved Israel and its position in the Middle East, an issue on which differences between the United States and its allies run well beyond arms control. In cases that did not involve Israel, the United States was joined by its allies only if they had specific interests at play. Second, in every case in which the United States stood nearly alone in voting no, most of its allies abstained. Japan was no different in that regard from the European states.

In a number of other cases, the United States voted no and was joined by most of its allies. These included votes on: a new nuclear disarmament initiative within the CD, including consideration of stopping development and deployment of new types of weapons; prohibiting the neutron weapon; prohibiting stationing of nuclear weapons in states where none are at present (all allies save Greece voted no, and Greece abstained); and condemning any doctrine of the first use of nuclear weapons (all save Greece voted no). Again, Japan's voting pattern was no different from the European states. What is striking, but hardly surprising, about these cases is that inter-allied unity was strongest when resolutions went explicitly against NATO strategy (and the logic of the US-Japan mutual security treaty) or against weapons options the US and its allies might still have wished to retain.

In a larger number of cases, the United States abstained rather than vote against particular resolutions. Again, most of the time it was joined by most of its allies. However, in abstaining, the United States presumably was taking a stand in principle, but a fairly weak one. Hence it would come as little surprise if allies felt freer to break ranks with the United States, and that in fact occurred. Those breaking rank were not the central members of the alliance, but rather, as the logic of the free riding would suggest, the smaller allies, especially those with special traditions and constituencies (the Nordics plus Iceland) or those with particular political problems (Greece and Turkey). Japan, for example, voted with the United States in these cases more often than those countries.

Beyond these few indications, recent experience says relatively little about Japan's interests in multilateral arms control. Japanese public opinion paid scant attention to the "old" agenda of nuclear arms control between the superpowers.[22] The nation's preoccupations were internal and economic, and the postwar anti-military feeling reinforced the sense that any security threat to Japan was far away. Those attitudes have changed only slowly and partially. Four events were important in that change. The 1975 debate over the Non-Proliferation Treaty (NPT) was a bridge between the "old" agenda and newer concerns; it raised more explicitly than before the issue of Japan's security and the role of nuclear weapons in it. The Soviet military build-up in Asia and on the Japanese-claimed islands gradually brought home that the threat was perhaps not so abstract after all. American Defense Secretary James Schlesinger's suggestion in 1975 that nuclear weapons might be used in Korea, coupled with the subsequent decision by the Carter Administration to reduce American ground forces in Korea, added urgency to the Japanese security debate and indicated that Japan might have a concrete interest in non-proliferation. Finally, the row with the Carter Administration over breeder reactors suggested that arms control could affect specific Japanese interests beyond military defense.

Still, Japan's interests in multilateral arms control seem largely those of principle and rhetoric. That will be the case unless a few specific interests come to be at play: in INF if NATO appears willing to diminish the Soviet nuclear threat to Europe by forcing Soviet systems eastward; in non-proliferation if the status of Korea or Japan's energy security seem at issue. Only then will Japan become involved in more restricted multilateral forums. In more universal gatherings, it will continue to behave much like the Europeans: occasionally playing to third world galleries, especially on issues that relate to larger differences of view with the United States (the Middle East), but closing ranks when proposals bear on the requisites of the US-Japan treaty.

IMPLICATIONS FOR UNITED STATES POLICY

This review of recent cases, both in universal and in more restricted multilateral forums, suggests broad lessons familiar to the management of American relations with allies: to be attentive to differences among types of negotiations labelled "multilateral," to ask how important unity is in different cases, and to limit demands made on the domestic politics of allied countries. Some degree of free riding is inevitable, especially in universal forums, but also in more restricted gatherings. The paradox, and from the American perspective, the frustration, is that most efforts to prevent free riding amount to cutting off one's nose to spite the face. The collective good provided by current security arrangements is in the United States interest. If the United States, as the dominant partner, provides less of that good simply because its smaller partners do, there will be less security and the United States will suffer accordingly. That fact is independent of what the smaller partners do. Thus, American threats to withdraw nuclear protection from Europe, or to withdraw American forces, are not very credible. They certainly are not very credible in response to deviations by allies on secondary issues, which include most of those under consideration in multilateral arms control.

In most of the universal arms control forums most of the time, complete unity among the United States and its allies in Europe and Japan will not be all that important. Often those differences that arise will be related to issues where broader disagreements exist, such as the Middle East. In those cases, it hardly makes sense to put much pressure on the allies or to pay much to bring them into line. When proposals in universal forums bear directly on NATO strategy or alliance interests and thus make unity more important— no-first-use, for example—unity should be easier to achieve.

If the United States sought dramatic initiatives for universal gatherings like the Special Sessions, the goal of allied unity would become a constraint on American action, and the United States would have to ask how much it valued unity. Most dramatic initiatives— NFU, nuclear-free zones, proposals to constrain arms transfers— raise concerns in American allies (or virtual allies like Israel). They could be expected to press those concerns on the United States and would be likely to succeed, for in the end the United States values allied unity more than a dramatic proposal for a Special Session. That has been clear in the last two SSODs. The result in 1978 was the "some" first use pledge, probably worth doing but hardly impressive either as arms control or as an appeal to the third world gallery. In 1982 the US opposed an NFU pledge for many reasons, but central among them was the reaction of the allies. Since the purpose of an NFU pledge in Europe would be to improve the climate for European support of NATO and its doctrine, such a pledge was hardly attractive if it appeared likely to have just the opposite effect, at least if presented as a dramatic US initiative. It appeared less likely to reassure Europeans than to make them jittery by suggesting that the United States was abandoning their defense.

Other initiatives could, if carefully crafted, be accepted by American allies. They probably could not, however, be made acceptable to the American government itself. That would be true for most proposals on arms transfers. A proposal that made responsibility for action commensurate with the size of transfers—thus putting most of the pressure on the United States and the Soviet Union—would not be easy for America's allies to criticize, even if Britain and France worried about the eventual impact of such measures given their disproportionate economic dependence on arms transfers. Yet it is hard to imagine such a proposal emerging from the bureaucratic machine in Washington. Similarly, US allies could not oppose, and many might welcome, American support for an international satellite verification agency, an area in which the United States retains a virtual monopoly on the technology. There, too, initiatives are unlikely for reasons less of allied interests than of American ones.

In the near term, the most pressing "multilateral" issues will be dealing with the implications for allies of bilateral arms control. Given European (and in a more muted way, Japanese) political interests in some movement in arms control, their immediate reaction to any American proposal for negotiation will be positive. That was the case with the Reagan Administration's "zero option" offer in INF and its "deep cuts" proposal for START. Yet over the longer run the allies, especially the Europeans, will react to how any particular initiative seems to affect their interests. That was clear in the instance of the SALT II negotiations. During 1977 and 1978 Europeans saw in American proposals for dealing with cruise missiles or with Backfire bombers a willingness to trade "European" interests for "American."

Similar strains could arise all too easily in START. This is not the place to catalogue them, but several examples will reinforce the point. Suppose, for instance, that the Soviet Union offered to make "deep cuts" in strategic systems the central objective of the negotiations, but only if NATO dropped its plan to deploy cruise and Pershing missiles in Western Europe. An American administration committed to deep cuts might be tempted to agree, but that would look to many in Western Europe like a particularly stark form of selling European interests for American interests.

More generally, the prospect of deep cuts in aggregate strategic launchers or warheads inevitably will make Europeans more attentive to the nuclear balance in Europe. President Reagan's Eureka College speech in May 1982 called for a limit of 5,000 on the land- and sea-based intercontinental ballistic missile warheads of the United States and the Soviet Union. In military terms, that would not solve the problem of the theoretical vulnerability of American land-based missiles to a Soviet first strike, and it might make it worse; thus American strategic analysts would remain concerned over that vulnerability, and their lack of confidence would reinforce European qualms over the reliability of the American nuclear guarantee to Europe. Also, modernization plans for French and British forces could give them over 500 warheads each within a decade; those increases by contrast to the prospect of "deep cuts" in Soviet and American forces would make it harder for Britain and France to resist Soviet pressure to take part in INF or START.

In the end, however, the European concern over deep cuts probably derives less from the principle or the military specifics than from a fear that to obtain Soviet agreement the United States would have to pay an unacceptable price in terms of systems of particular concern to Western Europe. Europeans would be more comfortable with a START approach that focused on stability—for instance, trying to reduce the prominence of land-based MIRVed ICBMs— than on deep cuts in numbers, again, however, with the residual concern over what the United States would have to pay to reach such an outcome.

The implications for the allies of the INF talks are even more direct. There, outcomes are politically charged and matter to NATO doctrine and cohesion. That makes sustaining the unity of the NATO allies an imperative; the political objective overshadows any more narrow military interests at play. Put bluntly, the cohesion of the Alliance matters much more than 572 new missiles. That suggests that the United States should press hard to move forward with deploying the missiles, in order to put pressure on the Soviets to negotiate seriously; in the end, however, the United States should be willing to fall back, even at the sacrifice of the 572 missiles, if continued pressure threatens to crack the Alliance.

The INF negotiations cannot, in that sense, be primarily about Western unity, as are the MBFR talks; not, at any rate, if the result is immobilism. INF talks that merely drag on and on will not serve even as a cover for the deployment of the 572 missiles. Such talks would end up producing serious strain between the United States and its European allies. Immobilism is acceptable in the case of MBFR for three reasons: MBFR long ago slipped to back pages of Western newspapers; conventional weapons are much less emotive than nuclear ones; and an agreement could be a source of strain within West German politics. It is not acceptable in INF.

The future of CSCE, and thus of any European disarmament conference, is hard to predict. In past review conferences, the United States and its allies have given precedence to maintaining their unity. That has probably been reasonable, especially in the security area given the limited possibilities for movement there. But there have been costs to that approach as well as gains: it has helped convert the process into a bloc-to-bloc discussion, thus making it harder for neutrals or for venturesome Warsaw Pact members to side with the Western nations.

With regard to arms control issues like non-proliferation and arms transfers, discussions that often are West-West in form as well as fact, the lessons of recent experience seem clearer. Some of the European states do regard themselves as having somewhat different interests from those of the United States. They tend to see those differences in economic terms. They may also be somewhat more willing to articulate differences in the absence of a negotiating opposite from the "East." In these circumstances, American pressure has not been strikingly effective, and a more patient approach is preferable. US pressures on allies in the arms transfer area during the Carter Administration failed, and the Reagan Administration has reversed course, making greater efforts to sell arms than to restrain their transfer. The more dangerous aspects of the German-Brazilian nuclear deal seem to have withered away of their own accord, at least for the time being, due to a combination of Brazilian economic problems, German reluctance, and technical problems. If anything, American pressure during 1977–78 probably served, by raising public attention, to commit Germany all the more to fulfilling its obligations under the deal.

For American policy, there is no alternative to patience and a sense of proportion. Most of the time, differences between the United States and its Western European and Japanese allies in universal arms control forums will not matter much. By the same token, American attempts to compel unity will be counterproductive, inducing the United States to take actions that are not in its interest, straining relations with allies for little benefit, or damaging the domestic climate in the United States for sensibly handling US relations with allies more generally. Allied unity with regard to negotiations that are in form bilateral—INF and START in particular—is much more critical. It will also be harder. The interests of both the United States and its allies are more important and more concrete. The US will be able to sustain tolerable unity but only if it gives its allies a measure of real influence in American decision-making; that, however, runs against ingrained habits in both the United States and its allies.

NOTES

1. See, for example, Mancur Olson, Jr. and Richard Zeckhauser, "An Economic Theory of Alliances," *The Review of Economics and Statistics*, XLVIII:3 (August, 1966), pp. 266–279.

2. For a general review of the MBFR negotiations, see John G. Keliher, *The Negotiations on Mutual and Balanced Force Reductions: The Search for Arms Control in Central Europe* (New York: Pergamon Press, 1980).

3. This point is made strongly by Christoph Bertram in *Mutual Force Reductions in Europe: Political Aspects*, Adelphi Paper No. 84 (London: International Institute for Strategic Studies [IISS], 1972).

4. See Jane M.O. Sharp, "MBFR as Arms Control?" in *Negotiating Security: An Arms Control Reader*, ed. by William H. Kincade and Jeffrey

D. Porro (Washington: The Carnegie Endowment for International Peace, 1979), p. 225.

5. For a general discussion of the military aspects of CSCE, see Stephen J. Flanagan, "The CSCE and the Development of European Security: A Post-Belgrade View," (unpublished paper, Center for Science and International Affairs, Harvard University, 1978).

6. There are many useful sources on INF. For a general background to the issues and the negotiations, see my study, *Nuclear Weapons in Europe,* Adelphi Paper No. 168 (London: IISS, 1981).

7. Christoph Bertram makes the argument that existing mechanisms are inadequate and that Europeans ought to participate more directly. See his article "The Implications of Theater Nuclear Weapons in Europe," *Foreign Affairs* 60:2 (Winter, 1981/82), p. 323.

8. For an interesting discussion of the West German perspective, see Phillip Windsor, *Germany and the Western Alliance: Lessons from the 1980 Crisis,* Adelphi Paper No. 170 (London: IISS, 1980).

9. For commentaries on the threat, see recent Japanese White Papers on Defense, and Prime Minister Zenko Suzuki's speech on 9 June 1982 at SSOD–II in Document of the UNGA, A/S–12/PV.5, p. 26.

10. On this point, see Lawrence G. Franko, "Restraining Arms Exports to the Third World: Will Europe Agree?" *Survival,* 21:1 (January/February, 1979), pp. 14–25.

11. See, for example, Karl Kaiser, "The Great Nuclear Debate: German-American Disagreements," *Foreign Policy,* 30 (Spring, 1978), pp. 83–110.

12. For a description of the process and results of INFCE, see *Strategic Survey 1980–1981* (London: IISS, 1981), pp. 111 ff.

13. See Ryukichi Imai, "Commentary: Changing Conceptions of Arms Control," in *U.S.-Japan Relations and the Security of East Asia: The Next Decade,* ed. by Franklin B. Weinstein (Boulder, Colorado: Westview Press), pp. 45 ff.

14. This conclusion and the references in the following paragraphs to the 1982 Special Session are based on the speeches at SSOD–II by: Japanese Prime Minister Zenko Suzuki, 9 June 1982; Canadian Prime Minister Pierre Trudeau, 18 June 1982; Belgian Prime Minister Leo Tindemans, 8 June 1982; Danish Prime Minister Anker Jorgensen, 4 June 1982; British Prime Minister Margaret Thatcher, 23 June 1982; West German Chancellor Helmut Schmidt, 14 June 1982 and French Foreign Minister Claude Cheysson, 11 June 1982.

15. Soviet Foreign Minister Andrei Gromyko's speech on 15 June 1982 at SSOD–II. See Document of the UNGA, A/S–12, pp. 22–23.

16. McGeorge Bundy, et. al., "Nuclear Weapons and the Atlantic Alliance," *Foreign Affairs,* 60:4 (Spring, 1982), pp. 753–768.

17. Former US Secretary of State Cyrus Vance's statement, 12 June 1978; also see Document of the Ad Hoc Committee of SSOD–I (1978), A/S–10/AC.1/30, p. 1.

18. In his speech on 11 June 1982, cited above, Foreign Minister Cheysson pledged that France would "not use nuclear arms against a State that does not have them and has pledged not to seek them, except if an act of aggression is carried out in association or alliance with a nuclear-weapon State against France or against a State with which France has a security commitment." See Document of the UNGA, A/S–12/PV.9, p. 69.

19. For former President Giscard d'Estaing's speech, see *Documents on Disarmament, 1978,* (Washington, DC: US Arms Control and Disarmament Agency, 1980), p. 337.

20. On the Trudeau proposals, see Ann Hallan Lakhdhir, "The UN Special Session: An Evaluation," in Kincade and Porro, op. cit. note 4, p. 249.

21. This survey is from *Resolutions and Decisions Adopted by the UN General Assembly During the First Part of its Thirty-Sixth Session (15 September to 18 December 1981)* (New York: UN Department of Public Information, 1982).

22. This discussion owes much to Imai, op. cit. note 13.

THE BAD, THE DULL, AND THE EMPTY: MULTILATERAL ARMS CONTROL AND THE SOVIET UNION

MICHAEL NACHT

To the serious as well as to the casual student of arms control, the behavior of the Soviet Union in multilateral arms control negotiations has been a subject of modest interest at best. For more than a decade, attention has been riveted instead on the bilateral strategic arms limitation talks (SALT), the agreements that emerged and that failed to emerge from the SALT process, and the future prospects of these negotiations reformulated by the Reagan Administration as START, the Strategic Arms Reduction Talks.

The flurry of negotiated arms control efforts initiated by the Carter Administration in 1977–78, including the conventional arms transfer talks as well as negotiations on naval limitations in the Indian Ocean and on the control of antisatellite weapons, were all conducted in the bilateral US–Soviet mode. The Carter nuclear nonproliferation policies, it is true, were a quintessentially multilateral enterprise that sought to retard worldwide the development of the liquid metal fast breeder reactor and to raise global consciousness to the dangerous connections between nuclear energy technologies and nuclear weapons proliferation. Nonetheless, in practice the policies focused a great deal on the alteration of US domestic energy policies and on affecting the posture particularly of France and Germany as suppliers of nuclear energy technology to developing countries. The Soviet Union, while compliant with the general orientation of these policies, did not loom especially large in their actual implementation. Those multilateral arms control forums that have engaged both Soviet and American representatives since the SALT I agreements entered into force in 1972, including the Mutual and Balanced Force Reduction (MBFR) talks, the Conference on Security and Cooperation in Europe (CSCE), the trilateral discussions with the Soviets and the British on a comprehensive nuclear test ban, and the various United Nations-related activities centered in the work of the Geneva-based Committee on Disarmament, have much deliberation and little progress to show for their efforts.

Most recently, the Reagan Administration, seemingly far more skeptical than its immediate predecessors of the utility of negotiated arms control processes and agreements, has nonetheless been prodded into one new exercise: the bilateral Intermediate Nuclear Force (INF) negotiations with the Soviet Union. Despite the fact that the INF talks affect directly the security interests of many European states, it was widely held on both sides of the Atlantic that restricting the discussions to a Soviet-American framework could optimize the likelihood of substantive progress and would simplify the interactions between these negotiations and the START process.

The conclusions to be drawn from this past decade of arms control effort seem self-evident to most American observers: tangible progress in negotiated arms control is extraordinarily difficult to achieve even under the best of circumstances; the Soviets are formidable negotiators who over the years have done exceedingly well in protecting and promoting their national interests through the negotiation process; and the only serious negotiations are bilateral negotiations. The dominant American view is that to encounter the Soviets in multilateral contexts is to engage in laborious talkathons that are bound to produce nothing: a guaranteed exposure to the bad (the Soviets); the dull (the negotiating process); and the empty (the results).

How is this scene viewed from the Soviet perspective? What value does the Soviet leadership place in the multilateral arms control approach? What policies might they pursue in the future? What follows are some evidence, observations, and speculations in response to these questions.

NOTES FROM HISTORY

Even if one examines the historical record in a somewhat mechanistic and apolitical fashion, it is difficult to sustain the notion that multilateral arms control negotiations involving the Soviet Union have been as valueless either to the Soviets or to the West as the dominant American view suggests. From 1961 to 1972, six major treaties entered into force that were products of such negotiations:

- The Antarctic Treaty, 1961, which prohibits the region's use for military purposes and includes provisions for on-site inspection;
- The Limited Nuclear Test Ban Treaty, 1963, which effectively prohibits the United States, the United Kingdom, and the Soviet Union from conducting nuclear weapons tests except underground;
- The Outer Space Treaty, 1967, which prohibits the deployment of nuclear or other weapons of mass destruction on the moon or any other celestial body or in orbit around the earth;
- The Latin American Nuclear-Weapon-Free Zone Treaty, 1968, which prohibits states in the region from acquiring nuclear weapons of their own or on behalf of powers external to the region; [1]
- The Nuclear Non-Proliferation Treaty, 1970, which prohibits the acquisition of nuclear weapons by non-nuclear states that are parties to the treaty; and
- The Seabed Arms Control Treaty, 1972, which prohibits the emplacement of nuclear weapons or weapons of mass destruction on the seabed and the ocean floor beyond a 12-mile coastal zone.

Four of the six treaties establish what amount to zones of exclusion for nuclear weapons development. Their existence indicates that the Soviet Union has in the past judged it to be in its national interest to preclude nuclear weapons deployments in geographical areas that had not previously housed them and that it also assigned value to participating actively in an ongoing international dialogue whose stated purpose and whose appearance is to reduce armament stockpiles and, in the process, the reliance on force in international politics.

To be sure, none of these agreements struck at the heart of the principal political-military concerns of the Soviet Union (or of the United States). As one student of Soviet arms control policy has concluded:

> These agreements involved, for the most part, renunciation of activities in which neither of the great powers had important vested interests. . . . [These agreements] permitted the continuation, almost undisturbed, of the strategic military programs of the two major military rivals, the US and the USSR.[2]

In the early days of multilateral arms control negotiations, the Soviets proved to be not merely formidable but difficult and exasperating negotiating partners. Consider the observations of Ambassador Arthur H. Dean, who represented the United States in the Limited Test Ban negotiations from January 1961 to December 1962. Dean noted two prominent characteristics in the Soviet diplomatic style: dogmatic expectation of hostility from the outside world, and an iron determination to carry out Moscow-formulated programs and policies without variation by diplomats in the field.[3] Dean remarked that Soviet tactics included:

> 1. The "twisting technique" in which Soviet diplomats took advantage of any indiscretion or mistake and stretched or cut statements by other negotiators to fit their own political purposes.

> 2. The "manipulation of time" to wear down an adversary, win concessions through sheer fatigue and boredom on the other side, or reach an agreement for agreement's sake that would paper over deep differences.

> 3. The "agreement in principle" of sufficient vagueness that they could interpret it in their own way and act to their own advantage while professing to observe the agreement.

> 4. The "waiving" argument in which once a general agreement "in principle" was made and a matter of detail or a specific point had been deferred, it would be claimed that the other side had "waived" the point for all time.

Indeed, so different were Soviet negotiating tactics from what the West had expected in such settings that some had come to question the suitability of characterizing Soviet behavior as "diplomacy." Sir Harold Nicholson, perhaps this century's foremost student of the subject, after considering Soviet actions in the context of Marxist-Leninist theory, was moved to write almost three decades ago:

> I have not observed as yet that this dialectic has improved international relationships, or that the Soviet diplomatists and commissars have evolved any system of negotiation that might be called a diplomatic system. Their activity in foreign countries or at international conferences is formidable, disturbing, compulsive. I do not for one moment underestimate either its potency or its danger. But it is not diplomacy: it is something else.[4]

To be sure, much has changed in the intervening period. Soviet negotiators have become more flexible and less virulently ideological in their negotiating postures. American and other Western negotiators have come to understand Soviet negotiating tactics and have developed cordial and sometimes warm human relationships with their Soviet counterparts. Indeed, Nicholson is incorrect in claiming that Soviet behavior is not diplomacy. While their behavior is clearly dominated by the traits of Russian culture, the Soviets do communicate, they do bargain, they do compromise, and they do adhere to international agreements in the service of their national interests.

Recognizing that the multilateral arms control agreements involving Soviet participation have not dealt with central problems of international security—arguably the Nuclear Non-Proliferation Treaty is an exception—and that at times Soviet negotiating tactics have significantly impeded the development of mutual confidence among the negotiators, what can be said of the fundamental objectives behind Soviet policy? Five purposes stand out. The first is a matter of *political symbolism*. The Soviet Union, as Czarist Russia before it, has an unquenchable thirst to be accepted as an equal among the community of nations. To compensate for inherent streaks of inferiority that run deeply through Russian culture, the Soviet leadership is required to take a high profile in international arms control forums, persistently endorsing the platitudes of universal peace and general and complete disarmament. From the Soviet perspective, endorsing such notions places the state squarely in the center of international diplomacy and helps to reinforce Soviet superpower status by serving as a reminder that no meaningful negotiated arms control pacts can be reached without Soviet cooperation. Satisfying certain requirements of political symbolism may also be of marginal benefit to the political leadership at home. Given that a high degree of insecurity is built into the very essence of the Soviet political system, with no legitimized means established for political succession, the leadership may derive positive feedback from key elements in the society if the Soviet Union is listened to and even followed within the international community.

The second objective is one of exercising *ideological leadership*. The Soviet hierarchy sees itself very much as the leader of the socialist camp and since the early 1960s has been highly sensitive to the challenges to that leadership posed particularly by the People's Republic of China. By repetitively endorsing general principles of peace and disarmament the ruling Soviet elite hopes to reinforce the connection between the Soviet Union and peace in the minds of people throughout the world, to strengthen the mental association between pacific intentions and communist ideology, and to establish and reestablish ad infinitum the position of the Soviet Union as the undisputed leader of the international communist movement.

The third objective, closely related to the second, is *recruitment of allies among the developing countries*. Since the Soviet Union has long sought to promote social and political change in the newly independent countries of Asia, Africa, and Latin America, establishing a highly visible posture in support of the reduction of armaments and military budgets is designed to win the hearts and minds of citizens throughout the developing world. Many of these citizens retain strong feelings of resentment from the colonial period toward Britain, France, the other Western democracies, and, as leader of the capitalist world, the United States. The Soviet Union carries no such liability with many of these peoples and indeed very little is known about the Soviet system in many of the less developed countries. To the extent that the Soviets can paint a political picture of itself as the representative of arms reduction and a portrait of the United States as the bastion of militarism, such efforts serve the broader foreign policy goals of gaining influence with governments or opposition groups throughout the third world.

The fourth objective, one that has become more highly developed since the early 1970s, is to appeal to peace and other politically liberal groups in the West with the long-run goal of splitting the Western European democracies from the United States and *inculcating political paralysis within the North Atlantic Treaty Organization*. The Soviet Union remains permanently concerned, and with good reason, about an American-inspired encirclement strategy which would meld the United States, Western Europe, China, and Japan into an explicit anti-Soviet alliance. The forging of such an alliance would obviously be highly deleterious to Soviet interests and would in fact be seen in Moscow as a grave threat to Soviet national security. To preclude such an eventuality, the Soviet Union has become highly skilled at playing on the fissures of domestic politics within the Western democracies and spends large sums and exerts great efforts to project as favorable and reasonable an image as possible, particularly among Western European publics. Obviously this goal of building a moderate image is constrained by the practical steps the leadership takes in pursuit of concrete foreign and defense policy objectives, objectives that in fact emphasize military and coercive power through the deployment of potent armed forces, the utilization of proxy forces, and the skilled employment of military assistance as a means of gaining political influence. Nonetheless, perception can become reality in international politics, and the Soviet Union works hard to cloak its reliance on militarism in an enormous fig leaf of conciliatory rhetoric. It should be noted that this relationship is virtually the inverse of that adopted by Stalin, and for much of his tenure, Khrushchev. For the first fifteen-odd years of the postwar period, Soviet military weakness was covered by aggressive and threatening bombast. Now just the reverse is the case.

It is clear that these four objectives—political status-seeking, ideological leadership, alliance-building in the developing world, and Western alliance fragmentation—are central elements of Soviet foreign policy. It is not the case that the Soviet leadership views multilateral arms control negotiations and agreements in functional and technical terms (apparently quite similar to the approach of top officials in the Reagan Administration to the INF negotiations). Rather, they are viewed as means to broader and more significant political ends. Each of these objectives is pursued in many different fashions. Multilateral arms control processes are merely one of several instrumentalities in support of Soviet policy.

This does not mean, however, that *issue-specific considerations* never play a role in Soviet policy formulation. Most significantly, the prospect of nuclear weapons proliferation must be a source of continuing concern for the Soviet leadership since many of the potential candidates to acquire nuclear weapons—the Federal Republic of Germany in particular, but also Japan, Israel, and South Korea—are or could be in highly adversarial relationships with the Soviet Union. Consequently, Soviet multilateral arms control policies can derive from the substantive merits of the issues themselves and are not always divorced from legitimate Soviet security concerns. A desire for and an expectation of specific outcomes have been characteristic of selected Soviet involvement in multilateral arms control forums.

HISTORICAL PARALLELISM AND CURRENT CONSTRAINTS

If one takes a longer view of the role of the Soviet Union in multilateral arms control, there is somewhat more reason for optimism than the previous analysis might suggest. The Soviet political system is only now entering its third period of leadership succession in the postwar era. A clue to Soviet foreign policy in the immediate years ahead, say 1983–85, may be found in the historical record of Soviet politics following Stalin's death, 1953–55, and after Khrushchev's demise, 1964–66. After Stalin's death there was an uncertain groping for the reins of leadership within the Soviet Union until Khrushchev assumed a dominant position symbolized by his anti-Stalin speech at the Twentieth Party Congress of the Communist Party of the Soviet Union in 1956. This domestic indecision was reflected in a tentativeness and a discernible mellowing in foreign policy in contrast to the Stalin period. In essence, a new leadership provided a new opportunity, both for the Soviet Union and the United States. While no dramatic developments emerged, important steps were taken that set the stage for more significant measures later on. One of these steps was the complex series of contacts that led to the Geneva summit meeting in 1955 and President Eisenhower's Open Skies proposal.[5] There is little doubt that the faltering efforts of the 1950s were a necessary prelude to the more concrete improvement in Soviet-American relations that took shape in the 1960s.

Similarly, the ouster of Nikita Khrushchev in October 1964 was followed by a period of approximately two years before Leonid Brezhnev had clearly asserted his position of political supremacy. Once again, in this period of leadership succession and political consolidation, the Soviets took few major foreign policy initiatives, were far more reactive than adventurous, and were open to consider ways in which American preferences could be adapted to meet Soviet priorities. Recall the political climate in which Secretary of Defense Robert McNamara was able to hold a tutorial for Premier Alexei Kosygin at the Glassboro summit meeting in 1967 on strategic theory and the destabilizing potentialities of ballistic missile defenses. McNamara was able to conduct such a session despite the contemporaneous escalation of the American war effort in Vietnam, a concatenation of events that would have been unthinkable even a few years previously. And, after all, it was the meeting at Glassboro that set in motion the necessary preparations required to initiate the SALT process two years later.

With the death of Mr. Brezhnev and the emergence of Yuri Andropov as his apparent successor, there may be an opportunity for some new arms control initiatives whose positive effects might not be visible until the late 1980s. This brief spurt of cautious optimism is predicted not only on extrapolation from the past, but on a realization of the present constraints that are tending to influence Soviet international behavior. Four constraints are especially evident:

• The prolonged Soviet military involvement in Afghanistan has increased the difficulties for the Soviets to make an effective case as a symbol of moderation for the developing countries. It is one thing to support wars of national liberation with arms transfers and proxy forces. It is quite another to get bogged down in a difficult and bloody war with a poor and backward neighbor.

• The festering problems in Poland and the threat that this situation poses for the very control of Eastern Europe by the Soviet Union have already shattered the hopes of progress at the CSCE and have complicated still further the calculus that could be the basis for an MBFR agreement.

• Allegations by the Reagan Administration of Soviet involvement in the use of toxins and chemical weapons in Southeast Asia and Afghanistan have damaged Soviet credibility as a champion of the Geneva Protocol and the Biological Weapons Convention and have complicated the Soviet position in multilateral discussions on control of non-nuclear weapons of mass destruction.[6]

• The structural economic difficulties now visible in the Soviet economy and the potential of the Reagan rearmament program may together induce the Soviet leadership to slow the pace of military modernization in part through negotiated agreement. The Soviet leadership may be increasingly appreciative that stabilization of the existing military balances may be preferable to the direction in which highly energized military competition might lead.

The opportunities afforded by prospective leadership changes in and present policy constraints on the Soviet leadership do not point to any clear and obvious initiatives to expect from the Soviets in multilateral arms control. But this is no reason to denigrate the real opportunities they may in fact provide for the West.

CONTEMPORARY ISSUES

What are some of the emerging issues in multilateral arms control that would involve the Soviet Union?

NO FIRST USE OF NUCLEAR WEAPONS

The second Special Session of the General Assembly devoted to disarmament (SSOD–II) addressed a broad agenda, including a comprehensive test ban treaty, the linkages between disarmament and development, and the prospects of reducing military budgets. But more importantly in political terms the Soviets seized upon the opportunity to follow up on the celebrated no-first-use proposal of McGeorge Bundy, George Kennan, Robert McNamara, and Gerard Smith, and pressed home that the Soviet Union has pledged not to be the first to use nuclear weapons. In his address before the UN General Assembly, Soviet Foreign Minister Andrei Gromyko urged that

> . . . the peoples of the world have the right to expect the other nuclear states to take similar steps following the Soviet Union's decision. That would radically change for the better the entire military and political situation in the world.[7]

It would appear that Gromyko's speech achieved the desired political effect from the Soviet perspective, since it presented a challenge to the United States to follow suit that was sidestepped by President Reagan in his own speech before the Special Session. Among elites in the developing countries, the Soviet posture in adhering to a no-first-use pledge is a far more tangible contribution to international stability than the provocative, anti-Soviet rhetoric employed by the American President. Consequently, the issue of no-first-use may not disappear. Despite healthy skepticism of its merits within the Reagan Administration, by many members of the American strategic studies community, and among Europeans concerned about the credibility of US security guarantees, the pledge may develop a political life of its own. The Soviets can be expected to introduce the subject in the UN and other forums, thereby pressing the United States to respond in kind.

NUCLEAR NON-PROLIFERATION

Nuclear non-proliferation remains the strongest common link in the Soviet-American multilateral arms control agenda. As suggested recently by Joseph Nye, many opportunities exist for increased cooperation including more frequent consultations, the establishment of joint approaches to specific non-proliferation problems, completion of the Treaty of Tlatelolco, measures to promote the return of spent fuel, and the implementation of sanctions against countries developing weapons.[8] The Soviets have strong national incentives to see that non-proliferation policies are strengthened. And indeed Mr. Gromyko stated at the UN that the Soviet Union would consider opening up some of its nuclear facilities to inspection by the International Atomic Energy Agency. But the seemingly low priority given to the issue by President Reagan, reflected in the absence of American initiatives in the past two years, suggests that tangible progress may not be easily forthcoming.

MBFR

While Jonathan Dean has urged that an MBFR formula be found that could promote change in Poland acceptable to both East and West,[9] continuing difficulties in Poland suggest such an agreement will be very difficult to achieve. Progress in MBFR remains hostage to START and to the INF talks. That a specialist on German politics, Mr. Y. A. Kvitsinsky, leads the Soviet INF delegation suggests where Soviet priorities lie. It is probably the case that unless a useful start is made in START, progress on other arms control fronts in the near term will be modest.

CHEMICAL WEAPONS

In the area of chemical weapons control, the Soviets have again renewed their declaratory interest and can be expected to push this issue hard at the Committee on Disarmament in Geneva. In June 1982 Mr. Gromyko submitted to the UN the provisions of a convention on the prohibition of the development, production, and stockpiling of chemical weapons and on their destruction.[10] The convention addressed questions on the prohibition of transfer and non-stationing of chemical weapons and on the elimination of conversion of facilities which presently provide capacities for the production of such weapons. But the skepticism expressed by the US government about the seriousness of the proposal has been sufficiently strong that it is difficult to visualize tangible movement toward an agreement.

FUTURE PROJECTS

Future progress will clearly depend on American as well as Soviet attitudes, and it must be noted that the American approach to multilateral arms control has been on balance no more forthcoming than that of the Soviet Union. For example, "damage limitation" was the operational strategy for the Carter Administration's approach to the first UN Special Session and a similar approach was taken by the Reagan Administration at the second Special Session. Moreover, the very distinction between multilateral and bilateral negotiations is a blurry one. In many instances, such as the INF talks, bilateralism is multilateralism.[11]

The dominant consideration, however, is the health of the US-Soviet relationship. As long as high tensions persist, progress on the arms control front will be difficult. These last few points, each worthy of some elaboration, all point in a pessimistic direction concerning the prospective achievements of multilateral arms control negotiations involving the Soviet Union.

Consider the United Nations Special Sessions on disarmament. The first Special Session, held in 1978, generated pronounced enthusiasm among many UN delegations from less developed countries and from arms control proponents in the United States and Western Europe. The agenda for discussion was long and ambitious. It included consideration of the pledge of no first use of nuclear weapons by each of the superpowers; a total cessation of nuclear testing, including a ban on the detonation of peaceful nuclear explosions; the halting of the spread of nuclear weapons to nonnuclear states, in part by concrete superpower implementation of Article VI of the NPT; the establishment of new nuclear-weapon-free zones along the lines specified by the Treaty of Tlatelolco for Latin America; the strengthening of conventional arms transfer restraints; the explicit analytical consideration of the relationship between arms expenditures and economic growth and development; and the establishment of a global verification institution to permit all the countries of the world to benefit from satellite surveillance systems rather than limiting the primary beneficiaries to the superpowers. But the enthusiasm surrounding the discussion of these agenda items diminished rapidly when it became clear that neither the United States nor the Soviet government brought to the session any tangible initiatives for making progress on these thorny and often-discussed issues.

Of course, in the intervening period until the Second Session was convened in June 1982, the international situation had deteriorated considerably. Optimism was far less plentiful in the UN General Assembly than had been the case four years previously, and with ample justification. By the Session's end in early July, press accounts struck an appropriately gloomy note. One report characterized the product of this UN effort as

> . . . a vague blueprint for inaction, papering over the failure of consensus . . . dramatizing the collapse of an international consensus on the theoretical goals of arms control that had existed for more than a decade and that had been defined by the ''action program'' adopted by the General Assembly's first disarmament session in 1978.[12]

In sum, multilateral arms control through the auspices of the UN General Assembly is not desired by either East or West, but only by less developed countries (LDCs) from the South. Neither superpower really seeks to influence the posture of the other, but instead concentrates on scoring political propaganda points and in limiting the diplomatic embarrassment suffered as a consequence of LDC criticism.

The observation that the distinction between bilateralism and multilateralism is increasingly being blurred is also not a cause for optimism. Scratching the surface of political motivations not very deeply reveals that a principal Soviet motivation in helping to construct the NPT framework was to head off the development of a West German nuclear weapons program. Although the Soviet Union doubtlessly sees the nuclear non-proliferation regime as being consistent with its national interests, it was this German-specific concern far more than a commitment to global arms control that determined Soviet negotiating behavior. Similarly, it should be recalled, the Nixon Administration entered into MBFR negotiations in 1973 not to effectuate some sort of ephemeral ''military detente'' in Europe. Just the opposite, for the motivation was clearly to undercut politically the initiatives that had been launched by Senator Mike Mansfield for the unilateral withdrawal of American troops from Europe. The Nixon Administration argued that it was imprudent for the US to withdraw its forces unilaterally when it was in the midst of a delicate and complex multilateral arms control negotiation. The INF talks cited previously illustrate the point still further. The negotiation, on its face, is a bilateral exercise aimed at producing an agreement on the number of intermediate nuclear launchers and warheads that could be deployed in the European theatre. In political fact, of course, it is something quite different. For the Reagan Administration it is the fulfillment of the "arms control" track specified in the 1979 NATO decision that ostensibly would permit the implementation of the "deployment" track, namely the emplacement of 108 Pershing II and 464 ground-launched cruise missiles in Europe. For the Soviet government, it is an opportunity to buy time, to manipulate specifically West German, and more generally, West European public opinion in the hope of forestalling these NATO deployments, leaving the Soviets with their own SS-20 intermediate-range systems intact and unanswered by the West.

In Geneva, at the meetings of the Committee on Disarmament, the focus has been on bacteriological and chemical weapons, on radiological weapons, and on other weapons of "mass destruction." But for Washington, the exercise seems perfunctory. The principles enunciated in Geneva may be exemplary, but they are in stark contrast to what the Reagan Administration claims is incontrovertible evidence of: (a) Warsaw Pact forces trained and equipped to fight with chemical weapons; (b) Soviet involvement in the use of toxins in Southeast Asia and their use of chemical weapons in Afghanistan; and (c) manufacture of biological weapons within the Soviet Union. The prospects for negotiated agreement at Geneva, therefore, are dim.

Taken in a broader context, these arms control negotiations are swimming upstream against strong international currents marked by an intense superpower rivalry; a significant diffusion of global military power; an eruption into war of regional conflict situations that have in one year alone embroiled the South Atlantic, the Middle East, the Persian Gulf, and Southeast Asia; a breakdown in the ability of international institutions to achieve conflict resolution; and an absence of effective conceptual lenses to guide diplomatic behavior. No wonder, therefore, that "the bad, the dull, and the empty" is regrettably an apt description of the current state of affairs. It would require a bold political initiative, probably under-taken by new leadership, or a fundamental alteration of superpower perspectives to be otherwise.

NOTES

1. For various political and legal reasons that need not be cited here, it should be noted that key states of Latin America—Argentina, Brazil, Chile and Cuba—do not consider themselves bound by the treaty, thereby raising serious questions as to its effectiveness.

2. Thomas B. Larson, *Disarmament and Soviet Policy 1964–1968* (Englewood Cliffs, New Jersey: Prentice Hall, Inc., 1969), p. 136.

3. Dean's comments, drawn from Congressional testimony, are cited in *Soviet Diplomacy and Negotiating Behavior: Emerging New Context for U.S. Diplomacy,* A study prepared by the Senior Specialists Division, Congressional Research Service, Library of Congress (Washington, D.C.: US GPO, 1979), p. 363.

4. Harold Nicolson, *Evolution of Diplomatic Method,* p. 90, as cited in *Soviet Diplomacy and Negotiating Behavior,* ibid., p. 540.

5. This episode is discussed at length in Dwight D. Eisenhower, *Mandate for Change 1953–1956* (New York: Signet Books, 1965), pp. 600–632.

6. A wealth of data is presented in *Chemical Warfare in Southeast Asia and Afghanistan,* Report to the Congress from Secretary of State Alexander M. Haig, Jr. (Washington, D.C.: US GPO, 22 March, 1982), p. 32.

7. See "Letter Dated 16 June 1982 from the Minister for Foreign Affairs of the Union of Soviet Socialist Republics to the Secretary-General of the UN," Document of the Ad Hoc Committee of SSOD–II (1982), A/S–12/AC.1/11, p. 3.

8. See Joseph Nye, "Nuclear Talks Must Go On," *New York Times,* January 23, 1982.

9. See Jonathan Dean, "Promoting Change in Poland," *New York Times,* 20 March 1982.

10. This draft convention on the prohibition and destruction of chemical weapons is contained in another letter from Foreign Minister Gromyko, dated 16 June 1982, to the UN Secretary-General. See Document of the Ad Hoc Committee of SSOD–II (1982), A/S–12/AC.1/12.

11. See Gregory Treverton's chapter in this book.

12. See Michael J. Berlin, "Collapse of International Consensus Marked UN Disarmament Session," *International Herald Tribune,* 12 July 1982, p. 1.

THE NON-ALIGNED STATES
AND ARMS CONTROL

GEORGE H. QUESTER

Skeptics about the significance or seriousness of the non-aligned movement can cite many grounds for doubt, beginning even with the title chosen for the group. By what stretch of imagination can Cuba and North Korea be regarded as non-aligned? By what standard of fairness could North Korea be admitted to the group and not South Korea? Why does the group so regularly criticize the United States, and so much restrain itself with regard to parallel transgressions by the Soviet Union? Is not the non-aligned movement at best a naive indulgence in doublethink and hypocrisy, and at worst simply a subtle front-group operation for the Soviet bloc?[1]

The last fear certainly has to be discounted, for one can point out a number of issues, including issues of arms policy and arms control, where the non-aligned third world movement has indeed stood at odds with the USSR. The Group of 77 may, by historical happenstance or by the inexorable processes of historical evolution, be loaded toward sympathy for the "second world" of Marxist states, but it is hardly uniform in this regard. Cuba and North Korea are members, but so are Singapore, Argentina, and Morocco. With the exception of the few more explicitly Marxist states, the bulk recognize that they have some very important conflicts of interest with Moscow. It is a little more difficult to disprove the charge of naiveté, or hypocrisy, for many of the public pronouncements of these countries would seem to support such a charge.

Yet it should be assumed that much of what the representatives of the non-aligned states say at international gatherings—at Special Sessions on Disarmament, for example—is different from their true feelings on the subject, overstated for political effect or as a bargaining ploy. A diplomat is still someone sent abroad to lie on behalf of his country, and there is no reason why the non-aligned states should be cursed with diplomats any less competent than those of the superpowers.

Moreover, in addition to expecting some distortion and dissimulation, it must also be presumed that the non-aligned states, behind this mask, are quite realistically pursuing concrete interests of their own, interests that will include some very specific arms control objectives.

THE MEANING OF NON-ALIGNED

Strictly speaking, non-aligned would have to be defined as an absence of military alliances, joint defense arrangements with major powers, and the kinds of political coordination that mortgage the parties' freedom of maneuver. Non-aligned is similar to but not quite the same as "neutral," in the old legal sense of respect for the duties of neutrality during war.

However defined, non-aligned is the self-identification of a large group of nations, numbering more than ninety today. Most of these states share economic underdevelopment and an aversion to wholly capitalist or Marxist models of economic growth. The terms third world and non-aligned are thus at times interchangeable, and issues can be defined in terms of both "South vs. North" and "East vs. West."

The non-aligned nations have never been as united on arms control questions as they sometimes try to seem, but they are never quite so divided that it becomes pointless to generalize about them as a class of nations.

The most resounding votes and endorsements from the diplomatic spokesmen for such nations have come for measures such as a complete ban on nuclear testing, or substantial nuclear disarmament by the superpowers, or General and Complete Disarmament, (GCD) or a total halt to the arms race.[2] Any observer treating the pronouncements at international meetings as a literal rendering of the actual policy of these nations will thus quite naturally see them as moralistic, naive, and impractical. Yet the fine print and the lower-key asides emanating from such nations offer a much more rounded picture of far more sophisticated and realistic approaches.

There is little reason to doubt that the non-aligned states (except for the few who are still hoping somehow to acquire nuclear weapons for themselves) would welcome a total ban on nuclear testing and moderation of the Soviet-American competition in strategic arms. If nothing else, such steps would be an encouraging sign that detente had not totally eroded, and that nuclear war between the two superpowers was still highly unlikely. It might also lead to reductions in superpower arms expenditures, funds that ultimately could find their way into assistance for economic development in the South.

Yet relatively few non-aligned governments would ever take seriously the prospect of total nuclear disarmament by the US and the USSR (however much they would vote for resolutions endorsing this as a worthwhile goal), and most might indeed have concerns about the instability and unpredictability that would accompany any such drastic step. The prospect of General and Complete Disarmament must similarly appear risky. Would the non-aligned truly be prepared to strip themselves of all conventional armaments? Would they trust the unknowns of such an international system more than the current perils of the known system?

Endorsements of comprehensive disarmament are thus rituals that mean little more to the non-aligned than they do to the nations of the West or of the Soviet bloc. Non-aligned representatives, while rarely expressing any open skepticism about comprehensive or general disarmament, often add an observation that greater attention should be addressed to more immediate practical and partial steps. The argument against partial measures sometimes heard from the peace movement in the United States—that such measures are to be avoided because they sap the momentum required for a more total reform of the international system and its armed confrontations—is not visibly persuasive for most of the non-aligned states.

Proposals similarly abound at the United Nations for special sessions and conferences and study groups keyed to more substantial and less realistic disarmament measures. Yet the non-aligned supporters of such meetings see these as means of embarrassing and pressuring the US and USSR more than as direct steps toward disarmament. If such conferences help build diplomatic and political leverage that might be cashed in for concrete concessions elsewhere to the South, this is hardly a bad day's work for the diplomats of the non-aligned community.

POTENTIAL CONTRIBUTIONS OF THE NON-ALIGNED

As illustrated graphically by the commentary on the 1982 Special Session on Disarmament, few observers would rate the non-aligned movement as being in its prime today, or at its peak of world stature and influence. To begin, the sheer novelty of states expressing a viewpoint free of both Washington and Moscow has worn off. The non-aligned phrase, if it means anything, is negatively defined by what these states have stayed free of and by what is different about them. As people get used to the difference, it captures less attention.

Second, the personal charisma of the original leaders of the movement, persons like Nasser and Nehru and Tito, has not been matched in later generations. Having been a leader of an independence movement, or of a fight for freedom from foreign entanglements, gave these figures an international stature that could not be matched.

Perhaps the most visible leader of the non-aligned today is Fidel Castro, but this illustrates a third aspect of the loss of non-aligned stature. The movement is seen as hypocritical and as a sham by much of the world, since it pretends to be non-aligned, while all too often aligning itself with Moscow against the West. While this is a misleading conclusion, to the extent that it rings true to observers around the world it reduces the influence of non-aligned spokesmen, on arms control issues or on anything else.

Fourth, the non-aligned cannot exert moral influence on arms control, if members of the group continue to purchase increasing quantities of weapons and even to get into the business of weapons manufacture, preparing for wars with each other. Who will listen to a lecture on disarmament from a group of nations that itself shows signs of being just as prone to the weaknesses and follies of traditional members of the state system?

These factors help explain why the non-aligned states have become less influential on the arms control front, yet they nonetheless have an important contribution to make.

To begin, they are indeed *not* aligned. Their foreign and defense policies are not simply a carbon copy or offshoot of the foreign and defense policies of one of the major powers, such that all an observer would have to do is read the posture statements of Washington or Moscow to see the full picture. The concrete interests of these countries will have to be taken into account by any American or Soviet leader seeking to serve his own nation's interests.

Being non-aligned, moreover, such countries can still play a balancing or moderating role, not out of any particular high-mindedness or moral superiority, but simply because the third of any three actors in an international arena normally tends to serve as a balancer between the other two. As noted below, the interests of the non-aligned break in many directions, such that they will often present fourth, fifth, and further perspectives, rather than merely a third.

Detente between the United States and the Soviet Union is indeed in trouble. The explanations of the demise of detente are as varied as the original explanations for its beginning. Those who attributed detente to a greater morality and wisdom in either or both of the superpowers would now again indict the folly or power hunger of either or both of them. But some others would have based their hopes for a detente on a greater fractionation of the world, restoring some of what was called the balance of power system in an earlier time. If detente is in trouble, it may be so because the non-aligned countries did not amount to much as actors on the scene, not being able to tip the balance by lending their strength to one side or the other in Angola, Afghanistan, or elsewhere. Yet, conversely, the non-aligned states are not totally lacking in weight and influence here. If there is still some hope for detente and arms control, the weight and impact of the non-aligned states may still account for some of it.

It amounts to a truism that the non-aligned states will prefer a multipolar international system to one that looks more bipolar. By the very definition of their own stance, they have elected to be an independent third force, perhaps with a view to moderating the interactions of the two major blocs, but also with a view to advancing interests of their own. Not only are most non-aligned nations relatively poor, they have also classically been subject to humiliations and denials of status. They therefore are now playing the political game, just as other nations have always played it, for some enhancement of prestige and status, as well as for increased welfare and security.

Two questions on multipolarity arise: will there ever be instances, perhaps because of the very arms interactions discussed here, where some non-aligned states might prefer a more bipolar rather than multipolar world order? How does this normal preference for multipolarity translate into policy on armaments questions?

Instances where the non-aligned favor alignment are obviously rare, and show up only where some further breakdown of alliances threatens to push the world more into war than into peace, a war which might threaten the interests of all. The non-aligned thus look like hypocrites in not condemning resolutely enough Russian intervention in Hungary or Poland, but this is mostly because the consequences of a major unraveling of the Communist hold on Eastern Europe seem too unpredictable. Where a very irresponsible ruler turns out to be a major threat to peace (as in the Central African Empire or Uganda), the non-aligned similarly protest only half-heartedly about efforts orchestrated by one of the superpowers to depose him.

Yet the normal case is that the non-aligned can have their cake and eat it too, in endorsing a multipolar international system for its own sake, and in concluding that this tends to reinforce peace and to reinforce detente by bringing some of the old balance-of-power mechanism back into play.

THE MEANING OF ARMS CONTROL

Arms control is another term that may cause some tensions and confusions as writers differ on its use. At times, it is read to be a synonym for disarmament, and at other times as synonymous with formal negotiations for disarmament. Yet the original definition of the term, as developed at the end of the 1950s, is somewhat different (or else why would the US government have minted up an Arms Control *and* Disarmament Agency?).

Arms control will be taken here to refer to steps taken to improve the outputs of the military confrontation of nations, i.e., to reduce the likelihood of war, to reduce the destructiveness of war if it happens, and to reduce the burdens of armament in peacetime. Compared to such outputs, disarmament per se, or formal negotiation per se, can only be an input, something that only makes sense as it contributes to these outputs.[3]

The difference between arms control and disarmament is thus analogous to the difference between program budgeting and line-item budgeting, and any student of operations research might thus be quick to see the advantages of an arms control perspective fixed on the assessment of these *outputs,* rather than following the journalistic shorthand, which has slid back toward always equating arms control with negotiations and disarmament.

Not every form of disarmament is desirable in terms of human happiness, and not every form of formal disarmament negotiation is desirable. The desirability of such inputs must be assessed by the outputs, as noted. Any and all of the choices on disarmament, or weapons procurement, or formal negotiation, or informal and tacit bargaining exchange, thus become the arms control policy addressed in this essay, with a view to the interests and outlooks and participation of the non-aligned countries.

If arms control thus means something different, and something more profound than disarmament, the United Nations will not be the best place to find documents marking the difference.

It is an old story for the history of arms control that formal and public negotiations can generate problems. A contest of posturing, and presentation of unreal and unreasonable demands may emerge to block any progress toward serious arms restraint. The posturing may be for the benefit of constituencies at home, or for one's allies, or for the non-aligned gallery judging the parties as to which is more noble and concerned about peace. Tacit bargaining has thus often enough been recommended as the proper avenue for understandings between the United States and the USSR, or between any two powers; if tacit bargaining were too unstructured, the recommendation would have been at least to keep the negotiations quiet and secret until some agreement that could be announced had been reached.

Woodrow Wilson at the end of World War I proposed the idealistic formula of "open covenants, openly arrived at." The contrary advice here would be "open covenants, secretly arrived at." Just as progress in a domestic labor dispute usually does not come until the press is shut away from the negotiators, so there often is little progress in international dealings if public negotiations are the designated approach.[4]

Yet this is a little too pessimistic on the possibilities of more structured multilateral approaches. All nations, not just the non-aligned, posture at the United Nations, but they also sometimes surprise one and all by the degree to which they rein themselves in with a layer of decorum and gentlemanly mutual respect. Structured negotiations have all the difficulties of publicity, but this publicity at the same time may reduce the risk of misunderstanding, as contracts are made more explicit as they are made more formal.

Above all, some of the useful deals of arms restraint may make sense only if a larger number of states can be drawn in as part of some sort of grand package deal, with everyone making a separate sacrifice and contribution, and everyone exacting a separate gain. Tacit agreements may work much better when only two parties are involved than when twenty or so have a stake in the exchange.

SOME SPECIAL INTERESTS AMONG THE NON-ALIGNED

Except for those who see the non-aligned or third world countries as having some special moral insights on world problems (and see the two superpowers as the major cause of such problems), few analysts should ever fall into the trap of thinking of the non-aligned as a monolithic entity with a single viewpoint. There are a host of disparate, at times very antagonistic, interests too often masked by a false image of solidarity at international conferences.

The real spread of interests here thus alternates between common goals and disparate goals, at times taking the form of a common front of difference from both Moscow and Washington, at other times an identification with one superpower against the other, at some times even an identification with both superpowers (for example, in being averse to nuclear war, and to airliner highjackings), at still other times breaking into multiple conflicts of interest and disagreements among the non-aligned.

An attempt will be made now to outline some of the differences in objective national and regional situations that make for particular outlooks on arms control matters. Among the differentiating characteristics that may produce substantially different arms policies among the non-aligned states, this chapter comments on the following special categories:

The Latin American states
The African states
The Francophone states as a subgroup of the African
The Arab states
The oil-producers and the oil-consumers
The maritime non-aligned states
The more explicitly Marxist non-aligned states

LATIN AMERICA

Latin America is a special case for international arms control, just as it has been a special case for many decades for almost all of international politics.[5] There have been arms races from time to time in Latin America, but very few wars. When one notes how aircraft carriers have been procured without any aircraft to fly off their decks, one then wonders whether the arms race title should even apply. Journalists projecting from the patterns of other continents have been all too inclined to assume that the "inherent conflicts" between Brazil and Argentina have some kind of reality comparable to conflicts between France and Britain in the past, but for one reason or another, relations among Latin American countries have been far less violent.

It is too easy therefore for outsiders to snicker at the parade-ground armies of the Latin American states. In some cases these armies have been criticized as vehicles of social repression, but the worst criticisms of armed forces—that they terrify their neighbors and provoke wars—have rarely applied much to the Latin American case, and it might be better to applaud the subtle sophistication of the generals and regimes involved rather than snickering.

The 1982 South Atlantic war between Argentina and Britain about the future of the Falklands/Malvinas was all the more shocking because it did not fit the Latin American pattern. Born out of the domestic political difficulties of the Argentine junta, or of British muddling whereby inattention and the whims of 1,800 islanders wasted earlier opportunities to abandon the islands gracefully, the war produced enough death and destruction to strip Latin America of some of its status as an exception to the normal international pattern.

If such warfare becomes a more normal pattern for the future, with outright battles by the combat-tested Argentines against Chile or Brazil, or comparable shootouts between Latin American armed forces and European or North American "imperialists," a very different model of arms policy will have to be applied. Similarly troublesome would be a move by the Argentine military government to turn to a nuclear explosives program as a way to recover its image after its debacle in the Falklands.

AFRICA

Africa, like Latin America, has been relatively free of boundary disputes, but only by means of tacit understanding involving most of the African regimes. While Latin America largely shares a single language, Africa could be fractionated by hundreds of ethnic partitions, cutting across virtually all the current boundaries, and the worst fear of the leadership of the OAU (Organization of African Unity) is precisely that any process of irredentist national reunification, once begun, would never stop.

The arms control perspective of the black African states is thus twofold: to terminate the last of the white colonial presence as soon as possible (the white regime in South Africa), but otherwise to reinforce the mutual respect for existing sovereignties that has been a necessary modus vivendi for the past two decades. The two goals could easily be in tension, if the black states feel a need to invest in advanced conventional (or even nuclear) weapons as the way to push the South Africans out, for the same weaponry could thereafter be the vehicle for battles among themselves.[6]

If guerilla war is to be the primary weapon against South Africa (a big if) and if guerrilla war in Africa proves itself the weapon of those already in a territory (rather than a domino-effect tool for outside agitator/infiltrators), less tension would emerge. If more conventional armies become involved, much more will be at stake.

The entry of the Cuban forces flown into Angola by the USSR illustrates this tension. Such forces could be rationalized as needed to counteract interventions of the South Africans, but thereafter pose an Angolan threat to Zaire or Zambia, and from Ethiopia into Somalia, etc. Black African states might aspire to having as few boundary disputes and as few international wars as Latin American states have had, but the presence of the Pretoria apartheid regime adds a dangerous complicating factor here.

It is interesting how the professed policies of some of the western nations supplying arms to South Africa in the past decade have been in synchronization with the distinction between conventional and guerrilla war. Weapons for the repression of guerrilla insurrection were not to be sold, according to the policies of France, or of the United States at an earlier time, but weapons for defense against foreign conventional attack were to be made available.

Parenthetically, exactly the opposite has until recently been the professed US attitude with regard to arms sales to Latin American regimes. Here the threat of conventional warfare was deemed to be so small that countries in the region should be persuaded to avoid wasting money on preparing for such war, or to avoid somehow generating a reality by weapons deployments which otherwise would not have existed. Given the fear of Marxist-fomented guerrilla war, however, the United States has favored training and equipping the Latin American armies for counterinsurgency roles.

FRANCOPHONE AFRICA

The bloc of Francophone countries—mostly former colonies of France, which have displayed a special attachment to the French language and culture, and to continued ties to France itself, including a special tolerance of, and dependence on, the interventionary capabilities of the French armed forces—are a special case.[7] Indeed, if one wishes to become exercised at the alleged double standards of the non-aligned as they allocate criticism unevenly, it has not just been the Soviets who seem to get off easily, but also France, forgiven for the intrusion of its armed forces into various locations in Africa (often flown there by the transport aircraft of the US Air Force), forgiven also for having sold substantial quantities of arms to South Africa.

As long as French armed forces are not used in an effort to restore French sovereignty to any corner of Africa, the Francophone countries will probably quietly welcome the moderating and stabilizing impact of the prospect of such interventions, and the rest of Africa will go along with the preferences of the Francophones (even if they privately disapprove of such blatant reliance on European military skills). Just as Andrew Young once described the Cuban troops as providing a "stabilizing influence" on Angola, the French troops may be tolerated as long as they supply this. The unanswered question, as in the Shaba episode, is whether two or more such forces can remain stabilizing if they come into contact with each other, and also whether such forces can be counted upon to restrict themselves to the task of stabilization, in accord with the wishes of the people in the region itself.

THE ARAB STATES

Further complicating any generalizations about the non-aligned, of course, is the special enmity felt by the Arab states for Israel. While other non-aligned nations can often be brought along to vote for resolutions condemning Israel at the United Nations, most of them are situated in regions where the prospect of enduring peace is quite attractive and thinkable, making their ritual endorsements of "lasting peace" easier to accept. Arab statements about the future peace of the Middle East are far more convoluted, however, hinging peace on a "just claim," still often amounting to the end of the existence of Israel.[8]

Arab policies on the transfer of conventional arms can thus hardly be disapproving, since it has only been the massive transfer of such arms that has given them the prospect of applying pressure to Israel. By comparison, since Israel is generally suspected of having moved toward a nuclear weapons capability as the ultimate insurance against being "pushed into the sea," it is easier for the Arab states to endorse what other regions have endorsed in opposition to nuclear weapons. Proposals for nuclear-free zones get hung up on the fear of having to negotiate directly with, or diplomatically recognize, Israel. One way out for the Arabs is an imposition of a mandate for denuclearization through some outside body such as the United Nations.

THE OIL-DEPENDENT STATES

Yet another internal fractionation of the non-aligned movement, hardly a trivial one, divides those states that are oil-rich, mostly in the Arab Persian Gulf area, and those that are not.[9] This separates the very rich, which have large amounts of money to spend on weapons, from the very poor, desperate for foreign aid. In terms of arms control considerations, a finer distinction would be: oil-exporter, oil-importer, and those which neither export nor import very much oil. The first two of these categories, on opposite ends of the scale in terms of wealth, nonetheless share a very real and intense interest in heading off any deployments and uses of weapons that would interfere with commerce coming out of the Persian Gulf. By contrast, those states not involved in this particular flow of oil might be less intensely interested, for example, in preventing the spread of anti-ship guided missiles to nations or sub-national terrorist groups around the Straits of Hormuz.

THE MARITIME STATES

The interests of the maritime powers form another special case.[10] These states are privately very satisfied with one aspect of the status quo, namely that almost no warfare has occurred on the high seas since 1945, even while they press their claims on other sea issues where they are much less satisfied, issues of territorial extent, exploitation of fisheries and seabed, and risks of ecological damage from tanker passages (i.e., the Law of the Sea negotiations where the US and the Soviet Union have, interestingly, sometimes come together to defend the same status quo position).

With regard to arms control on the seas, the maritime non-aligned thus wish peace to continue, and wish to maintain their own political independence against any intimidation projected in from the sea. Since the non-aligned are also notoriously capable of threatening wars, or fighting wars, against each other, the list of arms control desires here presumably also includes heading off regional maritime hegemonic threats, so that Brazil's navy does not menace Uruguay, or India's Ceylon, etc.

Some of the most frustrating non-aligned behavior, to Western eyes, comes in the pronouncements made on naval matters, as Western ship deployments seem to draw much more criticism than parallel Soviet deployments. If Soviet ships are to cruise in the Indian Ocean, should it not be in the interest of the riparian states to have American naval forces in the same area checking and balancing them? Does not an elementary sense of balance of power suggest that countries like India and Algeria and Tanzania should want two navies on the horizon, rather than one?

The induction from traditional balance-of-power logic (Britain always wanted to see two large armies on the continent of Europe, rather than merely one) is obvious, but it may be misleading, for the seas affect life in ways very different from control over land masses. When Britain dominated the seas all by itself in the decades after Trafalgar, it did not need to seize so many bases on shore. Countries like the United States and Japan were relatively ready to tolerate this dominance, because commerce and fishing and the other uses of the seas could go ahead undisturbed, and life on land at home was also undisturbed. The American and Japanese decision to build navies, and take charge of their own seas, came only when the British monopoly began to slip, when the warships on the horizon could no longer be counted upon to be British, but might instead be German or French.

Once the British naval monopoly had eroded, the prospect emerged of disruptive naval battles being fought directly beyond a country's three-mile limit. Worse still, the prospect emerged that competing naval forces might seek to acquire coastal bases and coaling stations to reinforce themselves for coming naval battles.

The analogy with past Japanese and American attitudes may thus be all too relevant to the feelings of non-aligned countries around the shores of the world's major oceans today. The first choice of many of these countries, clearly stated because of its apparent moral commitment to worldwide disarmament, is that *no* foreign navies appear at all off their shores. Hence the repeated proposals that the Indian Ocean or the Mediterranean be made into a "zone of peace." A few of the riparian states, fearing the latent naval power of other riparian states, *might* not truly welcome this as a first choice, but have kept their comments more muted on the subject.

The second choice of most such states is not, however, that there be *two* naval powers in any sea to check each other, but rather paradoxically that there be only one. When there is only one, the chances of a shooting war on the high seas stay low, the pressures for basing privileges stay low. It is the on-shore intrusions of superpower navies that may be most feared by the non-aligned.

This second choice has not been enunciated with any great clarity, for it is the kind of sophisticated self-interest that a nation does not proclaim, and does not enhance a nation's apparent moral stature when it is enunciated. The evidence for it is rather in the double standard by which the US Navy is criticized for entering a body of water when the Soviet Navy is already there. The criticism here is hardly because the state involved is already a faithful Soviet puppet, but rather because it aspires never to being pressured to become host for Soviet military facilities. The preference of such states might thus be for the Soviets to stay out if the US Navy is already determined to deploy into an area, and vice versa. The broader double standard, by which the Soviet Union is never condemned as explicitly as the US, then explains the rest of this apparent paradox.

In terms of weapons policy, littoral countries may then welcome the technological developments that make ships more sinkable at sea, the precision-guided anti-ship munitions that now allow most coastal states to do better against a foreign fleet that has had to travel any great distance.

Whatever the rights and wrongs of the Argentine invasion of the Falklands as seen by countries around the world, a fair number of littoral countries may thus have been somewhat pleased to see the sinkings of modern British destroyers by anti-ship missiles Argentina had acquired earlier from France. Coming after a British submarine had torpedoed and sunk a much older Argentine cruiser (a sinking more reminiscent of the days when Britannia or other non-

Latin American navies ruled the waves), the loss of the British destroyer signals that foreign fleets in general will now be able to approach distant coasts only at some peril, facing missiles, ships, and airplanes launched from the dry land they are approaching. The sale of such anti-ship missile systems to countries like Argentina or Singapore can be predicted to increase.

THE NON-ALIGNED MOSCOW SATELLITES

Those formal members of the non-aligned that Westerners suspect to be more truly aligned with the Soviet Union also amount to a special interest group. Cuba, Vietnam, and North Korea would seem the most prominent among these, but Ethiopia and Mozambique might also be put on the list.

Is there any reality at all to the independence from Moscow that is suggested by their admission to the non-aligned movement? Perhaps there is a very little; but perhaps there is a bit more than a little, with one of the special interests of this subgroup then being to retain as much as they can of this independence, rather than simply becoming as faithful and predictable a Soviet ally as Bulgaria or Outer Mongolia.[11] North Korea's deployments of resources and influence in Africa, for example, have certainly not fit the model of faithful alignment with the USSR, or even of a nation trying to stay halfway between Beijing and Moscow. Fidel Castro's commitments to supporting and exporting revolution in the past decade make him look more totally in step with Soviet interests, but it is not known if he is being directed into this by Moscow, or whether it is not instead more his own enthusiasm and initiative that pulls Moscow along behind him.

THE SPREAD OF NUCLEAR WEAPONS

This analysis turns now, from sorting the separate kinds of national interests motivating the non-aligned states, to discussing a series of substantive arms control problems facing the non-aligned, and the whole world, beginning with perhaps the most serious problem of all, nuclear proliferation.[12]

The statement is too often advanced that nuclear non-proliferation is of interest only to the existing nuclear-weapons states (the "haves") and an imposition on all the other states (the "have nots"). Such an interpretation of the interests involved rings true for the analyst who sees everything in realpolitik terms of national power, but otherwise misses too much. Such an interpretation also amounts to a good bargaining line for any non-aligned diplomat. By pretending to care less about an issue on which Washington and Moscow in the past have made their feelings clear, he thus perhaps hopes to extract some greater concessions by making the superpowers feel more guilty or more unsure of their hand.

Yet the reality is of course that many more states around the globe stand to lose from further nuclear weapons spread then simply the original two possessors of such weapons. This reality is well understood by many or most of the countries around the globe, even if they will be slow to verbalize such an understanding for the record.

It might be very tempting for any potential "nth" nuclear weapons state to join the club if, and only if, it could be certain that it was to become the last member admitted. It might be far less tempting, however, to become an African nuclear-weapons state followed by other such African states, or a Latin American bomb possessor followed by a number more of Latin American states similarly equipped.

The strongest argument for nuclear proliferation may be that nuclear weapons potential is not a net drain for the civilian economy in peacetime, but rather a net plus. Because various countries so much need nuclear-generated electricity, it is alleged, they will have to acquire the reactors and plutonium reprocessing facilities and uranium enrichment facilities that so trouble and worry their neighbors.

Happily for the prospects of arms control among the non-aligned (although unhappily for the economic prospects and future of these countries) nuclear electric power production is no longer as promising for third-world economic advancement as was once supposed. Looking more and more like a waste of money in terms of civilian material returns, the nuclear approach thereby becomes a much more costly as well as a more destabilizing and more destructive system.

The major point here is not whether this picture of the impact of nuclear weapons spread is correct, but rather that this picture is indeed now widely accepted by the governments of the non-aligned states, even while their public statements often pretend otherwise.[13] There are many reasons to be pessimistic about slowing or stopping the spread of nuclear weapons, not the least being the continued and inexorable spread of the basic technology involved, a technology that hardly merits anymore a label of "secret." Yet one reason often offered for pessimism is largely spurious, namely that much of the world is indifferent to or even in favor of nuclear proliferation.

The Arab states, and other non-aligned states, were vehement in condemning the Israeli air attack on the Iraqi reactor in June of 1981, but privately many of them welcomed it, just as many had privately been expressing misgivings for some time about Iraqi intentions in the nuclear field. As France now backs away from some of its commitments, refusing to give Iraq an exact duplicate of what the Israelis destroyed, it will not suffer any criticism from the other non-aligned states but will actually draw encouragement and thanks from these states. Similarly, there appears to be no glee in the third world, or even in the Islamic world, about the prospect of an "Islamic bomb." There has been substantial precautionary infighting about such a prospect, amid hints that Saudi Arabia is seeking to veto any sharing of Pakistani nuclear technology with Libya.

Most of the Latin American states, moreover, are quietly letting Brazil and Argentina know that they would not be pleased by a move toward any form of nuclear explosives, peaceful or otherwise.

The non-aligned countries have thus been relatively strong supporters of the International Atomic Energy Agency (IAEA) with its safeguards systems, and inclined to support quiet pressures for the extension of full-scope safeguards over peaceful nuclear activities around the globe. The IAEA has become increasingly politicized in style, just as have all other international bodies, but the non-aligned have sufficient interest in the efficient functioning of the Vienna Agency to moderate the volume and pace of their political use of the IAEA, so that it will remain (at least by comparison) one of the most businesslike and sober components of the UN structure.

Despite periodic threats at NPT review conferences, no states have withdrawn from the treaty. As a worldwide international legal consensus slowly develops by which states become more burdened by a responsibility to reassure their neighbors about their nuclear intentions, the non-aligned nations, with rare exceptions, will play a positive role in the evolution of this consensus.

Aside from committing themselves to non-acquisition of nuclear weapons, and submitting to IAEA inspection, perhaps the most relevant aspect of nuclear arms control for the non-aligned powers will be their attitudes toward nuclear-weapon-free zones. The nuclear-free zone proposal normally includes most of what adherence to the NPT would entail and includes somewhat more.[14] Parties to a nuclear-free zone must promise also not to tolerate the deployment of anyone else's nuclear weapons on their territory. Parties possessing such weapons promise not to use them within the agreed zone, and again not to deploy them within the zone. The link between prewar deployment and intrawar use is hardly insignificant; when a war erupts, nuclear weapons in place within the war zone have a much higher chance of coming into use, because of the sheer confusion and fog of war, or the initiative of local commanders, even if the national authority in charge of them were in the mood to withhold such weapons from use at the last moment.

Non-aligned attitudes on nuclear-weapons-free zones in large measure are parallel to the attitudes of the major powers.

The Latin American states, as noted, have already moved toward endorsing such a zone. The attitudes of Brazil and Argentina, the two most significant states in the region in nuclear competence, remain complicated, withholding full adherence to the treaty at the moment; the influence of other Latin American states is clearly being applied to push Brazil and Argentina in this direction.

Attitudes on nuclear-free zones in other regions are complicated by India's status in having already acquired nuclear explosives, and by the deep enmity between Israel and the Arab states, amid persistent rumors that Israel clandestinely has equipped itself with nuclear weapons.

THE SPREAD OF CONVENTIONAL ARMS

While the evidence is thus strong that the non-aligned nations share in the aversion to the spread of nuclear weapons, their attitudes on the parallel spread of conventional weapons have to be rated as much more mixed. The non-aligned of course resent any open statements that they are not to be trusted with either category of weapons, thus leaving the United States (or the Soviet Union) to present such arguments openly. One senses a quiet behind-the-scenes acceptance of the anti-nuclear proliferation argument, but the resentment of proposed bans on the sales of conventional weaponry seems to be a little more genuine.[15]

Again, the non-aligned are more sensible here than they may feel it is politic to admit. Most of their governments (excepting those that have a surfeit of oil revenue) realize that the acquisition of substantial conventional arms inventories can be quite expensive, and can thus set back the achievement of various goals of economic development. Most of them also can perceive the possibilities that the spread of more modern conventional weaponry could make wars more likely, or more destructive.

At the same time, the objective case against such weapons in the last two categories of impact is more challengeable, and this is not lost on the national leaderships of the third world. Some kinds of conventional weapons will make war less likely when they reinforce the defense. Nuclear weapons might have a similar deterrent effect from time to time, but all concerned fear that primitive "nth" power nuclear weapons systems would tend instead to invite preemptive attack. Turning from the likelihood of war to the costliness of war when it happens, the case seems even clearer. Nuclear weapons most assuredly would make any war among the non-aligned powers much more destructive. By contrast, some kinds of modern conventional weapons have lent themselves to the moderation and limitation of destruction.

Regarding the issue of economic cost, a few non-aligned countries contend that the acquisition of conventional arms aids rather than burdens their economic development. This is especially so when such nations become proficient at the indigenous production of conventional arms, rather than having to import such weapons from abroad. However, the same kind of "cutting edge" or "lead industry" argument sometimes also gets made even for high-technology weapons that have to be obtained entirely from foreign sources.

This kind of argument is always to be cross-examined and challenged, for it is offered by spokesmen for weapons programs whether it is true or not. The parallel domestic argument shows up within the United States when the military-industrial complex touts all the spinoffs that have emerged for the civilian sector as a result of military procurement and military research and development.

If such arguments are often hogwash, however, they are not always so. For Brazil or India, or another developing country, to acquire the ability to produce combat aircraft and other weapons systems may lift the rest of their industrial systems to high planes of precision and competence, with spinoffs that for a change are genuine returns to the civilian economy, rather than a waste of economic potential. For Saudi Arabia to have to train its pilots to fly modern jet fighter aircraft may infuse its population with a similar upward push in education and technological competence, a push it might not have achieved otherwise.

The non-aligned countries, generally so distrustful of the international trade and international divisions of labor, which they label "dependencia," may thus welcome a number of artificial reinforcements for domestic self-sufficiency, including domestic weapons production, and this may thrust some considerations of economic development philosophy ahead of considerations of arms control.

DEFENSE OVER OFFENSE

It is a truism by now that the non-aligned states have shown an extraordinary attachment to the post-colonial status quo. While sanctioning all kinds of revolutionary insurrection and military activity against the colonial powers, when such powers tried to hang on to territories in Africa and Asia, the non-aligned have been very steadfast in supporting the boundaries inherited from these colonial powers, rejecting virtually every irredentist claim, however strong such claims might be on considerations of religion and ethnicity, and have been reasonably steady also in supporting existing regimes against military overthrow by neighbors. The continued recognition of the Pol Pot regime in Cambodia and the continued seating of that regime at the United Nations, illustrates this all too well, flying in the face of its horrendous domestic performance. Similarly illustrating the pattern was the condemnation of India at the United Nations for the liberation of Bangladesh, and the general African opposition to Biafran independence and then to Somalian irredentist claims to territories within Ethiopia. Translated into considerations of arms control, these attitudes suggest more than a little concern among the non-aligned that insurrection and boundary revision not be encouraged or facilitated by the flow of modern arms, and that defensive checks be placed on the offensive use of arms by any state wanting to challenge this status quo.

Quite parallel to this attachment to a tenuous legitimacy of territorial status quo are the deeper non-aligned attitudes toward any aspiring regional powers. When India moves to the forefront of South Asian states in terms of military capability, or Brazil moves to the forefront of Latin American states, or Iraq reaches for a nuclear weapons capability, they may not draw very much open censure from their neighbors, yet the other states in practice are likely to adopt policies characteristic of old-fashioned balance-of-power politics, i.e., looking to their defenses and reshuffling alliances to cooperate in circumscribing the power of the leader. The cooperation will come quietly, in sharing of competence in arms supply and arms maintenance, and in a quiet diplomacy intended to frustrate the initiatives and reduce the leverage of the erstwhile hegemon. With a view to making such regional dominance less easy, moves will be made to punish the leader on small points, as a deterrent to continued pursuit of the central dominating position.

Distrustful of local hegemonic threats, the non-aligned states will be still more distrustful and disapproving of local megalomaniacs, even if the disapproval continues to be lower key. Khaddafi supplies the best example for the moment, although Idi Amin supplied it earlier.

For anyone to entertain the vision of being a great ideological leader for the non-aligned states is almost to present a contradiction in terms, for to be non-aligned is in a sense to reject the leadership of any great centralizing force.

The arms control implications remain the same. There will be great unease about any move toward nuclear weapons by such leaders. There will be substantial unease also about any substantial augmentation of the conventional arms available to their armies. There will be an interest in the acquisition of the kinds of arms that tend to favor the defense, rather than those favoring the offense, the kinds of weapons and military arrangements that leave each of the so-called non-aligned states more securely master in its own house.

RAPID DEPLOYMENT FORCES

If it is reasonable to assume that the non-aligned states will wish to avoid quick-reaction offensively inclined forces in their own ranks, it is even more plausible that they will generally not welcome the development and deployment of such forces by the major powers, forces that might be dispatched on short notice into third-world territories.[16]

The augmentation of airlift and sealift capabilities for both the United States and the Soviet Union has made possible what the US for a time called the Rapid Deployment Force (RDF), and similarly made possible the Soviet dispatch of Cuban troops into Angola, and then into Ethiopia and Yemen. As on every other question, a double standard has applied, whereby American and other Western incarnations of such forces are condemned more openly than those of countries of the Soviet bloc, but the practical realities of the third world arms control policy would be that they might welcome reductions in both sides' capability here.

This problem is illustrated by the Organization of African Unity (OAU) postures on the Angolan civil war, at least until the intervention of South African forces on the side of UNITA and the FNLA brought in a new and unignorably obnoxious element. For much of the civil war, the OAU's position was to disapprove of all the interventions from outside of Angola on behalf of any of the factions, hoping that all three of the anti-Portugese resistance groups would compromise their claims into a single government, rather than betting on the temptations of dramatic rapidly deployable help from outside. The OAU's hopes were to be frustrated, in part simply because the very possibility of flying in help existed. The Angolan civil war, put simply, would not have been as violent and as prolonged except for the troop carrier aircraft that appeared on the scene over the 1970s, a troop carrier deployment capability that arms control had not headed off.

CHEMICAL AND BIOLOGICAL WARFARE

Chemical weapons carry more than the normal stigma for weaponry. While this stigma emerged from the "first world" after World War I, it is maintained by the non-aligned nations today.

Perhaps this is for foolish reasons, just as some analysts contend that the original ban on chemical weaponry was a foolish follow-on to anti-German World War I propaganda. Chemical weapons might be humane weapons, it is sometimes argued, weapons capable of knocking an enemy's soldiers out of combat without killing or permanently injuring them. Perhaps such weapons are banned today only because human beings wish to maintain the bans on *something* in warfare, and will clung to whatever meager "accomplishments" they have negotiated in the laws of warfare in the past.

There are better reasons than this for retaining the ban on Chemical and Biological Weapons (CBW), however. While some weapons in this category might be surprisingly humane, others promise to be enormously deadly, offering any and all nations enormous capacities for destructiveness, comparable ultimately even to nuclear weapons.

The underdeveloped countries share a special aversion to any further legitimation or development of chemical warfare capabilities, for the breaches of the ban on their use have tended to come precisely in the less-developed corners of the world: Italy against Ethiopia in 1935; Japan against China during World War II; the accusations of Soviet use against Afghanistan and Cambodia; the accusations of American use against Korea and Vietnam; and the accusations of Egyptian and Soviet use against Yemen.[17] Various forms of non-lethal chemical warfare have also been thought appropriate for counter-guerrilla operations in the past, and guerrilla wars tend to get fought more in jungle areas than in the fully industrialized zones of the world.

The non-aligned denunciations of chemical weapons are more than ritualistic cant, since they relate to the practical interests of the non-aligned nations. If a United Nations double standard seems to let the Soviet Union and its patrons get off easier, the interest directed to the charges of chemical warfare in Afghanistan and Cambodia nonetheless shows the limits of this double standard. If the use of lethal or non-lethal chemical agents, or any form of biological agents, were to prove decisive in establishing a Moscow-backed central authority in these countries, many other countries would be quite appalled at the precedent.

TERRORISM

A fair amount of what Americans regard as terrorism emerges from the third world, while its targets are often in the economically advanced first world.

Diplomats for the non-aligned are often reluctant to denounce terrorism with any fervor comparable to that of spokesmen for the West, which again might lead to some mistaken conclusions. Are the non-aligned nations really so much at ease with the prospect of continued terrorism around the globe? When the test comes to whether their airports will be available as safe havens for skyjackers, or whether their hotels can be used as training grounds and rest areas, it is clear that most nations of the world understand that terrorism is a threat to all. Reluctant to denounce the Palestinians because of the third world commitment to the Arab cause against Israel, reluctant to condemn most movements that label themselves leftist or anticolonial, the non-aligned governments nonetheless will be receptive to concrete steps designed to make terrorism less easy.[18]

The tougher question, for both developed and developing countries, comes in weighing how this consideration will balance against the desire for advanced conventional arms. The same surface-to-air missile (SAM) that can let an infantryman shoot down a jet fighter would allow a terrorist to down a jet airliner. An anti-tank guided missile can also be used to attack a police station or a presidential palace.

VERIFICATION

Soviet-American arms control debates frequently get hung up on issues of verification, with the US quite logically insisting that an unverified agreement is all too likely to be violated, while the Russians somewhat perversely argue that verification implies a distrust that has no place in international negotiation. Whether the two superpowers are likely to remain typecast in these two roles is itself not so certain anymore, as some subtle changes of issue have made the Soviets more verification-minded, and the US more a spokesman for trust.

The non-aligned nations, showing their independence from Moscow, have increasingly endorsed the need for verifiability in disarmament agreements. Perhaps the credit for this has to go to the American diplomats who have stressed year after year that an unverified agreement might well accelerate, rather than slow, an arms race.

Yet other realities intrude here, besides the persuasiveness of American government spokesmen over the years. Arab states are now genuinely concerned about verification with regard to the risks inherent in Israel's nuclear potential. Black African states are now genuinely concerned about verification, with regard to the risks of similar potential in South Africa. Even the Russians became more concerned about verification with the Nuclear Non-Proliferation Treaty in the late 1960s, suddenly demanding rather than scoffing at IAEA inspection of the peaceful nuclear facilities of West Germany, and of every other non-weapons state, and suddenly tolerating IAEA safeguards in East Germany and in each of the other Soviet satellites in Eastern Europe.

PEACEKEEPING AND CONFIDENCE-BUILDING

With only a few exceptions, the non-aligned nations do not welcome wars. In earlier times, by the fullest-blown version of balance of power logic, any state concerned with maintaining its independence might have welcomed a war between the countries potentially threatening its independence. A war between two continental powers might well have weakened the ability of either to attack Britain, or to attack the independent states of North and South America. Any such glee with a war in Europe had to fade, however, once the economies of the world became substantially intertwined such that a military disaster on one continent became an economic disaster for other continents.

With today's nuclear armaments, of course, a military disaster on one continent could become a military disaster on all continents, as weapons use escalates and as radioactive fallout is spread. Even if a war between the West and East were kept far more limited, moreover, the economic fallout would again be very damaging to the non-aligned, just as World War I was damaging to North and South America.

The non-aligned can thus generally be counted upon to retain their positive interest in peacekeeping and mediating operations, after a war has erupted, and in the installation of confidence-building measures (CBMs) to head off a war before it breaks out. The contributions here will come in the form of supportive votes in the General Assembly, and in the loan of military forces or experienced diplomats for the implementation of peacemaking.

A nation captures some international prestige and stature if its battalion does well in UN service, with the military commanders getting some actual field experience in the process, experience that could come in handy if the nation involved ever gets into a war. If a diplomat from a non-aligned nation does a good job and wins a Nobel Peace Prize, all the more prestige is to be had. If he subsequently becomes a contender for the post of Secretary-General of the United Nations, the returns for his nation are still greater.

The non-aligned states can also generally be counted upon to be supportive of research undertaken by the United Nations on disarmament and arms control, and with this, on the collection of data on arms acquisitions and military expenditures. The major exception to date has been on the question of conventional arms transfers, for reasons noted above.

The world is fully aware of the unreliability of unverified disarmament agreements, but many individual states continue to resist efforts to publicize their own arms acquisitions and programs. Resolutions calling for UN inventories of weapons will therefore continue to win overwhelming General Assembly votes, only to be followed by far less than overwhelming cooperation when the individual states are asked to supply information about their own programs. Yet this desire to know, but not to be known, is hardly a new feature in the world. Rather than originating with the non-aligned, it has been a part of the anarchic international system for as long as one can remember.

TRANSLATION INTO AMERICAN INTERESTS

How can the United States apply this analysis of the arms control interests of the non-aligned states to its own policy choices? The clearest form of advice has already been keynoted several times, namely that the public statements of these states should not be taken at face value. It does little good to become irritated at their apparent lack of candor or wisdom, for the actual policies of most of these states are characterized by a commonsense approach that offers opportunities to make some practical gains in the control of armaments. Rather than remembering the irrationality of the Ayatollah's Iran as a model of how the third world will behave, policymakers should remember the contribution of Algeria in ending the hostage crisis, and the cooperation of a great many of the non-aligned states in applying quiet pressures and ostracism against the Iranian regime.

The more recently admitted members of the international state system have hardly missed the practical realities of military policy and foreign policy. Whatever their high-minded or ideological rhetoric at Special Sessions on Disarmament, or ordinary General Assembly sessions, or anywhere else, the non-aligned countries, in truth, should be assumed to have a well-developed understanding of the realities of military force, the opportunities offered by the development of such forces, and the dangers and pitfalls in such development. These states, in short, have real interests with regard to the possibilities of multinational arms restraint; they are not merely posturing or game-playing, but pursuing objectives very materially linked to their own national safety and well-being. United States policy on arms control and the non-aligned will be successful only if it takes these real objectives into account.

NOTES

1. For a valuable general discussion of the non-aligned movement, see Ernest Corea, "Non-Alignment: The Dynamics of a Movement," *Behind the Headlines* XXXVI:1, June, 1977 (Toronto: Canadian Institute of International Affairs).

2. For a representative sampling of the official positions taken by the non-aligned states at the United Nations, the best place to begin would be

The United Nations Disarmament Yearbook (New York: United Nations), published annually.

3. A very useful introduction to what was significantly new about the concept of arms control can be found in Thomas C. Schelling and Morton H. Halperin, *Strategy and Arms Control* (New York: Twentieth Century Fund, 1961).

4. For a valuable discussion of the advantages of less than fully open diplomacy, see Harold Nicolson, *Diplomacy* (London: Oxford University Press, 1963).

5. Some interesting insights on the special character of Latin American arms control approaches can be found in John R. Redick, "The Tlatelolco Regime and Nonproliferation in Latin America," *International Organization,* 35:1 (Winter, 1981), pp. 103–134.

6. See Jennifer Seymour Whitaker, *Africa and the United States: Vital Interests* (New York: New York University Press, 1978) for a discussion of black African views on arms questions.

7. The special role of French interventionary forces in Africa and elsewhere is discussed in Pierre Lellouche and Dominique Moisi, "French Policy in Africa: A Lonely Battle against Destabilization." *International Security,* 3:4 (Spring, 1979), pp. 108–133.

8. A useful discussion of Arab attitudes on arms control can be found in Paul Jabber, *Not By War Alone* (Berkeley: University of California Press, 1981); see also Yair Evron, "Arms Control in the Middle East: Some Proposals and Their Confidence-Building Roles," in *Arms Control and Military Force,* ed. by Christoph Bertram (Totowa, NJ: Allanheld, Osmun and Co., 1980), pp. 213–222.

9. The military threat to oil shipments is discussed in *Oil Fields as Military Objectives: A Feasibility Study* (Washington: Congressional Research Service, 1975).

10. The maritime arms issue, as it affects smaller powers around the borders of the world's oceans, is discussed in Michael McGwire, "The Proliferation of Maritime Weapons Systems in the Indo-Pacific Region," in Robert O'Neill, *Insecurity!* (Canberra: Australian National University Press, 1978), pp. 77–107.

11. For an analysis of the special role of Cuba, see Jiri Valenta, "The Soviet-Cuban Alliance in Africa and the Caribbean," *The World Today,* 37:2 (February, 1981), pp. 45–53; for a similar analysis of North Korea, see Y. C. Kim, "Pyongyang, Moscow and Peking," *Problems of Communism,* 27:6 (November–December, 1978), pp. 54–58.

12. For a fuller discussion of the nuclear proliferation issue, see the chapter by Michael Brenner in this volume.

13. For a parallel analysis of non-aligned attitudes on nuclear prolifera-

tion, see Joseph S. Nye, "Maintaining a Nonproliferation Regime," *International Organization*, 36:1 (Winter, 1981), pp. 15–38.

14. In the case of Latin America—the one operational example of a nuclear-weapon-free zone—there is a disquieting tolerance of the possibility of "peaceful nuclear explosives," nuclear explosives somehow distinguishable from warheads designed for military use. See Alfonso García Robles, *The Latin American Nuclear-Weapon-Free Zone*, Occasional Paper No. 19 (Muscatine, Iowa: The Stanley Foundation, May, 1979).

15. On conventional arms spread, see Andrew J. Pierre, *The Global Politics of Arms Sales* (Princeton, New Jersey: Princeton University Press, 1982).

16. Some of the tensions caused by rapid-deployment capabilities are outlined in Abdul Mansur, "The American Threat to Saudi Arabia," *Survival* 23:1 (January/February, 1981), pp. 36–41.

17. For a comprehensive survey of the accusations of chemical warfare, see Stockholm International Peace Research Institute, *The Problem of Chemical and Biological Warfare* (in six volumes), (New York: Humanities Press, 1971).

18. The attitudes of the non-aligned on terrorism are discussed in John F. Murphy, "The United Nations Proposals on the Control and Repression of Terrorism," in *International Terrorism and Political Crimes,* ed. by M. Cherif Bassiouni (Springfield, Illinois: Charles C. Thomas, 1975), pp. 493–506.

III. LOOKING AHEAD: SOME ELEMENTS OF A FUTURE AGENDA

This section endeavors to apply the broad historical, institutional, strategic, and political perspectives of the first two sections to more specific areas of policy. The focus is on three subjects—nuclear non-proliferation, conventional arms control, and confidence-building measures and verification—that have important multilateral dimensions. The subjects were chosen to illustrate the potentially broad scope of multilateral approaches, rather than to give a comprehensive review of possible areas for multilateral action. In each case, the author assesses how multilateral efforts can contribute to (or detract from) the resolution of serious security problems.

After analyzing the unique nature of the non-proliferation regime, Michael Brenner suggests several reasons why the international consensus against further proliferation may be breaking down. He then presents a detailed assessment of the strengths and weaknesses of a series of multinational measures to limit proliferation. In addressing the broad subject of conventional arms control, Edward C. Luck cites a number of reasons why conventional arms, and their limitation, should receive a higher priority on the US, multilateral, and public agendas. A number of serious obstacles to progress in the near future are described, but the chapter suggests a series of steps that could provide the groundwork for substantive negotiations if political conditions improve. Steven Canby assesses the utility of various kinds of confidence-building measures and verification efforts, both for Europe and for parts of the third world. The benefits of these measures are frequently overstated and their liabilities overlooked, he points out, but the paper suggests several innovative proposals that would forward security, as well as political, goals.

In the final chapter, Edward C. Luck outlines a future role for multilateralism that takes into account both its current weaknesses and its long-term potential. He urges multilateral forums to focus on reducing the causes of insecurity rather than on abstract and mechanistic formulas for disarmament, and to pursue arms control where it is most needed rather than where it is most easily applied. In light of the failure of the second Special Session to foster a global consensus, he recommends that the focus of attention be shifted to regional problems. Major progress on the global level, he concludes, will require a relaxation of Soviet-American tensions, a reassertion of positive leadership by the superpowers, and a willingness on the part of non-nuclear countries to address seriously global issues—such as nuclear proliferation, conventional arms, chemical weapons, and verification—as well as the Soviet-American nuclear competition.

RENEWING THE NON-PROLIFERATION REGIME: A MULTINATIONAL APPROACH

MICHAEL J. BRENNER

The postwar era in international politics is, in large measure, a record of efforts by the world community—and especially the great powers—to come to grips with the sobering reality created by weapons of mass destruction. An appreciation of the unique threat they pose to orderly and peaceful inter-state relations has inspired a strenuous campaign to contain their spread. In the United States, nuclear arms have been viewed from their inception as something to be contained, guarded, and restricted.

Whatever the shifts in stress and accent, successive administrations have acknowledged the menace of nuclear proliferation. The threat it represents is exceptional; so too has been the challenge to prevent weapons spread.

As an arms control issue, nuclear proliferation has three singular characteristics. First, it aims beyond limiting the *number* of weapons that states are permitted to deploy, in the interest of a stable equilibrium. Rather, it seeks to outlaw an entire class of weapons and to impose an absolute prohibition on their acquisition—by those states that currently do not possess them. Strikingly, they are the most powerful, if not the most useful, arms now known. The governments that acceded to the Non-Proliferation Treaty (NPT) (as non-nuclear-weapons states), and those who are the object of entreaties to do so, are being asked or have agreed already to a self-denying injunction on a potentially crucial means of national defense. These are exceptional, probably unprecedented acts by sovereign states. For those who accept the realpolitik axiom that "arms make the state," it comes close to being an unnatural political act. Even those who interpret a rejection of the nuclear option as entirely consistent with national self-interest must consider the possibility that future security circumstances may compel a re-examination of that commitment.

Hence, the prudent policymaker cannot avoid confronting the question of how much political capital should be invested in diplomatic ventures intended to prevent the spread of atomic weapons. Logically, he is drawn to multilateral approaches that serve as a form of political load-sharing, while strengthening common norms on what constitutes proper nuclear (or non-nuclear) conduct.

Second, uncertainties associated with a voluntary renunciation of nuclear arms are accentuated by the element of discrimination in the Non-Proliferation Treaty and associated accords. The prohibitions and restrictions they register are not universal. Five states now have substantial nuclear arsenals, another has exploded a nuclear device, and one or two more are believed to have manufactured and stockpiled atomic weapons clandestinely. The pledges of abstinence already made speak to the extraordinary gravity with which states regard nuclear weapons. They also underscore the potential fragility of the bargain incorporated in the NPT whereby non-weapons states exchanged their pledge for a commitment by weapons states to make available the fruits of civilian nuclear power and to limit their own nuclear arsenals. The loud protests against steps taken by the United States under the Carter Administration to restrict access to plutonium fuels, and related technologies, testified to the sensitivities of non-weapons states who do not accept willingly any alteration in the terms of an agreement that already compromises their rights as independent countries.

Where non-proliferation objectives point to the imposition of new restraints and restrictions, the introduction of further elements of discrimination must be kept to a minimum, a consensus in support of them carefully cultivated, and appropriate compensation offered.

The third distinctive feature of non-proliferation efforts is that weapons control is very closely connected, if not inseparable, from deprivation of another highly valued national good: atomic power as an energy source. Where policy concentrates on restricting the diffusion of technological capabilities (and fuels), it at the same time reduces the freedom of states to utilize civilian nuclear energy as they might choose. The potential loss is perceived as all the greater in a world where energy security has everywhere become a cardinal concern. Nuclear power, popularly viewed as the crowning achievement of modern science and technology, has always promised many wondrous and bountiful things. To many governments, it offers the hope of energy independence: a still preeminent goal despite the improving outlook for oil consumers (and the concomitant softening of demand for atomic power plants). The willingness of non-weapons states to make fresh concessions, therefore, is reduced by practical need as well as principled national sovereignty.

This implicit penalty will only be acceptable when legitimate nuclear energy interests are officially recognized through international treaties and institutions. Some form of multinational arrangement to assure access to nuclear goods, while closing the fuel cycle internationally, is probably a condition for restricting sensitive technologies and controlling plutonium fuels.

RECENT HISTORY

Awareness of the proliferation problem's extraordinary challenge to arms controllers has been heightened in recent years. The pivotal date is 1974. Three coincidental events in that year combined to refocus attention on proliferation, highlighting new features of the problem and prompting major initiatives by four successive American administrations. These developments were: (1) the Indian nuclear explosion; (2) the oil embargo; and (3) the first contracts for sale of sensitive, fuel-producing technology. Their effects were synergistic, triggering an intense debate as to how great was the proliferation danger inherent in civilian nuclear facilities, and raising serious questions about the adequacy of the controls and restraints represented by the NPT and the International Atomic Energy Agency (IAEA) safeguards.

A review of these events provides a useful perspective on efforts aimed at tightening the constraints on the spread of sensitive nuclear materials. It also spotlights the obstacles that must be overcome to fashion a new consensus on the rules and norms governing the international transfer and use of fuels and technologies.[1]

The most stunning nuclear event of 1974 was India's detonation of a rudimentary atomic device. The act forced a new awareness of the unbreakable bond between peaceful atomic power programs and weapons manufacture, for India had used its civilian facilities as the fuel source and technological base for its bomb. Most worrisome, the critical technology employed, spent-fuel reprocessing, and the key material, plutonium, were on the point of becoming items of commercial exchange.

Moreover, India had neatly sidestepped the safeguards that were supposed to prevent the exploitation of civilian operations for military purposes. It was a sober reminder of the incompleteness of the non-proliferation regime built around the International Atomic Energy Agency and the Nuclear Non-Proliferation Treaty of 1968. There were three lessons to be learned. First, those non-signatories of the NPT, who were not subject to IAEA-administered full-scope safeguards, were in a position to exploit uncontrolled indigenous facilities to build a bomb even more easily and cheaply than many had presumed. Second, safeguarded facilities were more vulnerable to abuse when linked to unregulated capabilities (whether they be legal or illegal). Finally, the United States, and other concerned parties, were wholly unprepared to impose sanctions, official or otherwise, on a government that detonated a nuclear explosion, in what reasonably, if not indisputably, could be claimed was a violation of bilateral agreements (although not an international treaty).

The Arab oil embargo, and OPEC price hike, had a multitude of profound economic consequences. From a non-proliferation perspective, they were unvaryingly ominous.

All states were sensitized to the costs of energy dependence. Threatened disruption of access to critical oil supplies created powerful political and economic incentives to develop more independent energy sources, nuclear energy prominent among them. The drive to energy security, spurred by vulnerabilities manifest in 1973–74, has been a constant in world affairs ever since.

The burgeoning world market for nuclear technology was soon populated by new, aggressive sellers as well as new buyers. Suppliers were ready and willing to meet emerging demand. States proficient in nuclear technology saw sales abroad as essential to defray the heavy costs of their own ambitious atomic energy programs, as well as a means to earn back some of the foreign exchange needed to offset oil-induced balance-of-payments deficits. Finally, the strong incentive to sell in a highly competitive market led some suppliers to set less demanding terms of sale for conventional reactors, and to offer previously restricted technologies for fuel reprocessing and uranium enrichment. The strong economic pull of demand for secure energy, and the push to sell high-priced nuclear technologies in order to recoup a portion of their skyrocketing oil costs, combined to create market conditions that militated against the collective imposition of tighter controls on the reprocessing technology and plutonium fuels whose proliferation risk had been exposed by the Indian explosion.

Evidence was soon forthcoming that the worries about an international commerce in sensitive nuclear technologies and fuels were not misplaced. Revelation of France's agreement to sell reprocessing plants to Taiwan and South Korea, and of West Germany's multibillion dollar deal to provide Brazil with both reprocessing and enrichment technology, left no doubt that a competitive market logic was driving down restrictions on the critical "barrier" technologies. The risk was that widespread reprocessing would lead to general use of plutonium as reactor fuel.[2] Ready access to plutonium, in turn, removed the greatest technical obstacle to bomb manufacture. Thus, the gloomy prospect was that, if the trend continued, the question of whether a state had a weapons capability could be answered in terms of a production schedule.

LIMITS TO CONSENSUS

For the United States, these unprecedented nuclear transfer agreements carried two profound lessons. First, Washington alone could not prevent the spread of facilities and fuels contributing to weapons development. Firm understanding among all potential suppliers about the transfer of nuclear materials would have to be a key ingredient in an amended and updated non-proliferation regime. Success in negotiating supplier guidelines on that score have been only partially successful. There is now tacit agreement prohibiting outright sales of fuel producing technologies. However, significant gaps remain in the supposedly common front against nuclear exports. Among suppliers, only the United States, Canada, and Australia condition the export of nuclear materials on the recipient state's acceptance of full-scope safeguards. Loopholes in the composition of the list of prohibited export items, and slack enforcements, have permitted growth of a semi-illicit traffic in materials that can be used for weapons purposes. (The Pakistani atomic program provides the most striking evidence of how the current system can be exploited.) The slackening demand for nuclear power plants, in the last few years, has presented fewer occasions where transfer of sensitive technologies might come under serious discussion. Yet the financial incentives to sell these "big-ticket" items remain, as does latent interest in their acquisition.

The situation that has emerged since 1974 has affected Washington's approach to proliferation in a second respect. No non-proliferation strategy could hope for success unless it addressed the energy cum economic insecurities that color so much thinking about atomic power worldwide. The Carter Administration, which tried strenuously to alter the terms of availability of fuels and technology, belatedly realized that proliferation policy, inescapably, is going to be strongly influenced, if not dominated, by the broad struggle to cope with disordered world energy conditions. Its successor in Washington gives evidence of seeing the connection, but has yet to reconcile energy and non-proliferation considerations in a set of credible, persuasive policies. The best of intentions may not be enough. To the extent that the proliferation problem is linked to the spread of civilian facilities, the chances of reaching a general agreement on the nature and degree of risk, much less on the means for dealing with it, are reduced by the world's continuing preoccupation with energy questions.

For many observers, and for some governments (the United States outstanding among them), the existing arrangements for regulating the nuclear marketplace are defective in both structure and scope for dealing with the threat of weapons spread. But there is a distinct absence of agreement on either where the danger lies or how it should be addressed. A broad if not universal consensus *does* remain on the principles embodied in the NPT. Countries are not abrogating the NPT. None are preaching the virtues of nuclear weapons, and the vital importance of safeguards is recognized nearly everywhere. The cleavages have appeared on those issues that represent the "new agenda" created by the events of 1974. Three issues are most in dispute.

1. Does the spread of reprocessing plants and plutonium fuels carry with it a major increase in the danger of weapons proliferation? The US, under Jimmy Carter at least, answered with an alarmed "yes." Most fellow supplier states have been dubious, to varying degrees, while consumers deny outright that any threat exists.

2. Given some noteworthy level of risk, is the most effective approach to impose more stringent export conditions or, rather, to work toward keeping consumers within a strengthened IAEA safeguards system (even at the expense of less than airtight controls on nuclear materials) while exercising friendly persuasion on problem cases? US policy, as embodied in the Nuclear Non-Proliferation Act, leaned toward the former. The policy, if not the law, has now been modified by President Reagan. The West Europeans and Japanese strongly argue the virtues of tactful restraint.

3. What priority should be accorded non-proliferation, as compared to other foreign policy goals? Clearly, the US, even under Reagan, sees the problem as more important and feels greater responsibility for acting on it than do most of its allies and other suppliers. Consumers, and developing countries generally, believe the danger is overstated and the concern misplaced.

In the light of those basic differences in outlook, it is a formidable challenge to obtain agreement on rules of the road, beyond those that form the old, NPT/IAEA based regime. The paradox, and policy dilemma, is that a more embracing consensus covering plutonium fuels has only seemed attainable at the unacceptably high price of diluted standards and softer export conditions. The only way out of this box lies with multinational nuclear centers. They carry the potential of meeting practical needs for fuel assurances and waste management while serving as the core around which a broad consensus on further non-proliferation measures can develop.

ELEMENTS OF US POLICY

Although the United States has lost the power to control global nuclear affairs, it has continued to take the initiative in efforts at stemming the spread of atomic weapons. Since 1974 Washington has led the effort to divert the current trends in the direction of proliferating capabilities, if not bombs. Unavoidably, these have been exercises in multilateral arms control.

Multilateralism, insofar as non-proliferation is concerned, might be understood as the active, if not necessarily formal cooperation of states acting with the conscious intention of preventing or retarding the development and deployment of armaments. Whether the emphasis is on capabilities or motivations, whatever the mix of instruments, no non-proliferation policy can meet its objectives unless it achieves a high degree of concertation among major supplier states, cooperation between suppliers and consumers, and, in the longer run, a strong consensus on steps to be taken against states that violate non-proliferation norms.[3]

Recent American non-proliferation policy has emphasized the need to regain collective control over international civilian nuclear power. These efforts have had the interlocking objectives of (1) reshaping and tightening the system for transfer and use of nuclear materials; (2) reestablishing the consensus on ground rules embodied in the NPT and the IAEA to take account of shifting conditions and, in the eyes of some, especially the United States, new interpretations of the risk; and (3) addressing the legitimate energy needs of states without compromising commitment to non-proliferation. As amended and partially redirected by the Reagan Administration, Washington's approach has placed new stress on a fourth objective: relieving the security anxieties of non-weapons states that could put them on the road to bomb manufacture.[4]

Overall strategy has been a mix of four ingredients, the proportions varying according to an Administration's inclination and external circumstances.[5] One component is *denial*. Denial takes several forms: outright prohibitions on the sale or transfer of sensitive items (high-enriched uranium, fuel-manufacturing technologies); making exports contingent on acceptance of safeguards, or pledges to forego certain activities (reprocessing); and the requiring of "litmus tests" as the basis for approving certain actions (the "need standard" applied to requests for the recyling of plutonium). Unilaterally imposed controls by the United States are grounded on the consent right it holds over the disposition of American-supplied fuel and the use of American-supplied reactors. These controls were tightened by the Nuclear Non-Proliferation Act of 1978, and actively administered by the Carter Administration. Its goal of winning the cooperation of other suppliers in support of its strict denial strategy was, as noted, only partially successful.

A policy of denial, so construed, suffers from diminishing effectiveness due to the steady diffusion of nuclear knowledge and capabilities, and Washington's failure to persuade others of the workability of and critical need for more stringent controls, especially those on plutonium. The challenge now is to give institutional form to multilateral agreements on the proper conditions for the production, transfer, and use of plutonium fuels. Those discussions are likely to focus, as they properly should, on multinational facilities, where direction and ownership—but not necessarily operational responsibility—is shared.

Prevention, or more properly *detection,* is the second pillar of the current system for containing proliferation. Its keystone is the International Atomic Energy Agency's system of safeguards based on inspections and recordkeeping. Agency safeguards are intended not to create physical impediments to the abuse of civilian facilities but rather to provide warning where diversions or other illicit activity have occurred. Their effectiveness is premised on two beliefs. One is that detection will occur early enough to provide the timely warning that would enable the IAEA and its members to take appropriate action. The other crucial assumption is that the likelihood of detection is sufficiently high, and the possible penalties for cheating sufficiently great, that any prospective violator will be deterred.

The controversy recently engendered by claims of weakness in the safeguards system has raised some doubts about its technical efficiency, and, therefore, by implication, about its deterrent value.[6]

At a time when the agency is also suffering from a sharpening of political conflict, the launching of multinational enterprises under its auspices is jeopardized. Plans for establishing an International Plutonium Storage System, for example, envisage the IAEA as the custodial body. Any doubts about the agency's competence or organizational integrity feed skepticism, most widespread in the United States, about the desirability and workability of multinational schemes. Yet the IAEA remains the only vehicle for organizing large-scale multinational enterprises. Moreover, it is desirable for the agency to be given responsibility for positive undertakings that meet genuine member interests. It is the one conceivable means to mute rhetorical confrontation, and to reinforce the sense of collective interest.

Incentives constitute the third component of non-proliferation policy, including fuel assurances and assistance in managing reactor waste. A commitment to help in the acquisition of the benefits of civilian nuclear power has been part of the deal for acceptance of restraints and controls. It took on a new importance with the active Carter Administration campaign to curb the use of plutonium fuels. Incentives for consumer states (and for some suppliers as well, insofar as waste management is concerned) were much discussed as a way to get acceptance of proposed limitations on reprocessing and plutonium recycling.

The United States' failure to produce a credible set of concrete proposals hampered Carter's ambitious strategy. The lively debate engendered by the Administration's anti-plutonium campaign did give rise to a rich and varied menu of ideas for reinforcing the reliability of nuclear fuel supplies, and also for handling the mounting waste disposal problem. Many were aired and given close examination in the course of the International Nuclear Fuel Cycle Evaluation. None of any consequence have come into existence. They should be revived. The implementation of specific measures is badly needed in order to tighten the bonds between suppliers and consumers in a renewed nuclear compact and to deal with outstanding issues associated with reprocessing and waste repatriation.

Meeting *the legitimate security needs* of non-weapons states is another critical aspect of non-proliferation. Whereas the first three ingredients concentrate on issues of access and capability, this approach addresses intention and motivation. Ultimately, the decision to build the bomb will turn on estimates of national interest, and how security might be enhanced by its acquisition. However much that decision might be influenced by the availability of means, and the drift of policies evolving incrementally over time, considerations of military utility and diplomatic advantage can be expected to determine the final outcome. Clearly, there is an inverse relationship between how secure a country feels and its interest in developing a nuclear weapons capability.

REAGAN ADMINISTRATION POLICY

This last element has been given place of prominence in the non-proliferation policy of the Reagan Administration. While sharing most essential principles with that of President Carter, there have been shifts of accent, the emphasis on the security motivations of possible proliferators foremost among them. The elements of continuity include the following: commitment to strengthening and improving IAEA safeguards provisions; support for the NPT and encouragement to non-signatories to accede to it; and an insistence on full-scope IAEA safeguards as a condition for nuclear exports from the US to new recipients.

Differences appear in a number of areas. First, pressure on suppliers and consumers to impose stringent export conditions over the entire range of transfer agreements has been noticeably eased. Also, the current administration has adopted a highly political approach to nuclear exchanges, dealing with countries on a case-by-case basis that makes specific reference to estimations of proliferation risk understood with regard to intent more than capability. Second, Washington now takes a much more benign view of plutonium and reprocessing. The administration encourages the development of plutonium-related processes and technology at home, while largely abandoning the effort to restrict reprocessing abroad.

Above all, the Reagan Administration has tried to treat proliferation less in terms of controlling capabilities and more in terms of removing incentives. In the words of its chief official responsible for non-proliferation policy, the goal is to "remove motivations for nuclear weapons acquisition by moves to satisfy legitimate aspirations for a credible conventional defense capability . . . to strengthen . . . alliance guarantees . . . [and to] mediate and resolve disputes.''[7] These are laudable objectives; and there is much that can be accomplished by astute American diplomacy and a clear, consistent set of defense policies.

But the limitations of US power and influence are totally evident. Indeed, it can be argued that the gradual unravelling of the postwar security system of which Washington was architect and custodian has heightened the sense of vulnerability felt by candidate members to the nuclear club. Prominent on the list of states commonly viewed as potential weapons states are either uneasy former and present dependents of the US (Taiwan, South Korea, Pakistan) or those in regions that are unsettled and where American ability to contribute to stability appears diminished (e.g., Southern Africa, South Asia, and, of course, the Middle East).

In these areas, multilateral diplomacy is the only feasible approach—whether for settlement of disputes or for dissuading states from exercising the nuclear option. However, one cannot overstate the difficulties of collectively marshalling and deploying the political resources for accomplishing either task. Even in those instances where the major powers view the risk of nuclear weapons proliferation with equal concern, it does not automatically follow that they will take joint action. For the United States, as for other powers, the pursuit of non-proliferation inevitably means making tradeoffs among several objectives and interests. What it is prepared to do, much less capable of doing in any region, is dependent on a complex pattern of intersecting, crosscutting relationships. The policy decisions taken, whether forced by exigent circumstances or based on careful calculation, will not always be the ones that advance the cause of non-proliferation.

Reasonably, one can have only very modest expectations of conjectured multilateral diplomatic initiatives aimed at removing the underlying security causes for new nuclear arms programs. Improving the odds on a collective policy of dissuasion depends, above all, on a marked rise in the importance that key governments attach to the goal of removing the proliferation threat. A keener appreciation of the threat doubtless occurs with each successful entry into the nuclear club (and even more serious action might eventuate were a minor nuclear power actually to use a bomb in combat). Regrettably, tangible evidence of non-proliferation policy's past failure also serves to diminish the credibility of friendly persuasion, or less than friendly sanction.

Accentuation of non-proliferation as a goal of national policies, for non-weapons states as well as for the great powers, may happen in a less dramatic fashion. A renewed effort to refocus attention and energies on the prosaic yet essential tasks of reconstituting the international fuel cycle can pay the added dividend of strengthening collective norms against proliferation. Progress in dealing with the capabilities dimension of the problem could indirectly prepare the ground for concerted attempts to do something about incentives. Without neglecting security questions, a revival of multilateral programs to put civilian nuclear power in better order worldwide, making it as difficult and costly as possible for governments to get hold of the wherewithal for making bombs, seems the way to begin.

A MENU OF MULTILATERAL APPROACHES

The current state of affairs is clearly less than satisfactory. The "regime" that has been built up over the years reveals major weaknesses: imperfect safeguards, erosion of support for and confidence in the basic understanding between nuclear proficient and non-proficient states, and the inability to control satisfactorily the dissemination of sensitive nuclear materials. Strenuous attempts by the Carter Administration to remedy the situation did not succeed in restoring effectiveness and credibility to the global system of restraint and regulation, even though it did raise the consciousness of increasing risk. Its successor in Washington searches haltingly for a viable new approach.

Measures are urgently needed that not only will deal with the immediate issues of access to fuels and technologies, but will also encourage growth of a new consensus. Multilateral measures are the only ones that carry that seminal potential. They need not, and should not be exclusive of bilateral accords and regional understandings. They are, however, of central importance.

PLUTONIUM, FUEL ASSURANCES, AND WASTE MANAGEMENT

The most pressing set of problems centers on (1) demands for access to nuclear fuels, including plutonium; (2) the commercial pressures to reprocess generated by facilities in operation; and (3) the vulnerabilities associated with such access. The development of most national atomic power programs has been predicated on the reprocessing of reactor waste and the recycling of separated plutonium. Closure of the fuel cycle through reprocessing has been seen as a simple, safe, and cheap method. A generation of nuclear officials grew up believing that it would simultaneously solve the problem of waste disposal, extend fuel resources, and provide a valuable lead-in to fast breeder programs.

This was the chain of thinking that the Carter Administration set out to break. As two senior Carter officials have recently noted, "the linkage between the spread of civilian facilities and weapons potential" was "the cornerstone of the Carter Administration's approach" to non-proliferation. In the end, it was frustrated by an inability to solve the "basic conflict . . . between denial of access to nuclear materials and a companion emphasis on assuring access to reactor fuel."[8] The energy anxieties of consumers, as well as the terms of the nuclear "deal" embodied in the NPT, dictated that access to fuels be provided on a reliable and timely basis. The tentative and partial steps taken in that direction could not hope to satisfy nations made increasingly skeptical about the sanctity of trade agreements, a skepticism accentuated by the campaign against plutonium and by the more stringent export conditions advanced by the administration, which were codified in the Nuclear Non-Proliferation Act.

Theoretically, the best hope for reconciling these positions always has been through multilateral means. Carter recognized this truth in his early promises of forthright American proposals on internationalizing fuel assurances and plans for waste management. Congress backed the idea, affirming its support for a Multinational Fuel Bank and urging the creation of international facilities for spent-fuel storage. The concluding report of the International Nuclear Fuel Cycle Evaluation also spoke in terms of fuel banks, multinational facilities, and of a Uranium Emergency Safety Network including stockpiling, cross-contracting, and related confidence-building measures. Hardly an official report or academic analysis has failed to make the case for moving in the same direction.

The attractions of the multilateral alternative are considerable. Institutional arrangements that restrict the location and terms of access to legitimate but sensitive nuclear facilities serve several purposes.

They could allay some of the genuine concern about secure access to nuclear fuels, i.e., low enriched uranium (LEU) or natural uranium for the Canadian-designed CANDU for existing power-generating reactors. Concomitantly, they could satisfy, however imperfectly, the understandable desire to be in touch with advanced nuclear technology.

They could provide the basis for a reasonable exchange whereby consumers receive firm guarantees of access to waste-storage facilities, to reprocessing services, and to the fuel needed to meet their requirements (whether in the form of mixed oxide plutonium or its fuel value equivalent in LEU) in return for their relinquishing unrestricted national rights to the full panoply of nuclear technologies.

They could reduce the risk that sensitive nuclear facilities will be exploited for military purposes. Access to critical processes and materials is limited and controlled. By providing strong incentive for non-weapons states to circumscribe their own national programs, they also militate against the building of the kind of technical mobilization base on which a bomb-making program may be constructed (whether through a series of incremental actions taken over time, or based on a single clear-cut decision).

They could help to establish the credibility of technically proficient nuclear suppliers by giving concrete form to their avowals of support and sensitivity to the energy interests of dependent consumers.

They could extend and reaffirm the underlying agreement on the value of a global regime for the transfer and use of civilian nuclear power, and encourage the formation of a new consensus.

They could "reduce the cover" of prospective proliferators by exposing national programs in sensitive fields as lacking economic or energy justification.

As a corollary, by lowering the risks associated with spreading civilian capabilities, they could allow policymakers to concentrate on other more obviously intentional routes to bomb acquisition, and the motivations that might lead states to take them.

Pronouncing the goals and purposes of multilateral arrangements for providing fuel assurances and management of spent fuel is one thing. Designing specific proposals and mobilizing support for them is far more challenging. Any number of schemes have been outlined, some practical and appealing enough to raise hope of their acceptance.[9]

FUEL ASSURANCES

The most promising proposals seek to enhance the security of the LEU supply. They cover several elements that could be composed into a layered system of contracts, shareholdings, and fuel exchanges.

Cross-contracting entails engaging suppliers and consumers in multiparty contracts that reinforce the obligation to deliver set quantities on fixed schedules. To be credible, the scheme should encompass both natural uranium fuel and enrichment services. The commitment of a pre-determined quantity of "yellow-cake" to a reserve account would act as insurance against disruption of deliveries by the primary contractor. A similar arrangement for enrichment services would require American and European authorities to allot a small portion of their capacity (again, based on a given percentage of contracted demand) to be held available in the event that is is necessary to make up for inordinate delays or interruptions associated with supply bottlenecks.

A reserve, in some versions of the scheme, could take the form of an actual stockpile of fuel. Placing buffer stocks under the control of some sort of international nuclear fuel bank is a far more ambitious idea. It would mean transferring control to an international body, the IAEA being the most likely candidate, with attendant problems of location, organization, management, and operational control. Under either format, there is the thorny question of consumer rights and supplier obligations. Would the guarantee be limited or absolute? What conditions, if any, should be placed on a country's access to the buffer stock? In the INFCE, the United

States parted company from most other participants who believed that the transfer of fuel should be exempt from national rights of prior consent on nuclear transfers (such as those imposed by the Nuclear Non-Proliferation Act). The majority felt strongly that where there had been no breach of non-proliferation undertakings (i.e., no violation of NPT or IAEA treaty provisions—adhesion to which could be a requirement for participation), transfer would have to be prompt and automatic. No other arrangement is acceptable to fuel-dependent consumers. Therefore, an amendment of US statutes is a precondition to making the fuel bank aspect of an Uranium Emergency Safety Network workable. (A similar problem arises with regard to any fuel exchange arrangement or international plutonium storage system. A related plan is built on the idea of consumers' holding of equity shares in enrichment consortia in exchange for a right to a portion of the product. Iran's participation in the now-lapsed EURODIFF is a precedent. Organizationally and politically, it is simpler and cleaner than other schemes. It is, however, financially burdensome.)

Practical difficulties notwithstanding, there is good reason to quicken the pace of efforts to put in place LEU fuel assurances. The impediments, economic and legal in nature, are not insurmountable. Moreover, conditions are propitious for doing so. Today's market is a buyer's market. Demand has slackened while both uranium supply and enrichment have expanded. Gerard Smith and George Rathjens have argued that, "with currently low uranium prices, long-term contracts and stockpiling offer economic alternatives to thermal recycle and breeder options as ways to reduce dependence on others for fuel."[10] A prod to move suppliers and consumers in this favorable direction is in order.

There is another reason for taking the venturesome step of a multinational fuel bank, rather than resting content with less daunting multilateral arrangements. It is the value of establishing a precedent for the more difficult task of organizing multinational reprocessing centers. If problems of authority and organization can be resolved for an LEU fuel bank, both experience and confidence might be among the assets transferable to those tackling the plutonium problem.

WASTE MANAGEMENT

The management of reactor waste is a second promising area for multilateral cooperation. Here, there is a convergence of interest among nearly all nuclear parties. For one thing, the build-up of waste from thermal reactors is beginning to pose major environmental problems, especially in those countries with appreciable power-generating capacity already on line. Political activism by ecology groups and legal challenges have slowed nuclear programs in a number of places, most noteworthily West Germany and Japan. Although they are not problem countries from a non-proliferation viewpoint, any arrangements for repatriation and international management of spent fuel that might be worked out with them could set an example and perhaps lay the basis for more encompassing plans. Storage and disposal of irradiated reactor waste is proving a burden for everyone who operates nuclear power plants. There are sound, practical reasons to look sympathetically on any reasonable offer to be relieved of it.

The build-up of reactor waste under national control poses a proliferation risk, for it is a source of fissionable material. Stockpiles of spent fuel are in effect plutonium mines. A government bent on bomb manufacture might well consider diverting reactor waste to a clandestine separation plant (as did India) for the extraction of weapons-grade plutonium. Removing the material to secure, safeguarded sites would reduce temptation and cut proliferation risk associated with civilian facilities. A system for repatriation of reactor waste to Away From Reactor (AFR) sites should be a priority of non-proliferation policy.

The United States has affirmed its support to help out with spent-fuel storage and disposal through three administrations. Yet it has experienced singular difficulty in hammering out firm proposals that could be offered to other governments, much less moved to gain their participation. The greatest handicap is the failure to find safe, effective means for handling domestic waste, let alone other people's nuclear garbage. The plans generated encountered a host of problems: inflated economic costs, inflated political costs, and even higher technical standards. The Reagan Administration, taking a more tolerant view of environmental considerations and dealing with a more compliant Congress, has made greater progress toward giving form to a comprehensive waste-management program. Implementation is likely to be hampered, though, by yet another reorganization of the functions performed by the moribund Department of Energy.

For a brief time in the late 1970s, the United States engaged Japan in talks about the possibility of finding a home for accumulated waste on the Pacific atoll of Palmyra. That demarche eventually foundered on Congressional opposition and disagreement over the determination of the material's fuel value and cost-sharing. Its lamentable history should not be taken as incontrovertible evidence of the impracticality of a multilateral approach to the waste-management problem. Other transfer arrangements, not involving the US, have been worked out. At the moment, substantial amounts of reactor waste have been transferred to reprocessing facilities in France and the UK from Japan, Sweden, and Switzerland. They are in accord with contracts that foresee the retransfer of separated plutonium, or its energy value in LEU, to the owner pending US consent, in cases where American approval is legally required. (To date, the US has approved retransfer of small amounts of plutonium fuels to start up experimental breeders.) In effect, then, there are already bilateral, if not multinational, arrangements in place for the management of nuclear wastes. They are by no means a model, though, for they are centered essentially on reprocessing and not waste storage facilities. Before they can be given a wider role, three issues must be resolved: (1) the final disposition of the highly radioactive material that is the byproduct of the separation process; (2) storage capacity for unreprocessed spent fuel, given the uneasiness of France and UK for retaining it on their soil; and (3) the key issue of retransfer and recycling of plutonium.

Both the French and British governments are ambivalent about assuming the responsibility for final disposal, probably in vitrified form, of the waste from their reprocessing plants. In one sense, it is a condition of their selling reprocessing services and an incentive to purchasers to be relieved of the spent-fuel problem. But there are limits, practical and political, to how much they will be ready to handle. Moreover, they are no more willing than the US to act as a depository of unreprocessed spent fuel for indefinite periods. Other sites, and other institutional formats, remain to be found.

Clearly, a depository is needed that would be independent of a reprocessing operation.

The first objective should be to settle on an Away From Reactor site dedicated exclusively to the storage, for an indefinite period, of spent fuel. Palmyra, or a similar locale, suggests itself. The United States' non-proliferation interest would be well served by offering it as home for a *multinational* facility managed by the IAEA. Constituting the facility on a multinational basis has a number of major advantages. It would lend credibility to the enterprise. It could stand as a model of multinational organization, like an LEU fuel bank, for analogous efforts in the more sensitive area of plutonium storage. It would provide experience in dealing with the ticklish administrative, technical, and budgetary aspects of running such an operation. Furthermore, by according the IAEA a significant new responsibility, it could, with luck, help to counteract the trend toward politicization and fragmentation of the organization that was so disconcertingly in evidence at the 1981 annual meeting. Rhetoric flourishes where concrete tasks are absent.

There would remain the ubiquitous question of release criteria. Unless states were prepared to cede rights to their spent fuel in perpetuity (a highly desirable course in some instances), the issue of ownership and attendant prerogatives would have to be addressed. There are a number of ways to finesse the problem. First, the United States should set an example by committing itself to use the site for storage of a substantial portion of its own reactor waste, and should continue its moratorium on commercial reprocessing. It would thereby reinforce the principle of recycling only into breeder, not thermal, reactors. Second, fuel exchanges on attractive terms should be offered. Multilateral fuel assurance agreements, such as those outlined above, should be promoted and linked to participation in the multinational waste-storage system. Fuel exchanges, in which LEU is transferred in amounts equivalent to the fuel value of byproduct plutonium (and residual uranium) in the spent fuel, would be part of the plan. Methods developed to calculate those exchange values could be made applicable to multinational plutonium reprocessing centers.

Admittedly, there will be difficulties in determining equivalent energy values, in allocating transportation, storage, and other transaction costs. On this score, traditional American generosity is called for. The US should stand ready to make up for the diseconomies associated with transportation or exceptional maintenance costs. Any proposal along these lines would doubtless run into Congressional opposition. Financial concessions could not be open-ended or of unlimited duration. Even a limited amount of support that facilitates inauguration of the plan would be valuable, though. A readiness to defray a disproportionate share of the costs in order to make the scheme economically attractive represents an excellent investment, if the return is an appreciable non-proliferation dividend.

Finally, as for release criteria on spent fuel whose ownership has not been transferred, there seems no way that the United States can avoid biting the bullet by accepting less than absolute consent rights. While there is no reason why the United States should go so far as to acquiesce in a system that gives an unrestricted right of control to national owners, a compromise that grants the neutral managing board some measure of discretion is all that can be hoped for. Less stringent than is ideal, the trade-off is unavoidable in order to retain a modicum of international control over sensitive nuclear transactions.

PLUTONIUM RECYCLING

Plutonium poses a less tractable problem. The reason is self-evident. The risks attached to broad and easy access to plutonium are so high that any system acceptable from an arms control standpoint encounters resistance from consumers who find its terms onerous and discriminatory. Discussions of a proposed International Plutonium Storage System (IPS), which have been conducted for the past several years under IAEA auspices, exposed major differences among the United States, other technically proficient states, and technically dependent states. Washington insists on strict controls and consent rights on transfers. The West Europeans and Japanese agree on controls while acknowledging rights of ownership. (They equivocate on the question of whether recycling should be limited to breeder reactors.) These more liberal arrangements are acceptable to some potential customers of centralized reprocessing services. Others, such as India and Pakistan, are the core of a third faction that has opposed anything but the most perfunctory requirements for repatriation of plutonium that might be separated from their spent fuel.

The debate over the long-negotiated IPS turns on the issue of access. The United States has been wary of the scheme from the outset for this very reason. It opposes release of plutonium fuels unless a persuasive case has been made that it is required for recycling into experimental breeder reactors; it wants to prohibit recycling into conventional reactors. Furthermore, it resists reprocessing itself, short of a compelling need to relieve an unmanageable build-up of spent reactor fuel. Even then, it has preferred that arrangements be made for interim storage. (This last stricture is particularly difficult to maintain given the unavailability of AFR facilities.)

The US conception, especially the "means test" for plutonium, introduces a new element of discrimination. It is made only slightly more palatable by the assumption that the host state (France, the UK, possibly the US) for reprocessing plants cum IPS site would be a weapons state and the proprietor of a large civilian nuclear establishment that could make efficient use of plutonium fuels. Recognizing the impossibility of incorporating this distinction in the operating code of an IPS, and fearful that the very establishment of such a system would lend legitimacy to the reprocessing and development of a plutonium economy, the United States has been suspicious of the idea.

It is time for the United States to back an International Plutonium Storage System, one that would be organized around currently operating reprocessing facilities in Western Europe. (There are formidable contractual and political obstacles to the transformation of the controversial Barnwell plant in South Carolina into a multinational facility.) With further delay, developments may well push the idea beyond the realm of possibility. European and Japanese interest is waning as American pressure on their own reprocessing plans eases; India, Argentina, Pakistan, and other interested consumers, who have made known their rejection of American conceptions, could be in a position soon to go their own way on nuclear matters. Whatever the problems raised by the location and precise format of IPS, it is the better of two unsatisfactory alternatives. The other is to fight an increasingly costly and unproductive rear-guard action against reprocessing using diminishing powers of legal authority over American-supplied nuclear materials.

The exact organizational design and operational mode of multinational reprocessing centers cum an international plutonium storage system have been carefully examined elsewhere.[11] Whether set up on a regional or some other basis, nearly all variations of the idea share the same basic characteristics. (1) The fuel center would perform three activities: the maintenance of secure AFR (Away From Reactor) facilities for the short-term storage of nuclear wastes; the reprocessing of reactor spent fuel; and the fabrication of plutonium fuels. (2) Secure locations would have to be selected. These would normally be in non-weapons states who are signatories of the NPT, and, as a practical matter, probably would be those who are technically proficient and already have proven reprocessing capability. (3) Joint ownership would not presume joint operational control. For such a facility to serve its non-proliferation ends, control and decisionmaking must be carried out either by an international agency (as in the case of a multinational fuel cycle center established by the IAEA) or by nationals of a host state under IAEA authority or supervision. (4) In exchange for accepting the discrimination implied by a two-tiered governing structure that separates policy from operational functions, participants would have to be assured fuel supplies on an economically attractive basis. They could take the form of LEU carrying the energy equivalent of the spent fuel contributed to the system—much preferred from a non-proliferation perspective—or prefabricated plutonium. If the latter procedure were followed, the proper demand should be made that custody of the fuel remain in the hands of an authority other than the recipient state until it is actually reinserted into a power reactor.

Support for IPS should be coupled to a strenuous campaign to win acceptance of two critical conditions. One is full-scope safeguards. They become all the more urgent with the creation of an IPS. They are required to avoid both the risk of diverted plutonium being exploited for military purposes, and the danger that technology obtained through participation in multinational facilities might be applied in developing clandestine or illegal national facilities. In making their case for IPS, Smith and Rathjens have stressed the need for "a major effort to reach a consensus among supplier nations that all future commerce will be conditioned on the purchasers accepting IAEA safeguards on all their peaceful nuclear activities.''[12] Preferably, such an initiative first should be launched in the IAEA, and a conscientious attempt made to win at least tacit consumer acceptance of full-scope safeguards. The unilateral imposition of restrictive rules by suppliers would surely engender considerable ill-will, thereby squandering whatever political gains have been made through support of an IPS.

There is some small reason for optimism that support for full-scope safeguards may be forthcoming. At the last NPT Review Conference, a number of third world countries (especially from Africa) backed the principle. As governments contemplate the real prospect of nuclear weapons in their backyards, perspectives do begin to shift somewhat. Nonetheless, the rhetorical barrier raised by cries of discrimination remains a formidable one, and the pressures of third world solidarity are not to be underestimated. Clearly, though, the odds on acceptance of full-scope safeguards are likely to worsen in the future. Augmented national capabilities, and further erosion of the IAEA's credibility and effectiveness, soon could put agreement beyond reach. We are operating in a narrow envelope of time that must be used, and used quickly.

Similarly, the imperative of political conciliation dictates that consensus (or at least wide backing) be sought for a needs test as a standard for approving release of plutonium fuels. This is the second condition for supporting IPS. Even were it to prove impractical to write such a clause into a multinational organization's articles of incorporation, it would be beneficial to have some statement of understanding that criteria of waste backup, energy requirements, and economic incentive should be observed. It would strengthen the sense of collective commitment to common norms and objectives, and would raise the political costs for those who might act counter to it. (Agreement on the more restrictive condition that plutonium only be released for recycling into breeders is even more desirable, but less likely to be forthcoming.)

In the light of the substantial constraints on diplomatic efforts at building multinational facilities, what can reasonably be achieved? Complete multinationalization of the international fuel cycle almost certainly is not in the cards. Indeed, it is unlikely that even the most sensitive parts of it could ever be rendered entirely safe and effective. Yet marginal improvement in non-proliferation benefits, over critical elements of the system, is still a significant and reachable goal. Making the attempt is imperative.

Without any substantial progress on multilateral waste management and fuel assurances, civilian nuclear power threatens to spin out of the control of the US, other suppliers, and the IAEA. Rapid diffusion of dual-capable technology, improving levels of technical skill, and troubling loopholes in safeguards do not auger well for non-proliferation goals. Multilateral measures to keep ''barrier'' technology under some sort of restriction, and to limit access to sensitive materials, inspire a measure of hope that the non-proliferation norm can be maintained. The twin principles of equity and effectiveness can only be reconciled on a multilateral, preferably a multinational, basis. It is the sole means to meet genuine energy needs and earnest interest in advanced technology, while making some degree of discrimination palatable.

SUPPLY REGULATION

Reinforcement and extension of supplier rules is a necessary complement to measures aimed at regulating access to sensitive nuclear technologies. Evidence of loopholes in the guidelines set down by the London Nuclear Suppliers' Club, and the appearance of new sources of important component technology, provide ample cause for reopening the issue.

Admittedly, the appropriate vehicle for drafting and monitoring a new set of guidelines is not immediately evident. With the completion of their last round of deliberations, most Suppliers' Club members made known their strong conviction that all future discussion of technology transfer should take place in a wider forum, i.e., the IAEA. Agreement on new transfer regulations seems wildly unrealistic in the strained and at times acrimonious conditions that have prevailed at recent Vienna meetings. Certainly, it would be a fatal error to underestimate the divisions between nuclear dependent states and suppliers, not to speak of the serious differences in outlook among suppliers.

A more restricted, less formal forum should be sought. The disbanded Suppliers' Club could not be officially constituted. Another body, with broader membership, is perhaps more plausible. It would be essential that it encompass potential third-tier suppliers, including China, and even those consumer states with a major stake in international nuclear transactions. With regard to the latter, one can only hope that augmented capability and proficiency is accompanied by a greater sense of collective responsibility and a wider view of national interest.

High on the agenda of such a group (or, were it to prove impractical, that of a more narrowly constituted group) should be the question of *monitoring* the traffic in nuclear materials, under whatever rules are agreed upon. It should explore the idea of establishing a nuclear fact-finding and arbitration service to investigate claims of clandestine weapons activity. Ideally, such a service would be coupled with a streamlining of IAEA procedures for setting in motion the sanctions process. Unfortunately, the divisiveness that recently has hampered the agency, accompanied by increasing sensitivity to encroachments on national sovereignty, does not make this a propitious time to advance plans for a more assertive role for the organization.[13] The discrepancy between need and capability should elicit a redoubled commitment to an independent and tougher IAEA and serious consideration of ways to get the job done outside the agency.

THE REACTION

How might we expect near-nuclear countries, and other interested governments, to react to the proposals we have set forth? Much depends on the degree of unity demonstrated by the nuclear-proficient states, and the overall attractiveness of whatever package of proposals is placed on the table. The benefits and costs of joining the program, or staying outside, will look rather different if important suppliers choose to stand apart. Given a broad supplier consensus on major parts of the program outlined above, the reaction of non-suppliers can be expected to break down into three categories.

At one extreme, there are those states who would be unmoved by any new initiatives. Strong commitments to independent nuclear programs by South Africa, Israel, and Pakistan would seem to preclude their adherence to any scheme that threatens to restrict their freedom of action, and to jeopardize their evident interest in weapons development.

At the other end of the continuum are those countries (probably a majority, harboring no ulterior interest in the military applications of nuclear power) with limited ambitions as regional powers, that probably could be persuaded to participate in a comprehensive system that satisfies all their nuclear energy needs at no tangible cost. Simply put, they would have much to gain and little to lose.

In between are the key group of states that are large enough, and ambitious enough, to be sensitive about any infringements on national sovereignty and the stigma of discrimination. The message that should be conveyed to countries like Brazil or Mexico would emphasize the practical advantages and equity of the proposal being offered and the risks to them individually, and to global stability generally, of a collective failure to control nuclear power adequately. Countries that are embarking on major civilian nuclear power programs may well see important benefits in working out a set of multilateral arrangements that assure a predictable supply of fuel and open access to important technologies, and that provide for safe closure of the fuel cycle on an international basis.

EXOGENOUS FACTORS

The eventual outcome of the proposals outlined here will depend in large part on contextual elements. Some of them are economic or technical: the level of concern over energy shortages, the rate at which competence in advanced technology (and the hardware itself) gets dispersed, the financial pressures to push sales of services and technology. Other factors will be of a more decidedly political character. They include: the tenor of North-South relations generally; the intensity of security anxieties in proliferation-sensitive areas; the coloration given to perceptions of nuclear weapons' utility by doctrines emanating from Moscow and Washington; and the ability of the two superpowers to act together to dampen conflicts or to raise the costs of nuclear weapons development. The last-mentioned deserves special, albeit cursory, attention here.

PROLIFERATION AND THE NUCLEAR SUPERPOWERS

As noted earlier, one of the distinguishing features of non-proliferation as an arms control problem is presumption of a fundamental line of discrimination between those states that are allowed to retain nuclear weapons and those that are asked to abjure them. As a consequence, the behavior of weapons states is under constant scrutiny by non-weapons states. Vertical proliferation—that is, the expansion and qualitative improvement of the nuclear arsenals of the great powers—is frequently pointed to as undermining the force and credibility of the campaign against horizontal proliferation. While it has never been quite clear how dangerous arms-racing at one level could be used to justify the acquisition of these horrific weapons by others, there is no denying the emotional tie that is made in the thinking of governments that are candidate proliferators.

Strategic arms control may not be a logical precondition to strengthening prohibitions against weapons spread, but it undeniably helps. It performs its most valuable service by reinforcing the conviction that nuclear weapons are indeed something new under the sun, deserving to be treated with exceptional caution and requiring extraordinary action by the nations of the world. The collapse of SALT II, followed by a return to confrontational postures by the US and USSR, creates inauspicious conditions for the launching of other major arms control proposals. Revival of talks to control strategic arms, the START negotiations, is itself a favorable development. Further non-proliferation dividends would accrue were the superpowers to act positively on the one item that actually bridges the two levels of arms control, i.e., a Comprehensive Test Ban (CTB).

From a non-proliferation standpoint, the value of a CTB is considerable. A general prohibition on nuclear explosions means that the onus of breaking an international norm would fall on any state that tests a weapon, however it may be represented. (Such a ban would have the further effect of reinforcing the stigma that attaches to nuclear weapons generally.) The CTB would permit drawing an unmistakable line between acceptable and unacceptable behavior. Being able to draw such a line, it becomes possible at least to think in terms of collective sanctions against transgression of a non-proliferation norm. Without such a clear guidepost no such action is feasible, even were there a superpower disposition to oppose actively nuclear weapons proliferation.

Under any circumstances, mobilizing multilateral cooperation for the imposition of sanctions faces formidable obstacles. Mechanisms would have to be created for an equitable distribution of the burdens associated with sanctions, and for absorbing any countermeasures. The crucial political condition for putting in place the means for penalizing any country that explodes a nuclear device is a high degree of common interest in deterring proliferation. Agreements on methods and means must reflect this understanding; they cannot be expected to create the essential political agreement. In this respect, a CTB accord would have important symbolic value, for the superpowers and for third parties alike. An elusive arms control objective for a generation, its attainment should be seen as inspired in good part by a common great-power desire to raise the ante for prospective entrants into the nuclear club.

Organizing collective sanctions would be facilitated by another great-power accord calling for a "no-first-use of nuclear weapons" doctrine. It would have a two-fold effect. By implicitly rejecting a war-fighting role for nuclear weapons, it would diminish their theoretical attractiveness as a useful mode of arms. By pledging the US and the USSR (and, desirably, other nuclear weapons states as well) to refrain from initiating atomic warfare, it would strengthen collective norms as to what is and is not acceptable nuclear conduct.[14] To the extent that the utility of nuclear arms is thereby devalued, the interest in acquiring them may be somewhat muted. Similarly, the implied cost of violating a general prohibition on first use could help to discourage a minor nuclear power from employing them in battle (and reduce the risk that their successful use would spur near-nuclear states, with comparable security needs, to develop their own nuclear weapons).

The outlook for a great power agreement on the no-first-use principle is, unfortunately, not bright. At the Second UN Special Session on Disarmament in June, the Soviet Union declared that it "would not be the first to use nuclear weapons," apparently making its observance of such a pledge contingent upon a reciprocal move by the US, France, and the United Kingdom.[15] The Reagan Administration responded with considerable skepticism, questioning the credibility of such a Soviet commitment. Washington has demurred for obvious and predictable reasons. Given what is seen as a clear Warsaw Pact advantage in conventional arms, NATO military planning has always foreseen the possibility of a first resort to nuclear weapons. That option will not be relinquished unless there is an appreciable shift in the balance of forces in Europe. Serious consideration of a mutual pledge on no-first-use must await upon a successful outcome of the continuing talks on Mutual and Balanced Force Reductions, and those under way on controlling theater nuclear weapons as well. The non-proliferation factor surely will not be determining, but it can add impetus to a move toward conditions that favor no-first-use.

However distant these goals might seem in the atmosphere of renewed Cold War, and however formidable the hurdles to the more ambitious goal of establishing a system of collective sanctions, they are worth pursuing. The sure and certain opprobrium of the major powers may be one of the few effective deterrents against widespread proliferation as capabilities spread and security anxieties grow.[16]

The program of action sketched in this chapter poses a challenge, especially to the United States. Although reduced in status to primus inter pares, it remains the only government capable of serious initiative and with the power, however reduced, to set an agenda. The issues and the circumstances do not lend themselves to brilliant strokes and drastic initiatives. All the better; past dramatic steps have not fared very well. The characteristic case-by-case approach of Washington policymakers holds out no greater promise. The absence of formula answers suggests the appropriateness of neither diplomatic cavalry charges nor an exaggerated empiricism devoid of theme or consistent purpose. What is needed is design, patience, and skillful execution, the inescapable requirements for successful policy.

NOTES

1. The significance of these events and their consequences for US non-proliferation policy are examined in detail in my book, *Nuclear Energy and Non-Proliferation* (New York: Cambridge University Press, 1981).

2. The influential appraisal of the proliferation risk associated with the commercialization of plutonium was made in the Ford Foundation Nuclear Policy Study Group and Mitre Corporation Report, *Nuclear Power: Issues*

and Choices (Cambridge, Massachusetts: Ballinger, 1977). See also the incisive assessment of the Committee for Economic Development, *Nuclear Energy and National Security* (New York, 1976).

3. President Carter's policies, despite a number of striking unilateral steps, are no exception. Those measures were viewed as necessary prods and examples in a strategy aimed at gaining wider appreciation of the danger seen in existing trends, and for forcing collective decisions. The Reagan Administration, for its part, has shifted the stresses and accents, concentrating more on motivation and intent, less on constraints. It also advocates a case-by-case approach as opposed to the promulgation of universal rules and standards. It too, though, has become more cognizant that *ad hoc* measures, in and of themselves, are not sufficient. Bilateral accords and understandings must be placed in an institutional framework to have full force and effect.

4. These linkages are one of the themes developed in Lewis A. Dunn's excellent work, *Controlling the Bomb: Nuclear Proliferation in the 1980's* a Twentieth Century Fund report (New Haven and London: Yale University Press, 1982).

5. An insightful review of these elements of non-proliferation policy is provided by Lawrence Scheinman, ''Multinational Alternatives and Nuclear Non-Proliferation,'' in *Nuclear Proliferation: Breaking the Chain,* ed. by George H. Quester (Madison, Wisconsin: University of Wisconsin Press, 1981).

6. These doubts were the subject of hearings held by the US Senate Committee on Foreign Relations, 1–2 December 1981, Washington, DC.

7. Statement of Richard T. Kennedy, Under Secretary of State for Management, before the US Senate Committee on Foreign Relations, 2 December 1981, Washington, DC.

8. Gerard Smith and George Rathjens, ''Reassessing Nuclear Nonproliferation Policy,'' *Foreign Affairs,* 59:4 (Spring, 1981), pp. 875 and 886.

9. Among the admirable studies of multinational facilities are: Abram Chayes and W. Bennett Lewis, eds., *International Arrangements for Nuclear Fuel Reprocessing* (Cambridge, Massachusetts: Ballinger, 1977); Lewis A. Dunn, *Influence at the Margin: Alternative Institutional Options for Global Nuclear Activities,* report prepared for the US Department of Energy (New York: The Hudson Institute, December, 1979); and Scheinman, op. cit. note 4.

10. Smith and Rathjens, op. cit. note 7, p. 893.

11. Scheinman, op. cit. note 4; Dunn, op. cit. note 9; and Ted Greenwood and Robert Haffa, Jr., ''Supply-Side Non-Proliferation,'' *Foreign Policy,* 42 (Spring, 1981).

12. Smith and Rathjens, op. cit. note 7.

13. Political trends in the IAEA are the subject of a well-informed article, "US Perturbed with IAEA Politics, Examines Role in Agency," in *Nucleonics Week,* 22:44 (5 November 1981), p. 3.

14. There are other possible benefits from a no-first-use doctrine, as argued in the provocative article by McGeorge Bundy, et. al., "Nuclear Weapons and the Atlantic Alliance," *Foreign Affairs* 60:4 (Spring 1982), pp. 753–768.

15. Soviet Foreign Minister Andrei Gromyko's speech on 15 June 1982, at SSOD–II. See Document of the UNGA, A/S–12/PV.12, p. 23.

16. To have maximum impact, statements of displeasure would have to be backed by penalties. Realistically, they would be limited to economic and political action.

PLACING CONVENTIONAL ARMS ON THE MULTILATERAL AGENDA

EDWARD C. LUCK

Nuclear disarmament continues to dominate international attention and discussion, if not action, while the control of conventional arms largely remains hidden below the surface of international priorities. On the surface, little has changed. Like an iceberg, only the tip of the problem has been widely recognized and the full dimensions and implications of conventional arms issues have yet to be assessed. Discussions at the UN, where for many years conventional disarmament was a taboo subject, have been glaringly one-sided. The conclusions of the July 1982 final document of the second UN Special Session Devoted to Disarmament fail even to mention the subject.[1]

Compared to the tidal wave of public anxiety about nuclear weapons, conventional arms control has hardly stirred a ripple of concern. It still lacks a constituency during a period in which nuclear arms control has been gaining an enormous, if amorphous, public following. While hundreds of thousands of Europeans, Japanese, and Americans have turned out for anti-nuclear rallies, conventional arms issues have lacked the emotional appeal necessary to attract wide public attention.

There are signs, however, that governments in many parts of the world are beginning to recognize that the uncontrolled development and proliferation of conventional weapons poses a real danger to their security, political, and economic interests. These concerns, however, do not always surface in speeches to global forums, such as the two UN Special Sessions on Disarmament. These are basically political exercises and, without a public constituency, national leaders have little incentive to pledge their devotion to controlling conventional arms. Nevertheless, as discussed later in this chapter, references to the need to control conventional arms are beginning to appear with greater frequency in these national statements.

These nascent concerns have not led to the development of an international consensus either on the priority that the issue should be accorded or on the direction control efforts should take. Among the lengthy list of items that formed the Program of Action adopted at the first Special Session in 1978, Paragraph 81 called for the resolute pursuit of limitations and reductions of conventional arms "together with negotiations on nuclear disarmament measures."[2] While this was a major step toward giving the international community's blessing for conventional arms control efforts, it fell far short of giving them equal footing with nuclear issues. Moreover, whatever fragile and vague consensus existed in 1978 had disappeared by the time of the second Special Session in 1982. Given the political divisions and substantive complexities that surround discussions of conventional arms control, it will take considerable time to build an international consensus, if that is possible at all. The consensus-building process could be energized—as has happened on the nuclear level—if the public begins to take the lead, rather than to lag behind, on this issue.

This chapter takes a broad view of what constitutes conventional arms control, defining it to include measures to limit or reduce the development, procurement, deployment, or transfer of conventional weapons and armed forces. It addresses possible multilateral efforts on both the regional and global levels. In discussions and writings in this field, there has been an unfortunate tendency to equate conventional arms control with limits on international arms transfers, which is only one of many important sub-topics. This tendency has hindered diplomatic efforts to deal with conventional arms, because it has suggested to third world diplomats that the major powers are interested in limiting horizontal, but not vertical, proliferation.

There are five parts to this chapter: (1) an exposition of why conventional arms are central to the implementation of US security and foreign policy; (2) a discussion of the potential benefits of conventional arms control; (3) an assessment of the very serious obstacles to major multilateral progress in this field in the near future;

(4) a description of some criteria that should be taken into account in developing conventional arms control initiatives; and (5) an outline of a series of possible steps towards controlling conventional arms.

THE CENTRAL ROLE OF CONVENTIONAL ARMS

Conventional forces, much more than their nuclear counterparts, are useful and usable for forwarding a wide variety of foreign policy and security objectives. They are uniquely valuable in peacetime for showing the flag in distant but strategically vital regions; for demonstrating resolve and commitment in crises; for bolstering friendly governments in periods of instability; for protecting a nation's diplomats or citizens in chaotic situations abroad or from terrorists; for providing a neutral buffer—sometimes under international auspices—in local conflicts; for posing a credible threat of military involvement in regional conflicts; or, if necessary, for intervening in situations where a relatively modest presence could tip the balance in a favorable direction. In wartime, conventional forces are essential for seizing and holding territory, while nuclear weapons can only cause destruction.

In sum, for global powers like the US and Soviet Union, conventional forces provide a principal means for projecting influence far from home, as well as for protecting their own territorial integrity. As a Chinese working paper on conventional disarmament, submitted to the UN Disarmament Commission, commented:

> The super-powers have always regarded nuclear and conventional armaments as two inseparable components of their overall military strength. Nuclear weapons serve primarily as a deterrent and a means of blackmail while conventional arms have invariably been used in actual aggression. This is particularly true of the hegemonist super-power that has been using tanks, aircraft, artillery and warships rather than nuclear weapons in its military aggression. That is why China is in favour of giving equal importance to conventional and nuclear disarmament.[3]

The vast majority of countries, of course, have no ready alternative except to depend on conventional arms for both deterrence and defense.

Yet it should be emphasized that the use or threat to use conventional forces may be stabilizing, rather than destabilizing, depending on the circumstances. In theory, the application of conventional power can be graduated and controlled more easily than can nuclear power, if political conditions permit. Conventional options are generally more selective and incremental, in part because their range and yield are less, while their application usually unfolds deliberately enough to permit the decisionmaking processes on both sides to react. Some political and economic objectives may seem worth the risks and costs entailed in employing conventional force to get them, while nuclear options and threats appear irrational and incredible for any purpose other than deterring the massive use of force by potential aggressors. Conventional arms, therefore, are not only usable; they are used, again and again, throughout the world.

It seems safe to predict, after three turbulent years, that the 1980s will be an era in which conventional forces will be called upon repeatedly to play the central role in determining the outcomes of dozens of local conflicts. It is no longer fashionable to suggest that the use of military force has gone out of style as a means of settling international disputes. In mid-1982, major conventional conflicts were raging simultaneously in the South Atlantic, Middle East, Persian Gulf, Afghanistan, Indochina, Central America, and in several parts of Africa. The collapse of Soviet-American detente has eliminated what had sometimes been a key factor in facilitating the peaceful resolution of regional disputes, while the escalation of East-West tensions has tended to polarize and exacerbate local problems.

The East-West balance of conventional forces will also become increasingly critical as public pressures grow for substantial reductions of theater and strategic nuclear weapons. In each case that non-governmental groups have advocated bold steps designed to lessen NATO's dependence on nuclear weapons in Europe—no first use, a nuclear-free zone in Central Europe, or a freeze on further nuclear deployments—it has raised the thorny issues of NATO's flexible response doctrine and its capabilities for defending Western Europe from a conventional attack by the Warsaw Pact. Progress in the strategic arms reduction talks (START) and the intermediate nuclear force (INF) negotiations, therefore, may be slowed if there is not any significant positive movement in the talks on mutual and balanced force reductions (MBFR), which deal with conventional forces in Central Europe. MBFR progress, in turn, may be linked to movement in the INF and START negotiations. President Reagan tacitly recognized this three-stage interrelationship when he first announced in November 1981 that the US would seek agreements on all three levels.[4] While the public has failed to recognize this nuclear-conventional linkage, it will be a central concern of US negotiators, who must consider how to integrate and coordinate US policies in the three separate negotiations.

The peacetime uses of conventional arms, especially by major powers, often have far-reaching diplomatic and political repercussions. For the US, decisions about arms transfers and deployments have a direct effect on relations within the Western alliance and with friendly countries in other regions. Other governments watch very closely for shifts in US deployment and transfer patterns as concrete evidence of changes in American foreign policy priorities and commitments. In the Carter Administration, efforts to negotiate limits on arms transfers and Indian Ocean deployments, as well as unilateral plans to reduce US ground forces in South Korea, ran aground on these ubiquitous but uncharted diplomatic shoals. These diplomatic problems frequently have tangible military consequences, since neither the US nor the USSR can project conventional forces far from home for extended periods without the cooperation of other countries for access to naval bases, air strips and other facilities, and for permission to make overflights and to pass through restricted straits.

US arms transfer policies, whether intended to be restrictive, as in the Carter Administration, or more open as in the Reagan Administration, are constantly buffeted by competing political demands. In mid-1982, for example, the US was engaged in protracted and delicate discussions with China over the issue of continued arms sales to Taiwan and in a diplomatic dispute with Israel over its apparent use of cluster bombs in heavily populated areas of Lebanon. At the same time, France and the United Kingdom were squabbling about the degree of involvement of French technicians in helping Argentina to fit French-supplied Exocet missiles to French-built aircraft so that they could attack and sink British warships during the Falklands war.[5] As these examples suggest, bilateral arms transfers usually have serious multilateral implications.

This discussion suggests that decisions about the acquisition, deployment and transfer of conventional arms should be treated as matters of central importance to forwarding US security and foreign policy objectives. Yet, it might be asked, if conventional arms are so useful, then why should the US initiate or support multilateral efforts to limit them? Arms control, after all, as it has been practiced for the past two decades, has largely been the act of limiting precisely those weapons that were least useful and least likely to be used. Attempts to control conventional arms, on the other hand, could have far-reaching implications—positive or negative depending on the circumstances—for US national security and foreign policy. The next section argues that there are several strong reasons for the US to pursue at this time selected conventional arms control measures in multilateral forums. These need to be approached with considerable caution and after wide consultations, however, because limits on conventional forces could have a much greater potential impact on immediate US interests than would modest changes in the aggregate level of strategic nuclear forces.

THE POTENTIAL UTILITY OF CONVENTIONAL ARMS CONTROL

Limitations on conventional arms, if designed and monitored properly, can make major contributions toward advancing the three traditional goals of arms control. These are: (1) to make the outbreak of war less likely; (2) to decrease the probable damage if war should break out; and (3) to lessen the costs of peacetime preparations for war. In the conventional area, as in other aspects of arms control, agreements per se do not necessarily further any of these goals. If an agreement is poorly conceived or unverifiable, it could actually make war more likely or more destructive. Steven Canby illustrates this point well in this volume in his discussion of confidence-building measures.[6]

In order to reduce the likelihood of war, arms control measures must make recourse to war a less attractive option for potential aggressors. This can be done (1) by raising the aggressor's probable costs, which is the traditional concept of deterrence through assured retaliation, or (2) by decreasing his chances of achieving his desired objectives through military, instead of peaceful, means. Nuclear arms control has largely focused on the first goal through attempts to stabilize but retain the balance of terror, while limitations on conventional arms can contribute most directly to the second objective.

Conventional arms limitations have been most effective in discouraging the outbreak of conflict when they have been embedded in a larger framework of political and economic detente. The military aspects of the Sinai accord between Israel and Egypt, for example, have succeeded in keeping these two formerly bitter enemies at peace, despite the growing turmoil in the region, in large part because these measures reinforced an existing process of political detente.[7] If two nations (or a single aggressor) are determined to go to war, as seemingly has been the case with Iran and Iraq, arms control can at best delay its outbreak. But in cases where relations are improving, stable, or uncertain, arms control can be a stabilizing element: making surprise attacks and full-scale hostilities more difficult; reducing uncertainties about the current or future balance of forces; limiting the influx of extra-regional weapons, advisors, or combat forces; creating international norms about the acquisition and use of military force, while raising the political costs of violating them; and fostering a dialogue among national leaders that could facilitate parallel progress on political, cultural, and economic issues as well.

The second arms control goal—reducing the destructiveness of war should it occur—is usually cited as the primary reason to give a higher priority to nuclear than to conventional arms control. Individual conventional weapons are certainly much less destructive than their nuclear counterparts (though the trend toward area weapons such as cluster bombs, incendiaries, and fuel-air explosives may increase the number of civilian casualties and the amount of collateral damage in future large-scale conventional conflicts). Wars fought with conventional munitions nevertheless sometimes have been extremely destructive, as demonstrated by the tens of millions of casualties—a large proportion of whom were civilians—in World War II. Paradoxically, it is the memory of these enormous losses, as well as the horrible potential of nuclear weapons, that has shaped present perspectives of Soviet leaders regarding their security needs and has convinced many Western Europeans not to undertake determined preparations to resist a Warsaw Pact conventional attack, but rather to rely on the US nuclear umbrella for deterrence of either a conventional or nuclear strike.

As long as there are fairly large numbers of nuclear weapons in the world—a condition that will no doubt remain for many years since even a small fraction of existing warheads would be sufficient to kill tens of millions of people and destroy the US, the USSR, and Europe as functioning societies—the surest way to forward the goal of reducing wartime losses will be to avoid the outbreak of East-West conventional conflicts and to prevent their escalation to the nuclear level should they occur. (None of the Soviet or American proposals discussed so far in the SALT, START and INF negotiations would be radical enough to alter this fundamental reality.) This objective requires a combination of sufficient force deployments, vigilance, and arms control measures. Potential adversaries need to be convinced that surprise probably could not be achieved, aggression would be too costly, force would ultimately fail to achieve the desired purposes, escalating the level of conflict would not be worth the costs, and the dispute in question could be resolved by alternative peaceful means. Limitations on conventional arms can contribute to each of these elements of the equation, though they cannot compensate for a weak defense or lack of vigilance.

It is towards the third traditional arms control objective—reducing costs of defense preparations—that conventional arms limitations can make their greatest and most unambiguous contributions. At least 80 percent of global military outlays are devoted to conventional weapons and armed forces, including, of course, virtually all defense spending in the non-nuclear countries. The Reagan Administration defense program, contrary to the focus of public and media attention on its strategic nuclear components, has quite properly continued to emphasize spending for general purpose forces, personnel, and readiness.

Savings could someday accrue from START and INF agreements, at least in terms of foregone potential expenditures for new strategic systems, but over the long term the greatest untapped source for major savings would be through conventional arms control. If developing countries truly want to see the theoretical linkage between disarmament and development realized, they should begin to give a higher priority to conventional arms control efforts. In the short run, neither nuclear nor conventional arms control steps are likely to produce a bonanza of savings, in part because of the incremental and non-comprehensive nature of the enterprise. Moreover, this goal should continue to receive a lower priority than the first two traditional arms control objectives. Yet over the long term, it should be recognized that the limitation of conventional arms and forces is a prerequisite for major progress toward any of the three goals.

Conventional limitations should have a special appeal for the United States and its allies, which are faced with the substantial task of coping with the large and varied general purpose forces of the Soviet Union. For a number of interrelated reasons—geography, tradition, doctrine, numbers, and priorities—the Soviet Union has long possessed significant advantages in conventional forces, especially over its neighbors on the Eurasian continent. Perhaps just as importantly, the Soviet Union retains a psychological edge in that some of its neighbors—the Chinese and Afghans are among the exceptions—assume that the Red Army cannot be resisted successfully without the use of nuclear weapons, thus stressing nuclear deterrence over conventional defense. These perceptions of the conventional superiority of the Soviet Union are no doubt bloated, especially in light of the increasing restiveness of its Warsaw Pact comrades in Eastern Europe. Yet crippling Soviet capabilities for launching a sudden large-scale conventional assault on Western Europe should remain a top priority for Western arms control efforts.

The most troubling trend in Soviet foreign and military policies over the past decade has been their increasingly global dimensions. As the Soviet Union has sought to match the global reach of the

United States, its chief means of influencing events in distant (as well as nearby) regions has been conventional military power. This effort has entailed the development of a blue-water navy and a naval infantry, substantial increases in airlift and sealift capabilities, agreements on the use of facilities and bases in third world countries, large transfers of modern arms to friendly countries in the third world, and the support of proxy forces, especially in Africa and Asia.

The key question for US policy is not whether these are legitimate activities—indeed in many respects they resemble the way the US operated in the third world in the 1950s and 1960s—but how best to counter Soviet efforts to foster or support change in the third world through military means. Arms transfers and redeployments of US forces often provide a temporary answer, but over the long term they need to be supplemented by regional political, economic, and arms control initiatives. Many third world leaders share American apprehensions about the dangers of Soviet military involvement in the third world, but at the same time they are just as mistrustful of US military intentions. It is clearly in the US—and third world—interest to make every effort to shift the locus of East-West competition from military to non-military arenas, from an area of comparative Soviet advantage to an area of comparative Western advantage. Over the long run, regional arms control efforts that can dampen local disputes and reduce the opportunities for extra-regional military intervention would make an invaluable contribution to furthering this objective.

There continue to be strong reasons to pursue conventional arms control in Europe, the region that has received the most attention in the past. Any arms limitation, confidence-building measure, or verification arrangement that could reduce the feasibility of a Warsaw Pact surprise attack and provide more time for Western mobilization would be a step toward reducing the most direct threat to Western security. These steps would not eliminate the deficits in Western conventional forces, command structure, and doctrines, which are likely to persist for political reasons, and are no substitute for sound military planning and preparations. They could, however, lessen the impact of these deficits on Western security.

From the outset of the MBFR negotiations, political factors have provided a major impetus for arms control in Europe. While Congressional pressure to remove a portion of US troops from Europe is not nearly as strong today as it was at the time of the Mansfield Amendment, which was a primary motivation for launching the MBFR talks, it appears to be growing.[8] For some years, it has been an effective argument to note that it makes little sense to pull US forces out of Europe unilaterally when there is a possibility of achieving a quid pro quo from the Soviets through the negotiating process. The argument will begin to wear thin, however, if there is not more substantial progress in the negotiations. Putting forward new MBFR initiatives, as President Reagan did in July 1982, may also have a positive effect on public opinion in Western Europe. They serve to draw attention to the fundamental security problem in Europe—which is the imbalance in conventional forces—and away from the anti-nuclear movement.

These points underline the long-term importance of conventional arms control on the regional level, but do not answer why this issue should also be pursued more vigorously in global forums. It is true that most security problems relating to conventional forces arise in a regional context, among neighboring states, but there are global dimensions to the conventional arms competition as well. These relate primarily to arms transfers, to Soviet-American competition, and to North-South relations broadly conceived.

Over the past decade, the global arms trade has grown substantially in both the quantity and quality of arms shipments.[9] The chief direction of the trade has shifted from North-North to North-South, with developing countries purchasing the bulk of the arms from a handful of major arms producers, led by the US and the USSR. The flow of advanced, highly capable weapons from North to South has begun to produce subtle shifts in the balance of power between major and minor military actors and has complicated the prospects of military interventions in the third world. For example, a few advanced missiles allowed Argentina, which was no match for the United Kingdom in terms of overall military power, to raise significantly the costs and risks faced by the British in regaining the Falkland Islands. Moreover, a few developing countries with indigenous arms industries, such as Israel, Brazil, and India, have begun to export arms to other states in the third world, initiating a small but rapidly growing South-South arms flow. While the motivations for acquiring additional conventional arms may stem from regional conditions, the arms trade itself has in many respects taken on a global character. To be successful over the long run, arms transfer restraints would have to address both the regional and global aspects of the trade. Arms transfers are bilateral transactions with multilateral implications.

While regional disputes and arms races usually are caused by local conditions, they are frequently escalated and exacerbated by the injection of East-West tensions. It is hard to imagine, for example, any major arms control progress in unstable regions, such as the Middle East, Southeast Asia, North Africa, or Southern Africa, without the cooperation and involvement of the US, the Soviet Union, and some international institutions. Regional problems have a tendency to grow into global problems, especially during periods of high East-West tension, and can only be resolved through a blend of regional and global diplomacy. This is not to suggest that highly sensitive and controversial regional security issues should automatically be thrust into politicized UN forums, such as Special Sessions on Disarmament, but rather that norms and guidelines developed through global discussions could be helpful in providing points of reference in regional arms negotiations. Norms developed in global forums have unusually wide application and legitimacy, though their wording is sometimes vague or ambiguous, because they represent both a North-South and an East-West consensus.

It would clearly be in the US interest, moreover, if the focus of discussion in global forums began to shift away from nuclear towards conventional arms issues. A turn away from the present preoccupation with nuclear issues, however, seems improbable in the near future and the US has limited leverage for inducing such a change. The US should nevertheless encourage such a shift, because it would (1) draw attention to the role and responsibilities of third world countries in controlling regional arms competitions; (2) deflect some of the criticisms of the US and other nuclear powers for not making greater progress on nuclear arms control; and (3) provide the US with a fuller opportunity to explain its reluctance to move forward on some nuclear issues, such as a no-first-use pledge, because of Soviet advantages in conventional forces. Serious discussion of conventional arms problems in highly visible forums like the Special Session and the proposed World Disarmament Campaign, moreover, can perform a useful public education and consciousness-raising function both in the West and the third world at a time of growing anti-nuclear sentiment.

OBSTACLES TO MULTILATERAL PROGRESS

Despite these strong reasons to encourage greater multilateral efforts to control conventional arms, there are several major political, military, economic, and historical obstacles to achieving substantial progress in the near future. The results of the second Special Session made it painfully clear that there is little political momentum behind conventional arms control at this juncture. As noted earlier, the American and Western European publics have displayed relatively little interest in controlling conventional arms, except indirectly through concern about the level of overall military expenditures.

The non-nuclear countries as a whole have retained much of their traditional opposition to giving conventional arms a higher place on the international agenda. Without more rapid progress in nuclear and conventional arms control among the major powers, most non-nuclear countries will continue to be reluctant to embrace conventional arms limitations wholeheartedly. The countries of the third world never have been monolithic on this issue, however, and their differences are increasingly being aired in public forums.[10] Until the first Special Session gave its heavily qualified blessing to the pursuit of conventional arms control, every proposal in the UN even to study the issue had been thwarted by the third world majority. In 1981 in contrast, the General Assembly approved a broad study of conventional arms control. No countries voted against the resolution; the Soviet Union, its allies, and a few major non-aligned states abstained; and a large number of third world states joined the Western countries in voting approval.[11] Chinese diplomats, who have become increasingly active in international disarmament discussions since taking their seat in the Committee on Disarmament following the first Special Session, generally have spoken and voted in favor of conventional arms limitations. Their emphasis, however, has been on finding ways of restricting the forces of the two superpowers rather than on forwarding traditional arms control goals or developing a broad international consensus.

Western Europeans have been generally supportive of the MBFR negotiations, partly as a tool for fostering alliance unity and partly as a means of maintaining, not reducing, the US military presence. They were much less enthusiastic about President Carter's appeals for limiting arms transfers and are not eager to reopen the issue. The Soviet Union has kept a relatively low profile and has generally been unsupportive on conventional arms issues in multilateral forums, probably because it feels politically vulnerable on the issue and prefers to side with the majority of third world states on most issues before the UN.

The United States, on the other hand, is poorly positioned to take the lead in pushing initiatives in this field. As a leading nuclear power and the object of frequent criticism from the non-aligned on this score, the US would be accused of trying to divert attention from the lack of progress in nuclear arms control. As one of the world's two leading arms exporters, the US can hardly preach about the evils of the arms trade, especially since the Carter Administration approached arms transfer limitations in a clumsy, inconsistent, and ill-conceived manner; the Reagan Administration has abandoned the effort entirely.[12] Since the US is not in a good political position to take the lead, it should give strong support and encouragement to the efforts of other countries.

Because general purpose forces and arms transfers are useful in carrying out a wide spectrum of national security tasks, as noted earlier in this chapter, there will be strong reasons and influential constituencies in the US opposed to each proposed limitation measure. Limitations on general purpose forces are more likely to be challenged by the Navy and the Army than by the Air Force, whose interests (narrowly conceived) are threatened more directly in nuclear arms control. Military views on arms transfer talks have been mixed, blending serious concerns about the implications of the spread of advanced arms to the Third World with a deep skepticism about the utility of negotiations for enhancing national security.

Broad Soviet-American negotiations on limiting their conventional forces would quickly confront the problem of asymmetries between the structures and missions of the two opposing forces. This has already been a problem in MBFR, where the West at one point proposed a trade-off between reductions in Warsaw Pact armed forces and in NATO tactical nuclear weapons. This was seen as a way of going beyond establishing aggregate ceilings on the number of military personnel stationed in Central Europe, which was recognized as having little relationship to military missions and objectives. Globally, the missions of US conventional forces—such as aiding the defense of allies overseas, protecting the sea lanes, and projecting force far from home—are not symmetrical with those of the Soviet Union. As a result the compositions of their forces differ markedly. As the Soviet Union has become more of a global military power, however, these differences have begun to narrow.

Another obstacle that the US would face in entering international discussions of regional, deployment, or arms transfer limitations would be the likely negative reactions this would generate from some allies and friendly countries. Such a step might raise doubts about the credibility and reliability of US security assurances, especially in a period when neo-isolationist sentiment is growing in the US and a vocal minority in Congress is pressing for reductions in the US military presence in Europe and East Asia.

Finally, though regional initiatives sound promising on paper, there has been a long history of failure to achieve lasting accords in many areas and no region looks especially promising for such steps at the present time. Europe remains the most likely area for progress, but nine years of MBFR talks, seven years of CSCE dialogue, and almost a year of INF negotiations have not yielded any militarily significant results. Latin America has witnessed a myriad of arms control efforts over the past two decades, including the 1974 Ayacucho Declaration to limit conventional forces and arms outlays, but political conditions are souring in the region, which is now the site of several low-level armed conflicts. African and Middle Eastern issues are constantly addressed in the UN, but always with an anti-South African and anti-Israeli tinge. The numerous international initiatives regarding limitations in the Indian Ocean have failed consistently and current prospects are complicated by the Iran-

Iraq and Afghanistan conflicts. That leaves Northeast and Southeast Asia, both of which are split by deep political divisions and in neither of which is there any real interest in arms control measures.

CRITERIA FOR MULTILATERAL PROGRESS

For the foreseeable future, conventional arms control initiatives will face formidable obstacles in multilateral forums, so they ought to be designed in a way to maximize their slender prospects for success. In several respects, the Nuclear Non-Proliferation Treaty (NPT) provides a good analogy. The trade-off visualized in its Article VI—that the nuclear powers reverse the trend toward vertical proliferation in return for non-nuclear states undertaking to refrain from further horizontal proliferation—is particularly relevant to any multilateral discussions of restrictions on conventional arms transfers. Countries that depend on the major arms-producing nations for their means of self-defense are understandably hesitant about efforts to limit the arms trade. This not only would seem to them to be inequitable, as is the NPT, but also could affect their fundamental security interests. It would thus be most palatable politically if limits on horizontal proliferation (arms transfers) and on vertical proliferation (forces of major powers) were pursued simultaneously. While the linkage may not be logical in military terms, it is important for diplomatic reasons. Likewise, proposals for progress on conventional arms are most likely to be successful if there is simultaneous movement on nuclear issues. This would defuse some of the charges that the nuclear powers are trying to divert attention from nuclear questions.

The recent Convention on Excessively Injurious or Indiscriminate Weapons, which has quietly been endorsed by most third world states, provides another analogy. As the success of this agreement limiting a class of conventional weapons demonstrates, non-aligned states are most interested in limiting weapons that are frequently used in the third world, especially if they are chiefly produced by major powers. Chemical weapons are also analogous in this regard. Moreover, non-aligned states will be less suspicious of conventional arms initiatives that focus on specific kinds of weapons and that forward a clear and widely held arms control rationale than of vague talk of eliminating the evils of the arms trade.

Measures that would appeal to the interests of the less powerful, but more numerous, non-aligned countries would have some chance of success in global, one-country-one-vote, forums even if the major non-aligned countries continue to object. (This was the voting pattern, for example, when the General Assembly approved a UN study of conventional arms control in 1980 and 1981.) To this end, consideration should be given to arms control steps that are linked to economic assistance or collective security measures. Such an approach, however, would obviously require subtle diplomacy and would fare better with US support than with US leadership. At the same time, it is important to avoid approaches that could be readily politicized and that could lead to US isolation. Initiatives concerning Africa and the Middle East are clearly the most sensitive.

In considering possible initiatives, the focus should be on how the measures would serve security and arms control objectives, because the international and domestic political benefits are likely to be minimal, especially in the short run. It would be tempting to try to identify catchy slogans for sweeping US initiatives in the conventional arms field in order to stimulate greater public interest. The conventional arena, however, simply does not lend itself to simple formulas and the public does not feel a sense of urgency to limit conventional forces. Presidential leadership could be useful in drawing public attention to the issue, if it does not appear to be an attempt to defuse the anti-nuclear movement, but it would be hard to sustain public interest.

POSSIBLE STEPS

This analysis suggests that there is no single major initiative on the horizon that would be militarily desirable, politically feasible, and that could serve as a catalyst for a sudden reinvigoration of multilateral conventional arms control efforts. There are, however, a number of useful steps that could be taken whose aggregate impact could be substantial. These fall into four broad areas: (1) UN-related measures; (2) European regional action; (3) Soviet-American dialogue; and (4) arms transfer consultations.

The UN, for all its faults, and its sister organizations on the regional level, are well placed to serve two functions vital to successful arms control: (1) peacemaking and peacekeeping; and (2) international monitoring and verification of agreements. These functions should be more closely integrated with arms control efforts, especially on the regional level, if arms limitations are ever to be developed in the areas where they are most needed, rather than only in those where they can most easily be achieved. As a first step, the US should call for a review of fact-finding, mediation, and peacekeeping machinery, while announcing its intention to rely on these UN capabilities more frequently in the future. The US should repeat the offer made by Vice President Mondale at the first Special Session to provide logistical support for international peacekeeping operations, as it has done in regional efforts such as those that the OAU undertook in Chad.

Second, the US should encourage the UN and regional organizations to establish neutral international monitoring teams to help implement confidence-building measures and verify international arms control agreements. The current UN investigation of charges of Soviet and Vietnamese use of toxins and chemical weapons in Afghanistan and Southeast Asia represents an especially difficult test case. If the UN can retain some credibility after this challenging assignment, it should be given a larger role in policing future agreements.

The US should encourage the UN to play a greater role in publishing objective information and analyses of conventiontional arms control issues. The UN studies of confidence-building measures, regional disarmament, military budgets, and now conventional disarmament are steps in the right direction. The national military budget reporting instrument developed by a UN-appointed panel of experts provides a means for comparing national defense outlays in a standard format, but only a handful of countries, mostly Western, have undertaken to report their expenditures to the Secretary-General. If a large number of countries could be persuaded to do this annually, then this would put pressure on the Soviet Union and its allies to be more forthcoming and accurate in disclosing their military outlays.[13] Now that a World Disarmament Campaign has been approved in principle by the second Special Session, every effort should be made to insure that conventional arms issues are given equal weight with nuclear issues.

It is too early to tell whether President Reagan's recent MBFR initiative will revive the negotiations, but there are supplemental steps that could be taken in the meantime. Steven Canby, in the following chapter, suggests several innovative kinds of confidence-building measures. Two additional areas for further efforts involve crisis communications and military exchanges. Senators Sam Nunn and Henry Jackson have proposed that the US and the Soviet Union establish a bilateral crisis communications center in a neutral spot such as Geneva. The idea has considerable merit, but it could be enhanced by making it a multilateral enterprise. If it was staffed by military representatives from several NATO and Warsaw Pact countries, perhaps on a rotating basis, this would allow lengthier and more regularized contacts between Western and Eastern military officers on neutral territory. Other forms of East-West military exchanges should also be encouraged. It would be particularly valuable to foster a dialogue with military officers from Eastern Europe at this juncture, since other Warsaw Pact countries may someday follow the Polish example and give greater political power to the military. The role of the military in shaping Soviet arms control policies is unclear, but the military appears to be influential in discouraging greater openness and flexibility.

The time is not ripe for opening Soviet-American negotiations aimed at achieving additional conventional arms control agreements beyond MBFR. The US should consider, however, proposing a broad and continuing series of bilateral discussions, not negotiations, at the cabinet and chiefs of staff level on military and arms control problems relating to conventional forces. Among the topics for discussion could be lessening the risks of surprise attacks, qualitative or mission-oriented limitations, the roles of Soviet and American naval forces, and the use of major power forces or their proxies in the third world. The asymmetries between US and Soviet missions may hinder negotiations, but they would make this kind of discussion all the more interesting and important in laying the groundwork for future bilateral or multilateral negotiations.

Neither East-West, North-South, nor West-West negotiations on limiting arms transfers would be productive at the present time.

Moreover, as noted before, the US is poorly positioned to take the lead on this issue. In light of the controversies and confusions that surround many aspects of the arms trade, however, greater multi-lateral consultations on both the regional and global levels would be helpful. One possibility would be the development of regional consultative forums on security and arms transfer issues and of regional conferences between arms suppliers and recipients that would focus on enhancing local security and not just on possible limitations. The initiatives, however, should come from local states. Another possibility would be a conference of supplier states that would include the ''new'' suppliers, such as Israel, Brazil, and India, and would consider general arms trade problems, such as better coordination or regulation of the trade, and not just limitations.

These steps are intended to lay the groundwork for more concrete progress in the future, if conditions improve. Conventional arms control issues are extraordinarily complex, especially at the multi-lateral level, where the differences in interests and perspectives run deep and there is little prospect of dramatic breakthroughs in the foreseeable future. Yet Soviet-American relations have followed a cyclical pattern in the past and changes in the international climate are always possible. If and when the climate begins to thaw, conventional arms restraints should be one of the first steps towards building more constructive and enduring East-West and North-South relationships.

NOTES

1. See Document of the UNGA, A/S–12/32, pp. 21–23.

2. See UN Department of Public Information, ''Final Document—Special Session of the UN General Assembly on Disarmament 1978,'' (New York: UN, 1981), Paragraph 81, p. 15.

3. See Document of the UN Disarmament Commission titled, ''Views of the Chinese Delegation on Conventional Disarmament,'' A/CN.10/28 (29 May 1981).

4. See President Ronald Reagan's speech, ''U.S. Program for Peace and Arms Control,'' *Current Policy,* No. 346 (Washington, DC: US Department of State, 18 November, 1981).

5. Flora Lewis, ''Buyers of Death,'' *New York Times,* 29 July 1982.

6. See Steven Canby's chapter, "Arms Control, Confidence-Building Measures and Verification," which follows this chapter.

7. For a somewhat more negative assessment of the Sinai accords, see Steven Canby, op. cit. note 6.

8. For example, a measure introduced by Representative Patricia Schoeder, Democrat of Colorado, calling for a 50 percent reduction in US forces stationed overseas within four years, was defeated by the House of Representatives by a vote of 314 to 87 on 29 July 1982. See "House Approves 175.3 Billion Dollars Military Measure," *New York Times,* 30 July 1982.

9. For a detailed study, see Andrew J. Pierre, *The Global Politics of Arms Sales,* (Princeton, New Jersey: Princeton University Press, 1982). For statistical information, see US Arms Control and Disarmament Agency, *World Military Expenditures and Arms Transfers: 1970–1979* (Washington, DC: US GPO, March, 1982).

10. For a fuller discussion of this point, see my chapter "The Arms Trade," in *The Changing United Nations: Options for the US,* ed. by David A. Kay, *Proceedings* 32:4 (New York: The Academy of Political Science, 1977), pp. 170–183.

11. See UN General Assembly resolution 36/97A adopted on 9 December 1981 by 114–0 votes, with 26 countries abstaining. A proposal for such a study had been approved by the UN General Assembly on 12 December 1980, in resolution 35/156A. On this occasion, 14 countries, including the Soviet Union, its allies, and some important non-aligned countries voted against the resolution.

12. For a critique of the Carter Administration's approach, see my testimony before the Senate Foreign Relations Committee, "An Evaluation of US Conventional Arms Transfer Policies," March 4, 1980.

13. Undoubtedly, this was the rationale for President Reagan's proposal to the Second Special Session on Disarmament that an international conference be convened on the subject of military expenditures.

ARMS CONTROL, CONFIDENCE-BUILDING MEASURES, AND VERIFICATION

STEVEN L. CANBY

Arms control has existed for many years and its objectives are well-known: reducing the role of force and its associated peacetime and wartime costs. Its primary tool has been arms limitation. Verification, which consumes inordinate attention and which may well be a sine qua non of any agreement, serves this aspect.

In the last decade confidence-building measures (CBMs) have received prominence in arms control efforts. This prominence was initiated by the Conference on Security and Cooperation in Europe (CSCE) in Helsinki in 1975, and later in Belgrade and Madrid. In the ongoing Mutual and Balanced Force Reduction (MBFR) negotiations, CBMs are termed Associated Measures (AMs). Their prominence is due to the recognition that there is more to arms control than arms limitation and, even if limitations remain the practical goal, too much mutual distrust exists for an agreement in the near future. CBMs bridge this gap by providing mechanisms for:

1. Reducing misunderstandings that could degenerate into armed conflict;

2. Building relationships that could generate mutual trust; and

3. Hindering surprise and short-warning attacks.

Which of these mechanisms is the more important is situation-dependent. Certainly, the first would have eliminated the special circumstances (if not the cause) that led to the outbreak of World War I in August 1914. The first is obviously useful in situations of mutual hostility, but not necessarily where neither party has aggressive intentions (deterrence and the use of nuclear weapons being cases in point).

The second consumes much of the academic literature. Its orientation is the process of establishing contacts and momentum. Many believe a network of interaction will ineluctably lead to mutual trust and the realization that the costs of war exceed its benefits. This view, however, is hypothetical. Empirically the world has never been more interdependent—through marriage and the intimacy of ruling classes and political parties, capital flows, and trade—than the Europe of 1914. Another cautionary example is the recent breakdown in detente.

The third has been the main focus of Europe-oriented CBMs. It is the natural focus of the military, the institution most directly concerned with security. However, in practice, while most CBMs may have the intent of inhibiting surprise attack, their real impact in Europe has been the establishment of a network of relationships that could eventually be expanded into a major arms limitation agreement, such as a common ceiling.

Perhaps because their goals have been modest, CBMs have been widely acclaimed. The questions to be pursued in this chapter are:

1. Their effectiveness as surprise attack inhibitors; and

2. Their extensions abroad (the Middle East, Korea, and the generalized third world).

CENTRAL EUROPE

The following chart lists the CBMs and AMs that have been proposed for application in Europe. Most have the flavor of verification and inhibition of surprise attack. Neither would actually be accomplished. Verification, particularly of personnel strengths, is inordinately difficult. And the measures lack bite to be effective against surprise and short-warning attack. This effectively places their usefulness in the first two categories of reducing misunderstandings and establishing the process of confidence-building. While useful, it must nevertheless be recognized that the first may no longer be needed in Europe, and the second is dominated by the overall political milieu in Europe. What is needed are mutually acceptable measures with bite.

The military problem in Europe is NATO's conventional inferiority. MBFR cannot offset this inferiority because the Warsaw Pact's center of strength is outside the guidelines area, which is to NATO's detriment. As long as the focus is purely on this area, outside forces can always be reintroduced; and in most cases, forces can be mobilized internally too (a facet often neglected in Western analyses). Accordingly, the most MBFR can accomplish militarily is inhibiting surprise and short-warning attacks. The NATO goal of a common ceiling does not affect the overall balance. It simply concerns forces in place before reinforcement and mobilization. If these occur quickly or if one side can attack with forces in place, a common ceiling has in fact no practical military meaning. The corollary conclusion is that verification similarly assumes no meaning.

The conclusion is inescapable: whatever its political purposes, MBFR militarily can only limit surprise and short-warning attacks. Politically, force levels are useful for locking NATO countries into their "coupling" commitments, but its military role remains enhancing the difficulty of a surprise attack. In principle, as force levels drop unreinforced attacks become less feasible. This is due less to defending forces, which presumably also drop quantitatively, than to the need for the attacker to occupy and protect the territorial space gained by success. In this case, the lower the force levels and the greater the defense potential of mobilized regular forces or militia, the less feasible and likely an unreinforced attack. Moreover, this builds in a degree of robustness, which eliminates the military need for elaborate schemes for verification and warning.

Presently Soviet levels are sufficient to launch an unreinforced attack; even fewer troops are required if surprise could be orchestrated. The Soviets, in their modernizing, are reorganizing their forces for a fluid, granular form of non-linear, non-concentrated warfare that is entirely consistent with a preemptive surprise attack. In the revised Soviet approach, Group Soviet Forces Germany have

Proposed Confidence-Building Measures and Associated Measures

Confidence-Building Measures (CSCE)
1975

Measure 1. 21-day prior notification on maneuvers exceeding 25,000.
Measure 2. Notification of smaller maneuvers.
Measure 3. Exercise information.
Measure 4. Observers to attend maneuvers.

NATO Associated Measures (MBFR)
Tabled December 1979

Measure 1. Prior notification of out-of-garrison activities.
Measure 2. Exchange of observers at pre-notified out-of-garrison activities.
Measure 3. Prior notification of movements into the area of reductions.
Measure 4. Ground and aerial inspection (18 inspections per year).
Measure 5. Declared troop entry/exit points with observers.
Measure 6. Exchange of information on manpower and structure.
Measure 7. Noninterference with technical means of verification.

Warsaw Pact Associated Measures (MBFR)
Presented December 1980

Measure 1. Mutual notification of beginning and end of reductions.
Measure 2. Exchange of lists of reduced/withdrawn units and residual manpower strengths.
Measure 3. Temporary control points with observers during withdrawal period.
Measure 4. Exchange of information on compliance.
Measure 5. Exchange of lists of US/USSR reduced forces in Phase I.
Measure 6. Further exchanges of such information at specified intervals.
Measure 7. Prior notification of large (20,000 or more) exercises.
Measure 8. Prior notification of movements within area of 20,000 troops or more.
Measure 9. Notification of entry into and departure from reductions area.
Measure 10. Limitations (40,000–50,000) on military exercises.
Measure 11. Verification by national technical means, with reciprocal agreement not to interfere.
Measure 12. Consultations in event of doubts concerning compliance.
Measure 13. Temporary mixed commission to consider questions regarding implementation.

become the cutting edge of a Soviet attack. The reinforcing second strategic echelon billeted in the Western Military Districts has become a mere consolidating force, akin to the horse-drawn German infantry divisions in World War II, whose task was to follow in the wake of the Panzer divisions. The war cannot be won without them, but nevertheless everything rises and falls on the cutting-edge forces.

In this empirical situation, the present family of CBMs lacks military relevance. They may even be militarily counterproductive, though NATO may still desire them politically. They lack relevance and bite because the forces in place are already sufficiently large. Soviet forces do not need to move into exercise areas for launching a surprise attack. In fact, nowadays the very attempt to do so is a warning indicator in itself. The Soviets can "mobilize" within their barracks, and most barracks in the German Democratic Republic are, by definition, no more than 200 kilometers from the inter-German border. The dynamics of a surprise attack are such that main forces do not need to hit the border initially. That is the task of heliborne *desant* groupings, reconnaissance, special armor-raiding groups, and tactical airpower.

The present family of CBMs was not designed to cope with the dynamics of force, or more specifically the nature of its unfolding. Political scientists and foreign offices are unfamiliar with it; the military are protective and normally unwilling to consider any measure that could reduce their own flexibility, regardless of its effect upon opposing forces and overall political-military objectives.

Even if force levels were lower, the present family of CBMs amounts to a set of obstacles that complicate but do not stop an opponent intent upon circumventing them. Their weakness is that they are known "events," and their existence can therefore be taken into account. CBMs, to be effective, must therefore have an element of randomness or unpredictability; they should be difficult to skirt or outright crippling to a military force. An example of the first are unscheduled inspections. The second would be liaison officers attached to each regimental headquarters or major barracks. Techniques crippling an attack but not a defense offer the most bite.

Modern armies of the combined-arms armored variety are functionally specialized and similar to Swiss watches: take away one part, however small, and the watch stops. For instance, modern armies cannot operate without signals or artillery. Nowadays, without suppressing artillery fire against opposing anti-tank infantry, tanks and other armored vehicles are vulnerable; infantry concealed in the towns and forests that comprise 45 percent of the Federal Republic can stop them. However, commanders would resist removing such components even temporarily for arms control purposes. Their army could not attack, but they themselves would be vulnerable to attack.

The missing component must therefore be one that prevents attacking but allows defending. Bridging is the most obvious candidate. A tank army cannot advance without military bridging. It can fight within an area and even withdraw without bridging. By the time bridging might be needed, it would be reintroduced. The same could be said about reconnaissance (recce). A defender can operate without specialized recce. An attacker cannot. Of the two, bridging is the preferable restriction: its numbers are smaller and its absence is much easier to monitor.

While CBMs are in general stabilizing, they have destabilizing aspects also. They can induce complacency and it must be remembered that the adversary gains reciprocal access that could benefit a potential aggressor. In the absence of difficult-to-skirt or crippling variants, CBMs are not a substitute for vigilance. Yet because the latter is demanding, if not always costly, there is a tendency to yield to complacency. The danger of reciprocity is from mutual monitoring. If the Soviets are orchestrating a surprise attack, monitoring NATO's reactions is invaluable. If NATO is alert, and Soviet preparations are conducted in a non-obtrusive manner, the attack can be postponed and little is lost. If NATO is sensed to be not reacting, surprise is complete and the attack can be executed. Similarly, proposals such as those for visits between NATO and Warsaw Pact senior commanders and their staffs may be useful socially and politically, but they are not militarily meaningful and they can be dangerous if an aggressor confirms his hypothesis as to the nature of defensive preparations and the defender's likely reactions.

For NATO the inescapable conclusion is that more meaningful CBMs must be sought or unilateral steps taken to remove NATO's vulnerability to surprise attack in the first instance. Western Europe alone is almost as populous as the USSR and has significantly superior technological and industrial resources. In the MBFR guidelines area, NATO is outnumbered in personnel by 23 percent, 1,139,000 to 924,000.[1] If France is included as well, NATO outnumbers Warsaw Pact forces by 200,000. Overall, NATO has as many men under arms in peacetime and spends between ten (in dollars) and 40 (in rubles) percent more for defense. That for roughly equal manpower and costs, the Pact obtains three times the combat numbers is NATO's fault, not the East's. The Russians have traditionally held Western military prowess in awe. It is not their fault that in going about their military business (i.e., normal modernization), a windfall benefitting them has occurred due purely to Western military incompetence. At the same time, they can hardly be expected to give their advantage away, particularly when at any time the West could sort itself out and restore its prowess. After all, for a Russian, military equality can only mean some degree of numerical superiority to offset personnel and technological inferiorities.

In the same vein, it can be argued that CBMs for inhibiting surprise attack are not really necessary. And if they are not really necessary, negotiators should be careful in not compromising the long-term future of a Europe without America (that is, while America has committed troops to Europe for nearly half a century now, a century is a *long* time). While arms controllers and Foreign Offices have sought one-sided advantages vis-à-vis the USSR to reduce Western vulnerability to surprise attack, Western governments and militaries have done little unilaterally to remove their vulnerability to surprise attack, thereby themselves creating the opportunity and incentive for surprise attack and Soviet success at low costs to the Soviet leadership.

Surprise attacks are actually quite easy to stop. By definition, surprise connotes means other than outright force. Surprise attacks depend on confusion and the illusion of strength. The Warsaw Pact does not have the military forces in place in Eastern Europe to overwhelm deployed NATO forces. However, even these forces would be sufficient if NATO's formations were caught in garrison and if chaos and civilian panic were created so as to neutralize governments and inhibit formation deployments.

The chief instrument of the surprise attack nowadays is the transport helicopter. With present-style forces, these can only be stopped by deployed ground forces, or at a minimum the continuous peacetime deployment of most divisional low-level ground air defense. With present equipment, this is costly; worse, there is no indication that the NATO military command is even aware of the problem. Many NATO combat battalions in their barracks are vulnerable to assault by helicopter. Ironically, the US proposes to take steps that would actually increase its vulnerability to surprise attack by relocating combat battalions closer to the border and within easy pouncing range of Soviet helicopters. On the other hand, while US combat vehicles are at least partially combat loaded with ammunition (tanks in particular), none of the European armies are similarly combat loaded, and most European units are not even located with their ammunition. In at least one corps, the distance between tank units and tank ammunition for combat loading is 90 kilometers! Even more egregious, the I German Corps—NATO's largest and most proficient—literally ceases to exist every weekend from Friday afternoon to Monday morning, and cannot be readily recalled. German units are regionally recruited: I German Corps, however, is billeted in the thinly populated Luneburger Heide and its recruiting source is the Ruhr, several hundred kilometers away. In normal times, this is but several hours; in a surprise attack mounted with special operations troops (which the Soviets and East Germans emphasize) and pre-located saboteurs, return in a timely manner is impossible. Finally, of course, the list is much longer; for example, the prolonged deployment time of the Dutch and Belgian corps, vulnerability of power stations, and the like.

As for Warsaw Pact air forces, if these were used in a surprise onslaught, they could be trapped in the air by simultaneously attacking all main operating bases (there are roughly 60) with conventional cratering munitions from Pershing-like missiles (fired from fixed sites), forcing Pact air forces to recover on vulnerable dispersal bases. The technology is here and the cost is equivalent to a mere Pershing battalion. Yet the US and NATO Europe have done little to acquire the capability.

The point is simply that NATO has not taken measures unilaterally to correct its vulnerabilities to surprise attack, yet would inveigh against the Soviets and would have the Soviets make changes that NATO will itself not make. NATO can unilaterally eliminate its vulnerability to surprise attack;[2] CBMs can only make a surprise attack more difficult to design and prepare for, barring Soviet acceptance of a crippling variant like foregoing military bridging.

Militarily meaningful CBMs must take into account the changing nature of the Soviet threat, its capabilities, and in particular its approach to the problem of war. (This critique can also be applied to Northeast Asia or elsewhere, the problem being broadly based.) Thus, all arms control negotiations must be made within the context of opposing operational methods (OMs) and operational vulnerabilities. CBMs must go beyond the mechanics of inspection teams and verification procedures to an examination and adoption of measures that substantively reduce NATO vulnerability to surprise attack both by providing warning, and more significantly, increasing the resilience of NATO defenses, which, by preventing a rapid collapse, will reduce the benefits and incentives for a Soviet surprise attack in the first instance.

Increasing NATO defense resiliency in the context of arms limitation agreements requires an examination of Soviet OMs, their strengths and weaknesses, against the opposing NATO OMs. From such an examination the operating scenarios for Soviet surprise attacks can be determined as can the ability of NATO to counter them. Areas for enhancing NATO defensive resiliency can be pinpointed, possibly with concurrent reductions in force levels, as different OMs require different materiel and manpower commitments.

Verification teams, reconnaissance, and surveillance measures are obstacles to be accounted for in planning a surprise attack, as well as to be used in deceptive masking. Any (Soviet) surprise attack scenario must be fought with units in place, without significant mobilization or pre-concentration. The decision to attack will be of a go/no-go type, based upon Soviet judgment of Western alertness. Thus, there will be very little for NATO verification teams to report, but much to report for symmetrically applied Soviet verification teams (that is, removing the uncertainty of NATO readiness). In the event that NATO intelligence does perceive the beginning of a Soviet surprise attack, and NATO begins even a partial mobilization of forces, the Soviets, seeing the chance of surprise receding, can cancel the attack without changing the dispositions of their forces; the exercise can be continually repeated until NATO is detected unaware. The result of any NATO mobilization under these circumstances will be monetarily, politically, and diplomatically costly, as NATO will be cast, at worst, in the role of aggressor and at best as trigger-happy in an era of nuclear weapons. The surprise attack situation is akin to that of the October 1973 Middle East crisis. If an attack is contemplated, it will only be executed if no evidence of its detection is observed; if countermeasures to the planned attack are made, the threat disappears.

Accordingly, the allowance of Soviet verification teams in NATO forces could increase, rather than decrease, the likelihood of a Soviet surprise attack. Whereas Soviet preparations for a surprise attack on NATO would be largely undetectable to NATO verification teams, NATO preparations to meet a perceived Soviet surprise-attack threat would require significant mobilization and redeployment of forces, which would be obvious to Soviet observers. Thus Soviet verification teams can become the final trigger of a surprise attack by confirming the extent of NATO unreadiness to meet the onslaught. For these reasons, on-site inspection and verification are not absolutes as CBMs against Soviet surprise attack; rather they are additional obstacles to Soviet planning. At the same time, they present Soviet planners with a means to monitor NATO, and they can instill a false sense of security and thus serve to undermine the NATO defenses.

EXTENDING CBMs

Because they encompass most of the goals of arms control, save the consummating objective of lower force levels and its derived benefits, CBMs have wide applicability, can begin the process of arms control, and are relatively easy to initiate (even if the impact may be weak). The question is: are they applicable to other regions of the world?

KOREA

Korea would seem a natural candidate for bilateral implementation of CBMs. Meaningful CBMs would certainly ease the strain and tensions between the two Koreas. In this case, however, since the political climate is so adverse, no common ground may exist for even modest initiatives. The North, so long as Kim Il Sung lives, is too implacably hostile. A North Korea that continually probes southern defenses with infiltrations along the DMZ border and sends terrorists into the South by sea cannot be interested in processes for building mutual confidence, nor can it be interested in crippling CBMs. At most—and even this is problematical—the North might be interested in mechanisms for limiting situations escalating out of control. But for this case the long-standing Panmunjom mechanism exists.

A conflict in Korea could readily occur because of leadership ambitions in particular, and the natural pull of reunification and big-power politics in general. Yet arms control is unlikely to prevail in Korean conditions. On the other hand—as in Europe—a US ally has done little unilaterally to correct its military deficiencies. South Korea is weak purely because of its style of war. It has, relative to the much smaller North, few combat forces for its military manpower. Worse, South Korean forces are deployed in mountainous terrain in a tactically passive cordon defense, characterized by a linear line of battalion strongpoints on forward slopes of low mountains. The North is known to possess heavy artillery for smashing such positions, and light infantry for infiltrating gaps and flowing around static reserve positions, collapsing the defense in the familiar tactic of 30 years ago in the Korean War.

A South organized for war in this mode will always be vulnerable to attack, barring major increases in peacetime military forces. In this case, arms control would be called upon to make up for self-inflicted inferiority.

With the South's vulnerabilities unilaterally eliminated, the North has little chance of succeeding in a surprise attack and none in a long conflict. With the artillery smashing and light infantry undermining schemes foreclosed, any attack must be frontal and therefore asymmetrically costly. There is no opportunity for deploying tanks down the corridors to Seoul; they remain, as in 1950, mere distractions for the light infantry and a subsequent coup de grace force against a collapsed defense.

A military balance in Korea requires no additional resources. Indeed, some can be saved by de-emphasizing heavy firepower and anti-tank weaponry. Politically, the doctrinal revisions would be a signal to the North: it is no longer feasible to attack except by bruising frontal assaults. This is a form of war the North, with its inferior population and industry, cannot win. For the US, it also suggests US ground forces are militarily superfluous, while their deterrent value could be replaced by greater air and naval forces that could be militarily very useful in the overall global equation.

THE MIDDLE EAST

The Sinai accord between Israel and Egypt highlights another strength and weakness of arms control and CBMs. In disentangling Egypt and Israel, the CBMs adopted for the Sinai can be considered highly successful. It can be plausibly argued that without them, the Egyptian-Israeli accord could not have been engineered regardless of the best intentions of the two governments and coinciding fundamental interests.

On the other hand, the accord displays a second weakness of arms control: it is purely "micro" oriented and lacks "macro" perspective. (The first weakness is the previously discussed lack of attention to military detail and the dynamics and nature of military force.) The very success of CBMs in the Sinai also removed the constraints upon Israeli military actions elsewhere, which was of course the major Arab objection to the Camp David process in the first instance. Even worse, the United Nations instrumentality for enforcing peace—multinational forces—has been pushed aside and discredited by Israel in its invasion of Lebanon.

The Egyptian-Israeli accord suggests CBMs can be a major instrumentality for peace in the Middle East once the Palestinian question is resolved. The latter is a pre-condition; without its resolution, success simply shifts violence elsewhere. A second caveat is that the Sinai accord was ideal for CBMs: militarily, the Sinai is a buffer; the issue was surprise attack, not the overall military balance. A comprehensive Middle East settlement requires that the latter must be addressed. CBMs are mainly attuned to short-warning attacks. Unfortunately for arms control in the eastern Mediterranean, the two cannot be separated. Distances are too compressed and Israel has repeatedly demonstrated military competence in the best German tradition: rapid mobilization and preemptive strike.

Because of its quantitative disadvantages in resources and numbers, Israel is unlikely to accept limitations on its qualitative advantages in organization, tactics, and technology in the absence of a comprehensive peace settlement. In Europe the reintroduction of engineers or other vital parts necessary for attack provide warning time. In the Middle East, such variants could hobble Israel's Arab adversaries, but they probably would not hobble Israel sufficiently (they can be internally mobilized), nor is Israel likely to ever accept a CBM crippling its capacity for preemption. This relegates CBMs to mechanisms for defusing misunderstandings and generating mutual trust. However, normal intelligence in the porous Middle East can adequately monitor events, and CBMs are unlikely to more than marginally offset generations of mutual hostility, especially as long as the Palestinian question remains unresolved.

Intra-Arab wars are a different breed of conflict. Few Arab military forces are noted for military competence. In most cases too (except for the small Persian Gulf states), the centers of political power are widely spaced and protected by vast desert barriers. Ground attack and invasion are not a serious proposition. CBMs, being NATO-derived, have been oriented to this scenario. The threat to an Arab government is internal. All Arab governments are authoritarian and brittle. They are vulnerable to coups sponsored abroad and to loss of legitimacy, such as an inability to defend against attack by air. CBMs affecting destructive firepower and tactical air power would have distinctive merit. Otherwise, the network of relationships among Arab countries is sufficient and the balance-of-power mechanism among them ensures a measure of equilibrium against overt force. Coups are a different matter, but this domain is not amenable to CBMs and arms control.

THE THIRD WORLD IN GENERAL

The four cases cited—NATO, Korea, and two in the Middle East—suggest CBMs can be useful. There are limits to their usefulness and no single solution suffices for all. Each situation is different. In the third world, a still different pattern is likely to prevail: border adjustment and irredentism. Fundamental issues of survival may not exist; combat itself, however, may be no less intense because of long-standing, righteous emotionalism. A second consideration is that most armies are oriented to internal security, not force projection and war fighting. Few have the competence and the means to invade more than border regions. For these countries air forces are the instrument of projecting power. Such projection normally has little military content; though destructive, its purpose is political signalling and terrorizing.

Except for controlling air forces, normal CBMs are not applicable. Mechanisms for defusing misperceptions and misunderstandings are useful. This is also the function of foreign offices. Nor is there much point in establishing a process for confidence-building, since it is unlikely to overcome the emotions of centuries. Crippling mechanisms for ground forces in border regions would be effective in some regions (e.g., the India-Pakistan border). In other regions, however, such provisions would have little impact because of compressed distances or the rudimentary functional specialization and military competence of the armies involved.

In former times, demilitarization of border areas would have sufficed to provide sufficient warning for the defender. Today, outside forces can move too quickly through border provinces. The CBMs useful in these cases are those focusing the attention of world opinion and the major powers. This mechanism is often not effective against strong, self-confident powers (e.g., Israel). In most cases, however, countries do value outside opinion and do feel inhibited by the possibility of outside sanctions, including unilateral intervention by former colonial powers and the interspersion of UN peace-keeping forces.

Everywhere there is a case for publicity, which is an effective pressuring device on most countries, large and small. Many third world countries, however, are habitually neglected by the world press. Peacetime military movements and arms sales should be monitored and the results disseminated widely. The effect can be only positive. Publicity can substitute for bureaucratic arrangements; it is like Adam Smith's Invisible Hand: every action will be contained by an effective reaction. Similarly, multinational inspection teams with official status, monitoring conflicts wherever they occur, could be useful, and certain areas (for instance, the Middle East) should be monitored on a full-time basis. Monitoring and publicity is a CBM of sorts and for the third world, in addition, serves the very useful purpose of insuring more careful adherence to the laws of war, a task only imperfectly served by the mass media.

CBMs can be a useful arms control instrument. Their weakness derives from their mechanistic application. Their application rarely has strategic perspective and their application is often oblivious to the nature of military operations. This approach is suitable for use in strategic arms negotiations and verification, but it is unsuited for dealing with unfolding military operations. A mechanistic approach relegates opposing forces to inanimate, passive participants upon whom a series of verification measures are imposed. This implies the opponent will accept their intent, and will have neither the will nor the ability to manipulate them for advantage. In war, the opponent is rarely passive.

NOTES

1. Jeffrey Record, *Force Reductions in Europe,* Institute for Foreign Policy Analysis, 1980, p. 29.

2. For a cataloging of measures, see Steven L. Canby, *Short and (Long) War Responses, Restructuring, Border Defense, and Reserve Mobilization for Armored Warfare,* Technology Service Corporation, March 1978.

A FUTURE FOR MULTILATERAL
ARMS CONTROL

EDWARD C. LUCK

This has not been a good year for multilateral arms control. The most spectacular event, the second UN Special Session on Disarmament, not surprisingly proved to be the least productive. It failed even to build upon the modest accomplishments of the first Special Session that was held four years earlier. The trilateral negotiations on a Comprehensive Test Ban remain suspended indefinitely as the US government reviews the potential utility and verifiability of such an agreement and the Vienna negotiations on Mutual and Balanced Force Reductions quietly entered their tenth year without agreement, despite a new Western proposal and a slight narrowing of the differences that have so long separated the two sides. It is understandable, then, why challenging questions are being raised about the utility, purposes, and future of multilateral efforts to curb the arms race. In this atmosphere it would be tempting, but shortsighted, to join the chorus of skeptics who have long dismissed multilateral mechanisms as irrelevant, irresponsible, and ineffective, and as long on rhetoric and short on substance.

There is considerable confusion on both the official and public levels about the purposes and activities of multilateral forums. In part, this stems from the general failure of international agencies to define a clear role for themselves. They appear to be malleable, serving whatever purposes their member states want them to, and

This essay draws on some of the themes raised in the meetings of the UNA-USA Study Group on Multilateral Approaches to Arms Control, but it does not necessarily reflect the views of any of its individual members. The author is grateful to John B. McGrath, who served as Rapporteur of the Group, for his careful summaries of the Study Group discussions.

accomplishing no more than their members will permit. In diplomacy this is a virtue, as well as a prerequisite for institutional survival in a world of sovereign nation-states. But it does prevent multilateral institutions from seizing the initiative or from taking independent action. They exist largely to reflect and implement the will of the international community.

The most visible multilateral forums, such as the UN Special Session, are designed more for discussion than action. The smaller, more specialized and less publicized bodies, such as the Committee on Disarmament in Geneva and the MBFR talks in Vienna, do the most serious negotiating. There is a broad range of multilateral bodies, forming a continuum of regional, functional, and global institutions. At one end of the spectrum, the second Special Session seemed to many observers to epitomize all that is wrong with multilateralism. The frustrations and complexities of dealing simultaneously with 157 sovereign nations on crucial and highly technical security issues were painfully evident. Rather than fostering an international consensus, the Session served to underline how deep the cleavages—East-West, North-South, and intra-regional—have grown since the first Special Session in 1978.

Among the many lessons that can be derived from the failure of the second Special Session, seven interrelated themes stand out:

> 1. Without a propitious international political climate, major positive results are unlikely. The general atmosphere has a decisive influence on the prospects for agreement, while the process of multilateral discussion and negotiation itself can at best have a marginal impact on an unfavorable political climate. The growing public interest in nuclear disarmament in the West has so far had little positive influence on the underlying issues that divide East and West.

> 2. The timing of major events is a key factor in determining their success or failure, and their planning should be based on a realistic evaluation of international political trends. The advocates of holding the second Special Session in mid–1982 contended that such an event is most needed at times of international tension and discord. If a particular multilateral discus-

sion holds real promise of bridging the gaps between countries and of reducing the sources of tension, then it makes sense to proceed. However, if the more likely results are an increase in the volume of propaganda and mutual incriminations, widening fissures in consensus positions previously agreed upon, and public disillusionment with the process of inter-governmental negotiation—as was the case with the second Special Session—then it would be better to postpone such a large public forum until a more propitious time.

3. Major multilateral forums require very extensive and careful preparations with the active participation of all of the major actors. Unless there is general prior agreement on basic principles and objectives, especially among the key players, it will be extraordinarily difficult to reach a consensus in the conference or negotiation itself. The inability to reach even a modest degree of agreement before the session on the outline of a major item, such as the proposed Comprehensive Program on Disarmament, should have been a clear signal that a consensus was unlikely to be achieved on that issue.

4. Serious and constructive consultations among the US, the USSR, and other major actors before and during the event are essential if issues of real substantive importance are to be addressed. The key decisions on security and arms control are made in national capitals, not in New York or Geneva, and bilateral understandings are needed to lay the foundations for multilateral agreements. When the two key countries cannot find any basis for cooperation in a multilateral arena, as happened in the second Special Session, there is little chance for a positive or constructive outcome.

5. In global disarmament discussions, the best tends to be the enemy of the good. In the wake of the rhetorical flourishes of the General Debate speeches and the public cries for action, it is extraordinarily difficult to formulate a realistic set of goals and expectations for multilateral efforts. As long as unrealistically high standards of accomplishment are posed for global

forums, public disillusionment will inevitably follow and their real though modest achievements will be ignored or demeaned. Perhaps failure will now breed realism, though the current domestic and international political atmosphere may instead encourage demagogy, hypocrisy, and a general round of finger-pointing as each side looks for someone else to blame.

6. As a corollary, multilateral discussions need to focus to a much greater extent on why nations acquire arms and how their security needs can be met at lower levels, rather than on abstract formulas and timetables for disarmament. In the West, there is increasing recognition that arms control policies will be more viable over the long term if they are integrated into overall security policies and strategies. Arms control, especially on the multilateral level, has become increasingly mechanistic and opportunistic, focusing more on what appears feasible than on what is urgently necessary to enhance international security. The central goal of disarmament is greater security for all countries, and this objective will not be well served if nations continue to talk one way in the UN for largely political reasons and to act another way in their unilateral defense planning.

7. Since the most urgent security issues arise among neighboring states, there should be a renewed emphasis on regional approaches and negotiations, which can complement and reinforce global discussions. The UN's frequently successful work on peacekeeping and its less productive discussions of disarmament have been compartmentalized as if they were unrelated subjects rather than two interrelated aspects of the same subject: international security. This tendency has contributed to the air of unreality that surrounds vague discussions of global disarmament.

Most of these points seem obvious and ought to be standard principles for any successful international negotiation, yet they have frequently been ignored by the advocates of multilateral disarmament. On most of these counts, the first Special Session was better prepared, better timed and more successful than its successor. The fundamental lesson, therefore, is not that global forums are inherently useless, but that their future utility will depend on whether they can be reoriented and planned more realistically.

The history of both bilateral and multilateral arms control negotiations suggests that talks are unlikely to bear fruit in a period of declining East-West relations and, if they do, that the resulting agreements stand little chance of ratification. Ironically, like other forms of international cooperation, arms control is least likely to succeed when it is most needed. The mutual mistrust that spurs the arms race also acts to discourage flexibility and openness in negotiations.

Yet a basic premise of global negotiations, on the other hand, is that the negotiating process itself can foster the conditions necessary for agreement by bringing political pressures from the third world, allies, and public opinion to bear on the recalcitrant major powers. If multilateral mechanisms cannot yet offer security incentives for nations to moderate their policies, then at least they can raise the political costs of appearing uncooperative or unconcerned about the dangers of the arms competition. If multilateral negotiations are unpromising and unwieldly, then at least they can stimulate progress elsewhere in more restricted or specialized forums. As Alan Neidle points out, bringing contentious issues to multilateral forums has the advantages of defusing bilateral political tensions and eliminating zero-sum bargaining.

Global approaches have sometimes served to defuse tensions among regional rivals or lesser powers. For example, addressing nuclear proliferation in a global treaty helped overcome the political problems inherent in obtaining a separate agreement for the Middle East. When Soviet-American tensions are high, however, these forums tend to become arenas in which the superpowers compete for influence and propaganda points. The US and USSR have apparently adopted similar strategies of advancing major arms control initiatives while seeking to embarrass the other side. Attempting to undermine one's potential bargaining partner may not be the surest way to instill mutual confidence and promote the negotiating process, but it has become a common tactic in politically oriented forums like the Special Session.

At the first Special Session the debates were largely North-South, with the superpowers sharing the brunt of third world criticism, while the second Session was dominated by sharp East-West differences. The non-aligned movement no longer speaks with a single clear voice on disarmament issues and the deep fissures in its ranks have sapped its influence and effectiveness as a prod to the major powers. This has further complicated the task of consensus-building, a process that is especially difficult in forums where North-South and East-West differences have to be reconciled simultaneously.

Whatever its procedural and substantive shortcomings, the second Special Session did attract nineteen heads of state, including President Reagan, forty-five foreign ministers, and the largest peace demonstration ever held in the US. It provided an opportunity for countless bilateral meetings at the foreign minister level, including one between Secretary of State Haig and Soviet Foreign Minister Gromyko. The US and the USSR decided to time the opening of their START negotiations to coincide with the session, and President Reagan used the occasion as the basis for an invitation to meet with Soviet President Brezhnev.

The event was clearly perceived by many people at high levels as being important at least for political, if not substantive, reasons. While few states accord multilateral efforts a high priority, even fewer are prepared to express their doubts publicly. Reflecting the role of public opinion and the fear of appearing reluctant about disarmament at a time of growing public interest, almost all of the heads of state to appear were from Western countries.

Global arms talks have survived an uneven history spanning nearly a century to become an integral part of the fabric of international life. Multilateral arms control on the global level is inevitably an unsatisfactory exercise for most of the participants, with no single countries or blocs completely pleased by the outcomes. The rule of consensus not only insures the survival of the process, but also guarantees its glacially slow pace, its lack of clear direction, and its tendency to shun innovation and fresh perspectives. To idealists global negotiations and discussions are a means to achieve global disarmament, to cynics they are a relatively harmless way to pacify the idealists, and to pragmatists they are a tool for drawing attention to arms control problems of global scope and for beginning to develop international norms about armaments and their use.

Despite their political underpinnings, multilateral efforts on both the global and regional levels have not just been talk and window-dressing. Most public attention has been drawn to spectacular events, like the Special Session, that are deliberations or discussions more than true negotiations. The work of the 40-member Committee on Disarmament in Geneva, the chief multilateral negotiating body, receives little public notice. While suffering many of the drawbacks of other mechanisms with broad representation, it is still a place for serious business and has served as a useful link between bilateral and global activities.

Through the creative interaction of bilateral, regional, and global efforts, eleven multilateral treaties and conventions have been adopted over the last two decades, including the crucial Nuclear Non-Proliferation Treaty and restrictions on weapons deployments in several areas. While these steps have not placed strict limitations on existing arsenals or qualitative improvements, they have channelled the arms competition in certain directions and have precluded its spread into other areas. Moreover, the multilateral record compares favorably with the achievements of bilateral negotiations over the same period. Yet as Alan Neidle points out, most of the progress occurred during a period of improving East-West relations in the 1960s and early 1970s.

It is easier to define the differences between bilateral and multilateral negotiations in theory than in practice. The relationship between these two levels of diplomacy is complex, varying from case to case, but frequently symbiotic and mutually reinforcing. Many substantive issues are addressed at several levels simultaneously, sometimes ranging from bilateral negotiations to multilateral exhortations. Several multilateral treaties have been the products of a three-tiered process: bilateral or trilateral negotiations to produce a draft convention or general principles; discussion and revision in the Committee on Disarmament or its predecessors; and an adoption by a large number of states. At other times the bilateral-multilateral interactions do not proceed smoothly, as in the cases of the Environmental Modifications Convention and the stalled negotiations on a radiological weapons ban, in which strong third world objections to Soviet-American drafts slowed or halted the process. Agreement between the superpowers is apparently a necessary, but not sufficient, condition for multilateral agreement.

Inter-alliance negotiations, so far largely restricted to Europe, have elements of both bilateralism and multilateralism. MBFR is officially a multilateral negotiation involving 19 countries, yet in practice the Soviet Union dominates the Eastern side and the US and West Germany, with the most at stake, take the lead for the West. INF and START, on the other hand, are conducted formally as bilateral Soviet-American negotiations, yet, at least on the Western side, the US positions are put forward after a series of bilateral and multilateral consultations within the alliance. In reality, there are few East-West arms control problems that are the sole concern of two or three countries, while, on the other hand, there are few global security issues that concern all states equally. As Gregory Treverton points out, on any given topic the arms control process forms a continuum, with the forums determined both by which countries are needed for agreement and which insist on having some indirect voice in the outcome.

In part, because of this overlapping of bilateral and multilateral concerns and negotiations, global forums have suffered from something of a political identity crisis. They have addressed almost all arms control issues, while having sole responsibility for almost none. The Special Sessions have largely been devoted to determining agendas and setting priorities, tasks at which large committees are not especially adept. Universality and purposefulness are both admirable traits, especially in dealing with global problems, but they are frequently incompatible. It is essential that agenda-setting and debates not become further politicized, which is a common tendency in UN bodies when their substantive work is frustrated. This would do irreparable damage to an already crippled process.

With the superpowers at loggerheads and the non-aligned divided and discouraged, what constructive role can be played by multilateral negotiations in the 1980s? Multilateral bodies should not lack important issues to deal with, since many of the most persistent and potentially explosive topics on the arms control agenda are inherently regional or global in scope. The diffusion of military, political, and economic power in recent years has meant that few security problems can be handled successfully by the US and Soviet Union alone. At the same time, multilateral efforts can accomplish little without prior US-Soviet agreement in principle.

Among the most obvious multilateral problems are nuclear proliferation, a comprehensive nuclear test ban, chemical weapons, conventional arms transfers, regional arms deployments, military budget reductions, and further arms deployments in outer space. Global and regional bodies could play major roles in verification, confidence-building measures, peacekeeping and peacemaking, research, data collection and publication, and public education and training, especially in the third world where there is comparatively little expertise in arms control problems. Yet none of this potential will be realized unless there are dramatic shifts in policies and attitudes on the part of all the parties. There could be a resurgence of interest among the non-aligned in regional measures now that global discussions are at an impasse. Policymakers in third world capitals, as noted by George Quester, certainly recognize that security begins at home and that nuclear weapons of the major powers represent less of a security threat than do the conventional arms of neighboring countries. Yet their concerns, voiced at multilateral forums, tend to be quite different from those expressed in bilateral meetings with the major powers.

While multilateral arms control efforts have generally received a low priority from US decisionmakers, these issues are of great importance to the United States. If multilateral bodies could handle these issues more effectively and equitably, then American leaders would be more supportive of their activities. On the other hand, multilateral efforts will not be successful without greater support from the US, the USSR and their allies. The optimal answer to this dilemma would be for multilateral bodies to put less stress on Soviet-American problems and more on global and regional issues, and for the major powers to play more of a leadership role by offering imaginative, innovative, and far-reaching proposals for coping with multilateral security problems. So far, neither party has been willing to take the first step and the prospects for such a global bargain are dim.

There is no simple formula for quickly reviving multilateral arms control. Its problems are deeply rooted in the nature of the enterprise and in the state of world politics. It would be misleading and eventually counterproductive to encourage public opinion to expect much concrete progress in the near future. What is badly needed, however, is a long-term public and official constituency in support of multilateral approaches that recognizes both their weaknesses and potentials. The long-term process of reinvigorating and strengthening multilateral bodies needs to be undertaken soon if they are to be in a position to make a positive contribution when the international climate improves sufficiently to make real progress possible again.

APPENDIX A
AUTHORS' BIOGRAPHICAL SKETCHES

Richard E. Bissell is currently Professorial Lecturer at the Johns Hopkins School of Advanced International Studies. He is former Managing Editor of *Orbis* and Director of Economic Security Studies at the Foreign Policy Research Institute, Philadelphia. Bissell is a graduate of Stanford University and the Fletcher School of Law and Diplomacy. He is the author of *South Africa and the United States: Erosion of an Economic Relationship* and a forthcoming book, *Strategic Dimensions of Economic Behavior.*

Michael J. Brenner is Associate Professor of International Affairs at the University of Pittsburgh's Graduate School of Public and International Affairs. His previous academic appointments include teaching positions at Cornell, Stanford, and the University of California, Berkeley. He has also held research fellowships at Harvard University and the Brookings Institution. Professor Brenner has recently published *Nuclear Power and Non-Proliferation: The Remaking of U.S. Policy* with Cambridge University Press. A critical account of the evolution of government policy since 1974, it was written with support from the Ford Foundation's Arms Control and International Security Program.

Steven L. Canby is a Defense Analyst with C & L Associates. A graduate of the United States Military Academy at West Point, he has a Ph.D. from Harvard University. Canby is the author of numerous studies on military strategy, tactics, organization, and manpower.

Edward C. Luck is Executive Vice President of the United Nations Association of the USA which conducts research programs on economic issues, Soviet-American relations, Japanese-American relations, Chinese-American relations, arms control and national security problems, and UN affairs. From 1974 to 1977 he served as Project Director of the UNA-USA National Policy Panel on Conventional Arms Control. He formerly served as a consultant for the Social Science Department of the Rand Corporation. He has published and testified widely in the fields of arms control, national security policy and Soviet foreign policy. He holds a B.A. from Dartmouth College, M.A., M.I.A., and M.Ph. degreees from Columbia University, and the Certificate of Columbia's Russian Institute.

Charles William Maynes is currently editor of *Foreign Policy* magazine. He received his B.A. from Harvard University in 1960 and an M.A. from Oxford University in 1962. He joined the Department of State in 1962 and served as UN Political Affairs Officer, 1962–65. He was Chief Economist in the US AID Mission in Laos for non-project aid from 1965–67; Economic Officer for the American Embassy in Moscow, 1968–70; and Assistant Secretary for International Organization Affairs, 1977–80. Besides work with the State Department, Mr. Maynes was a Congressional Fellow, 1972; Senior Legislative Assistant to Senator Fred R. Harris, 1972; and Secretary for the Carnegie Endowment for International Peace, 1972–76.

John B. McGrath, who served as Research Associate on this project, specializes in West European and East Asian politics and in arms control, defense, and energy policy. He received an M. Phil. in Political Science from Columbia University in 1982 and is now engaged in doctoral dissertation research. In addition to work with the United Nations Association, he has served as consultant with the Japan Society and the Atlantic Council and has completed internships with the US Department of State and the UN Secretariat.

Michael Nacht is Associate Professor of Public Policy and Associate Director of the Kennedy School of Government's Center for Science and International Affairs at Harvard University. Trained in aeronautics and astronautics, he holds graduate degrees in statistics, operations research, and political science. Professor Nacht teaches in the areas of international affairs and security and in public management. He has been at Harvard since 1973 and a member of the faculty since 1975. Previously he served as an aerospace engineer with NASA Lewis Research Center and then worked for a private consulting firm on a variety of military and civilian projects. Professor Nacht has written widely on American foreign and defense policy, regional security problems in Europe, East Asia, and the Middle East, anticipating regime changes in developing countries, and management issues in the making of national security policy. He is co-editor of the quarterly *International Security* and is presently directing the US-Japan security project in Harvard's program on US-Japan relations. His most recent publication is "ABM ABCs," *Foreign Policy,* Spring 1982.

Alan F. Neidle was visiting Tom Slick Professor of World Peace at the Lyndon B. Johnson School of Public Affairs, University of Texas at Austin, from 1981–82. Prior to this position, he served for twenty-four years in the US Department of State and the Arms Control and Disarmament Agency. He has been an international lawyer, negotiator, and policy planner. He has conducted treaty negotiations with the Soviet Union, US allies, and non-aligned nations on a variety of arms control subjects, including limitations on nuclear testing, preventing nuclear weapons proliferation, and controlling chemical and biological weapons. He has also been responsible for formulating US policy for participation in the United Nations. For five years he was a member of the US delegation to the UN General Assembly.

George H. Quester is Chairman of the Department of Government and Politics at the University of Maryland, where he teaches courses in international politics and defense policy. Prior to coming to Maryland, he taught at Cornell University, Harvard University, University of California at Los Angeles, and the National War College. He is the author of *The Politics of Nuclear Proliferation, Offense and Defense in the International System,* and many other works.

Elliot L. Richardson is currently Chairman of the United Nations Association–USA and the senior resident partner in the Washington office of Milbank, Tweed, Hadley & McCloy, a New York law firm engaging in a diversified domestic and international practice. Ambassador Richardson graduated from Harvard College in 1941, and received his law degree from Harvard Law School in 1947. He has served as Lieutenant Governor of Massachusetts, 1965–67; Attorney General of Massachusetts, 1967–69; Under Secretary of State, 1969–70; Secretary of Health, Education and Welfare, 1970–73; Secretary of Defense, January to May, 1973; Attorney General of the US, May to October, 1973; Fellow of the Woodrow Wilson International Center for Scholars, 1974–75; Ambassador to the Court of St. James's, 1975–76; Secretary of Commerce, 1976–77; and Ambassador-at-Large and Special Representative of the President to the Law of the Sea Conference, 1977–80.

W. Scott Thompson is currently serving at the US International Communication Agency, on leave from his position as Professor at the Fletcher School of Law and Diplomacy. He served as an official advisor to the US delegation to the second Special Session on Disarmament in June–July, 1982. The first draft of his paper was prepared before the session and it was updated and revised after the session was concluded. Professor Thompson received his B.A. with Great Distinction from Stanford University in 1963 and later completed his doctorate of philosophy at Oxford University in 1967. From 1975 to 1976 he served as Assistant to the Secretary of Defense while serving as a White House Fellow. He recently served as Senior Fellow, Political-Military Studies, at the Center for Strategic and International Studies, Georgetown University. He is the author and co-author of various books, including *From Weakness to Strength: National Strategy in the 1980s,* and is the editor of *World Politics and Soviet Power Projection,* which he completed while serving as principal investigator for the US Navy.

Gregory F. Treverton is Lecturer in Public Policy, Kennedy School of Government, Harvard University. He received his B.A. in Public and International Affairs from Princeton University and his Master of Public Policy and Ph.D. degrees from Harvard University.

Prior to his current position, Dr. Treverton was Assistant Director of the International Institute for Strategic Studies in London as well as Staff Member for Western Europe at the National Security Council. He is the author and editor of numerous articles, reports, and books.

APPENDIX B
UNA-USA STUDY GROUP ON MULTILATERAL APPROACHES TO ARMS CONTROL

Chairman: **James F. Leonard**
Chairman
Committee for National Security

David Adamson
Advisor
Political and Security Affairs
United States Mission to the UN

Kenneth Adelman
Deputy Permanent Representative of the United States to the UN
United States Mission to the UN

Steven Aoki
Foreign Affairs Officer
Bureau of Politico-Military Affairs
Department of State

Leslie H. Brown
Deputy Director
Bureau of Politico-Military Affairs
Department of State

Sheila Buckley
Director, Multilateral Negotiations
Office of the Secretary of Defense
Department of Defense

Susan Burk
Assistant for Multilateral Negotiations
Office of the Secretary of Defense
Department of Defense

Albert Carnesale
Professor and Academic Dean
Kennedy School of Government
Harvard University

Jonathan Dean
Senior Associate
Carnegie Endowment for International Peace

James Dobbins
Director, Office of Theater Military Policy
Bureau of Politico-Military Affairs
Department of State

Donald Easum
President
African-American Institute

Robert Einhorn
Strategic Programs Bureau
US Arms Control and Disarmament Agency

Charles Flowerree
Former US Representative to the Committee on Disarmament

Richard N. Gardner
Henry L. Moses Professor of Law and International Organization
Columbia University

James George
Assistant Director
Multilateral Affairs Bureau
US Arms Control and Disarmament Agency

Alex Glicksman
Professional Staff Member
Senate Foreign Relations Committee

Michael Guhin
Staff Member
National Security Council

Lynn Hansen
Chief, Regional Division
US Arms Control and Disarmament Agency

Thor Hanson
Vice Admiral
United States Navy (Retired)

Mary Elizabeth Hoinkes
Deputy Assistant Director
Multilateral Affairs Bureau
US Arms Control and Disarmament Agency

Betty Jane Jones
Chief, International Relations Division
Multilateral Affairs Bureau
US Arms Control and Disarmament Agency

Sven Kraemer
Staff Member
National Security Council

Paul Kreisberg
Director of Studies
Council on Foreign Relations

Betty Lall
Director, Labor Programs and Urban Affairs
New York State School of Industrial and Labor Relations
Cornell University

Alexander T. Liebowitz
Foreign Service Officer
Office of Theater Military Policy
Department of State

Edward Malloy
Director, Office of Nuclear Policy and Operations
Bureau of Politico-Military Affairs
Department of State

Andrew Pierre
Senior Fellow
Council on Foreign Relations

Nicholas Platt
Deputy Assistant Secretary
Bureau of International Organization Affairs
Department of State

John Pustay
Lieutenant General, USAF
President
National Defense University

Stanley Resor
Partner
Debevoise and Plimpton

Elliot L. Richardson
Partner
Milbank, Tweed, Hadley & McCloy
Chairman, UNA-USA

Eugene Rostow
Director
US Arms Control and Disarmament Agency

Richard Slott
Deputy Chief, International Relations Division
Multilateral Affairs Bureau
US Arms Control and Disarmament Agency

Ivo Spalatin
Staff Director
Subcommittee on International Security and Scientific Affairs
House Committee on Foreign Affairs

Peter Swiers
Deputy Director, Office of Theater Military Policy
Bureau of Politico-Military Affairs
Department of State

John Tierney
Special Assistant
Multilateral Affairs Bureau
US Arms Control and Disarmament Agency

Philip Wilcox
Deputy Director
Office of UN Political Affairs
Bureau of International Organization Affairs
Department of State

UNA-USA STAFF

Edward C. Luck
Executive Vice President

Steven Dimoff
Director
Washington Office

John B. McGrath
Rapporteur and Research Associate

APPENDIX C
CHRONOLOGY OF
MULTILATERAL ARMS CONTROL
IN THE POSTWAR ERA

PREPARED BY JOHN B. MC GRATH

1946   Baruch Plan proposed by the United States for international control of nuclear materials and technology. Rejected by the Soviet Union.

1946–52   Deliberations of the UN Atomic Energy Commission and the UN Commission for Conventional Armaments. Merged in 1952 to form the UN Disarmament Commission.

1953–65   Deliberations of the UN Disarmament Commission. Resumed in 1979 on the recommendation of the first UN Special Session on Disarmament.

1953   "Atoms for Peace" plan proposed by President Eisenhower at the UN. Provided for the dissemination and use of nuclear technology for peaceful purposes and called for an international agency to monitor these activities.

1954   Subcommittee on Disarmament of the UN Disarmament Commission established in London. Members included the United States, the Soviet Union, the United Kingdom, France, and Canada.

1954   General disarmament program proposed by Britain and France in the Subcommittee on Disarmament.

1955   Anglo-French plan supported by the United States and Canada. General disarmament program submitted by the Soviet Union accepting a number of Western positions.

1955   Geneva Summit. General disarmament proposals stalled, in part because of US concerns for inadequate inspection and verification. US "Open Skies" proposal for aerial inspection of military installations to reduce the danger of surprise attack in Europe.

1957   Deliberations of the Subcommittee on Disarmament suspended.

1957   International Atomic Energy Agency established in Vienna.

1958   Surprise Attack Conference between representatives of NATO and the Warsaw Pact.

1958   Conference of experts on the detection and verification of nuclear weapons tests, involving scientists and other experts from four NATO and four Warsaw Pact countries.

1958–62   Tripartite negotiations for a nuclear test ban between the United States, the Soviet Union, and the United Kingdom.

1958–61   US-Soviet moratorium on the testing of nuclear weapons. Tripartite negotiations ended shortly after the moratorium was broken by both sides.

1959–60   Ten Nation Disarmament Committee created as successor to the Subcommittee on Disarmament but existed for less than a year. Members included five NATO and five Warsaw Pact countries.

1959   Antarctic Treaty signed, prohibiting military activities in the region. By October 1981, twenty-four states had become parties to the treaty.

1961   US-Soviet Joint Statement of Agreed Principles for disarmament negotiations (the McCloy-Zorin Agreed Principles), calling for efforts to achieve general and complete disarmament and for the creation of a new negotiating body.

1962   Eighteen Nation Disarmament Committee established in Geneva. In addition to the five NATO and five Warsaw Pact members, eight nonaligned or neutral states included. Body expanded to 26 members and renamed the Conference of the Committee on Disarmament, 1969. At the first Special Session on Disarmament in 1978, enlarged again to 40 members and renamed Committee on Disarmament. France and China subsequently agreed to join the negotiations; for the first time, all the nuclear-weapon states are represented at Geneva.

1963   After tripartite talks resumed, US, UK, and USSR concluded the Limited or Partial Test Ban Treaty (Treaty Banning Nuclear Weapon Tests in the Atmosphere, in Outer Space, and Under Water). Underground testing permitted to continue. By October 1981, 112 states had become parties.

1963–67   Deliberations of the Preparatory Commission for the Denuclearization of Latin America resulted in 1967 in the Treaty of Tlatelolco (Treaty for the Prohibition of Nuclear Weapons in Latin America). Also known as the Latin American Nuclear-Weapon-Free Zone Treaty. Under a protocol, the nuclear-weapon states agreed to respect the provisions of the treaty.

1967   Outer Space Treaty signed (Treaty on Principles Governing the Activities of States in the Exploration and Use of Outer Space, Including the Moon and Other Celestial Bodies). Prohibited the deployment of nuclear weapons in orbit around the earth or on the moon.

1968   Treaty on the Non-Proliferation of Nuclear Weapons signed, regulating the peaceful use of nuclear technology and forbidding its military use by non-nuclear-weapon states. Also including pledge by nuclear-weapon states to seek nuclear disarmament. Conference of Non-

Nuclear-Weapon States on the treaty held in Geneva after the signing. By October 1981, 116 states had become parties.

1969–79   Strategic Arms Limitation Talks (SALT) between the United States and the Soviet Union. Although the talks were bilateral in structure, many countries in Europe and among the non-aligned felt that their interests would be affected by the outcome. The talks were discussed regularly in different multilateral bodies. In 1972, the SALT I accords included a treaty limiting the deployment of anti-ballistic missile systems (the ABM Treaty) and an agreement (the Interim Agreement) freezing, for five years, the number of strategic weapons launchers—ICBMs and SLBMs, but not bombers—of the two parties. In 1979 the SALT II Treaty established a ceiling of 2,400 strategic delivery vehicles, including bombers, and a subceiling limiting MIRVed missiles and bombers carrying cruise missiles to 1,320. The treaty was never submitted to the US Senate for ratification because of strong domestic opposition and the Soviet invasion of Afghanistan.

1971   Seabed Arms Control Treaty Signed (Treaty on the Prohibition of the Emplacement of Nuclear Weapons and Other Weapons of Mass Destruction on the Seabed and the Ocean Floor and in the Subsoil Thereof).

1972   Biological Weapons Convention signed (Convention on the Prohibition of the Development, Production and Stockpiling of Bacteriological [Biological] and Toxin Weapons and on Their Destruction). With the 1925 Geneva Protocol, prohibited chemical and biological warfare. By October 1981, 94 states had become parties.

1973   Negotiations on Mutual and Balanced Force Reductions in Europe begun in Vienna, continuing throughout the decade. New proposals submitted by the Reagan Administration in mid-1982. NATO and the Warsaw Pact have been unable to concur on each other's force levels.

1973–75   Conference on Security and Cooperation in Europe convened in Helsinki with 35 countries, including the United States and Canada, participating. Final Act in 1975 provided for confidence-building measures between NATO and Warsaw Pact forces. Review conferences held at Belgrade in 1977 and at Madrid in 1980.

1975   First Review Conference of the Non-Proliferation Treaty held, with broad disagreement between the non-aligned and the nuclear-weapon states about the progress made towards achieving disarmament, as pledged under the treaty.

1977   Review Conference of the Seabed Arms Control Treaty held.

1977   Environmental Modification Convention signed (Convention on the Prohibition of Military or Any Other Hostile Use of Environmental Modification Techniques).

1977–80   Tripartite talks for a comprehensive nuclear test ban begun between the United States, the United Kingdom, and the Soviet Union. Talks suspended in 1980, with a decision not to resume them made by the United States in 1982.
Two treaties signed by the United States and the Soviet Union in 1974 and 1976 prohibited underground nuclear tests and single nuclear explosions for peaceful purposes with yields of more than 150 kilotons (Threshold Test Ban Treaty, Peaceful Nuclear Explosions Treaty). Neither treaty has been ratified by the US Senate.

1977–80   Talks between the United States and the Soviet Union initiated on controlling chemical weapons, radiological weapons, and forces in the Indian Ocean. Bilateral efforts stalled by 1979–80, but discussion of the issues continued in the Committee on Disarmament and at the United Nations. Concurrent bilateral talks on anti-satellite weapons and conventional arms transfers also stalled without further action in multilateral forums.

1977   London Nuclear Suppliers' Club, composed of the major
            nuclear supplier states meeting since 1975, agreed on
            Guidelines for Nuclear Transfers with a trigger list of
            controls on the transfer of materials, equipment, and
            technology to non-nuclear-weapon states.

1977–80   International Nuclear Fuel Cycle Evaluation conference
            held in Vienna, with 66 countries participating. Confer-
            ence initiated by the United States to consider the grow-
            ing availability of nuclear technology and materials, in-
            cluding plutonium, throughout the world.

1978   First UN Special Session on Disarmament convened. Fi-
            nal document of the session contained a number of agreed
            principles and priorities for disarmament. Major devel-
            opments, in addition to changes in the Committee on
            Disarmament and the Disarmament Commission, in-
            cluded a decision to focus the work of the First Com-
            mittee of the General Assembly solely on disarmament
            matters and the establishment of a Centre for Disarma-
            ment in the UN Secretariat by expanding existing staff
            and resources devoted to disarmament work.

1980   Review Conference of the Biological Weapons Conven-
            tion held. Second Review Conference of the Non-Prolif-
            eration Treaty held with continuing disagreement be-
            tween nuclear-weapon and non-nuclear-weapon states.

1981   Convention on Inhumane Weapons signed (Convention
            on Prohibitions or Restrictions on the Use of Certain
            Conventional Weapons Which May Be Deemed to Be
            Excessively Injurious or to Have Indiscriminate Ef-
            fects). Drafted by a UN conference in 1979 and 1980,
            the convention limits the use of such weapons as incen-
            diary bombs and land mines.

1981   The United States and the Soviet Union begin talks on
            limiting the Intermediate Nuclear Forces of NATO and
            the Warsaw Pact.

1982   Second UN Special Session on Disarmament convened. Delegates unable to agree on a program for comprehensive disarmament. The United States and the Soviet Union resume efforts for strategic nuclear arms control in the Strategic Arms Reduction Talks (START).

SELECTED BIBLIOGRAPHY, 1976–82

PREPARED BY JOHN B. McGRATH

I. GENERAL WORKS AND ANTHOLOGIES ON ARMS CONTROL

Barton, John H., and Weiler, Lawrence D., eds. *International Arms Control: Issues and Agreements*. Stanford, California: Stanford University Press, 1976.

Brodie, Bernard. "On the Objectives of Arms Control." *International Security*, 1:1 (Summer, 1976).

Goldblat, Josef. *Agreements for Arms Control: A Critical Survey*. London: Taylor and Francis, for the Stockholm International Peace Research Institute, 1982.

Hanrieder, Wolfram, F., ed. *Arms Control and Security: Current Issues*. Boulder, Colorado: Westview Press, 1979.

Kincade, William H. and Porro, Jeffrey D., eds. *Negotiating Security: An Arms Control Reader*. Washington, DC: The Carnegie Endowment for International Peace, 1979.

Myrdal, Alva. *The Game of Disarmament*. New York: Pantheon Books, 1976.

Ranger, Robin. *Arms and Politics: 1958–78*. Toronto: Macmillan Company of Canada, 1979.

II. GENERAL WORKS ON MULTILATERAL ARMS CONTROL

Epstein, William. "UN Special Session on Disarmament: How Much Progress?" *Survival*, 20:6 (November/December, 1978).

Goldman, Ralph. *Arms Control and Peacekeeping*. New York: Random House, 1982.

International Security, 2:4 (Spring, 1978). Section on "The UN Special Session: Another Shot at Disarmament," with articles by Louis B. Sohn, Lincoln P. Bloomfield and Harlan Cleveland, and Tariq Osman Hyder.

Sharp, Jane M.O. *Opportunities for Disarmament: A Preview of the 1978 United Nations Special Session on Disarmament*. New York: The Carnegie Endowment for International Peace, 1978.

Stanley, C. Maxwell. *Multilateral Disarmament: Conspiracy for Common*

Sense. Occasional Paper No. 31. Muscatine, Iowa: The Stanley Foundation, May, 1982.

Stanley Foundation Reports on the United Nations of the Next Decade:
Multilateral Disarmament and the Special Session. 12th Conference Report. Muscatine, Iowa: The Stanley Foundation, June, 1977.
The Multilateral Disarmament Process. 16th Conference Report. Muscatine, Iowa: The Stanley Foundation, June, 1981.

Stanley Foundation Reports on United Nations Procedures:
UN Special Session on Disarmament. 8th Conference Report. May, 1977.
UN Special Session on Disarmament. 9th Conference Report. May, 1978.
Comprehensive Programme of Disarmament. 10th Conference Report. May, 1979.
United Nations Second Special Session on Disarmament. 12th Conference Report. May, 1981.
The UN Second Special Session on Disarmament and Beyond. 13th Conference Report. May, 1982.
All: Muscatine, Iowa: The Stanley Foundation, dates as given.

Stockholm International Peace Research Institute. *Arms Control: A Survey and Appraisal of Multilateral Agreements*. London: Taylor and Francis, 1978.

Survival, 20:5 (September/October, 1978). "The UN Special Session on Disarmament: Documentation."

Towle, Philip. "The UN Special Session on Disarmament: In Retrospect." *World Today*, 35:5 (May, 1979).

Verona, Sergui. "The Geneva Disarmament Negotiations as a Learning Process." *Arms Control*, 1:1 (May, 1980).

Weiler, Lawrence. "Reflections on the Disarmament Session." *The Bulletin of the Atomic Scientists*, 34:10 (December, 1978).

Zacher, Mark W. *International Conflicts and Collective Security: 1946–77*. New York: Praeger Publishers, 1979.

III. WORKS CONCERNING NUCLEAR NON-PROLIFERATION ISSUES

Brenner, Michael J. *Nuclear Power and Non-Proliferation*. New York: Cambridge University Press, 1982.

Chayes, Abram and Lewis, W. Bennett, eds. *International Arrangements for Nuclear Fuel Reprocessing*. Cambridge, Massachusetts: Ballinger, 1977.

Dunn, Lewis A. *Controlling the Bomb: Nuclear Proliferation in the 1980s*. Twentieth Century Fund Report. New Haven and London: Yale University Press, 1982.

Epstein, William. *The Last Chance: Nuclear Proliferation and Arms Control*. New York: Free Press, 1976.

Greenwood, Ted; Feiveson, Harold; and Taylor, Theodore. *Nuclear Proliferation Motivations, Capabilities, and Strategies for Control.* New York: McGraw-Hill, 1977.

Imai, Ryukichi, and Rowen, Henry S. *Nuclear Energy and Nuclear Proliferation: Japanese and American Views.* Boulder, Colorado: Westview Press, 1980.

Kapur, Ashok. *International Nuclear Proliferation: Multilateral Diplomacy and Regional Aspects.* New York: Praeger Publishers, 1979.

————. "The Nuclear Spread: A Third World View." *Third World Quarterly,* 2:1 (January, 1980).

King, John Kerry, ed. *International Political Effects of the Spread of Nuclear Weapons.* Washington, DC: US GPO, April, 1979.

Nye, Joseph S. "Nonproliferation: A Long-Term Strategy." *Foreign Affairs,* 56:3 (April, 1978).

————. "Sustaining Non-Proliferation in the 1980s." *Survival,* 23:3 (May/June, 1981).

Quester, George H., ed. *Nuclear Proliferation: Breaking the Chain.* Madison, Wisconsin: University of Wisconsin Press, 1981. Also published as Vol. 35, No. 1, of *International Organization.*

Smith, Gerard, and Rathjens, George. "Reassessing Nuclear Nonproliferation Policy." *Foreign Affairs,* 59:4 (Spring, 1981).

Stockholm International Peace Research Institute (SIPRI):
Internationalization to Prevent the Spread of Nuclear Weapons. London: Taylor and Francis, 1980.
Nuclear Energy and Nuclear Weapons Proliferation. London: Taylor and Francis, 1979.
NPT: The Main Political Barrier to Nuclear Weapon Proliferation. London: Taylor and Francis, 1980.

Waltz, Kenneth N. *The Spread of Nuclear Weapons: More May Be Better.* Adelphi Paper No. 171. London: International Institute for Strategic Studies, Autumn, 1981.

Wohlstetter, Albert. "Spreading the Bomb Without Quite Breaking the Rules." *Foreign Policy,* 25 (Winter, 1976–77).

Yager, Joseph A. *International Cooperation in Nuclear Energy.* Washington, DC: The Brookings Institution, 1981.

Yager, Joseph A. ed. *Nonproliferation and U.S. Foreign Policy.* Washington, DC: The Brookings Institution, 1980.

IV. WORKS ON CONVENTIONAL ARMS CONTROL ISSUES

Alford, Jonathan, ed. *The Future of Arms Control: Part III: Confidence-Building Measures.* Adelphi Paper No. 149. London: International Institute for Strategic Studies, Spring, 1979.

Baxter, Richard R. "Conventional Weapons Under Legal Prohibitions." *International Security*, 1:3 (Winter, 1977).

Burt, Richard. *Nuclear Proliferation and Conventional Arms Transfers: The Missing Link*. Santa Monica, California: California Seminar on Arms Control and Foreign Policy, 1977.

Burt, Richard. "Proliferation and the Spread of New Conventional Weapons Technology." *International Security*, 1:3 (Winter, 1977).

Cahn, Anne Hessing, et. al. *Controlling Future Arms Trade*. New York: McGraw-Hill, 1977.

Dudzinsky, S.J., and Digby, James. "New Technology and the Control of Conventional Arms." *International Security*, 1:4 (Spring, 1977).

Ehni, Reinhard W. "Confidence-Building Measures: A Task for Arms Control and Disarmament Policy." *NATO Review*, 28:3 (June, 1980).

Farley, Philip J.; Kaplan, Stephen S; and Lewis, William H. *Arms Across the Sea*. Washington, DC: The Brookings Institution, 1978.

Franko, Lawrence G. "Restraining Arms Exports to the Third World: Will Europe Agree?" *Survival*, 21:1 (January/February, 1979).

Hammond, Paul Y. "Controlling U.S. Arms Transfers: The Emerging System," *Orbis*, 23:2 (Summer, 1979).

Holst, Johan J., and Melander, Karen A. "European Security and Confidence-Building Measures." *Survival*, 19:4 (July/August, 1977).

Kearns, Graham. "CAT and Dogma: The Future of Multilateral Arms Transfer Restraint." *Arms Control*, 2:1 (May, 1981).

Macdonald, Hugh. "Conventional Arms Control in Europe." *Arms Control*, 2:3 (December, 1981).

Neuman, Stephanie G. and Harkavy, Robert E. *Arms Transfers in the Modern World*. New York: Praeger Publishers, 1979.

Pearson, Frederic S. "U.S. Arms Transfer Policy: The Feasibility of Restraint." *Arms Control*, 2:1 (May, 1981).

Pierre, Andrew J., ed. *Arms Transfers and American Foreign Policy*. New York: New York University Press, 1979.

Pierre, Andrew J. *The Global Politics of Arms Sales*. Princeton, New Jersey: Princeton University Press, 1982.

Ra'anan, Uri, et. al. *Arms Transfers to the Third World*. Boulder, Colorado: Westview Press, 1978.

Salomon, Michael D.; Louscher, David J.; and Hammond, Paul Y. "Lessons of the Carter Approach to Restraining Arms Transfers." *Survival*, 23:5 (September/October, 1981).

Stanford Journal of International Studies. Issue devoted to "Conventional Arms Control," 14 (Spring, 1979).

UNA-USA National Policy Panel on Conventional Arms Control. *Controlling the Conventional Arms Race*. New York: UNA-USA, 1976.

V. WORKS ON OTHER FUNCTIONAL ARMS CONTROL ISSUES

Becker, Abraham, S. *Military Expenditure Limitation for Arms Control: Problems and Prospects.* Cambridge, Massachusetts: Ballinger, 1977.

Blechman, Barry. "The Comprehensive Test Ban Negotiations: Can They Be Revitalized?" *Arms Control Today,* 11:5 (June, 1981).

Brennan, Donald. "A Comprehensive Test Ban: Everybody or Nobody." *International Security,* 1:1 (Summer, 1976).

Bundy, McGeorge, et. al. "Nuclear Weapons and the Atlantic Alliance." *Foreign Affairs,* 60:4 (Spring, 1981).

Crawford, Alan, et. al. *Compendium of Arms Control Verification Proposals.* Ottawa: Department of National Defense, 1980.

Garthoff, Raymond L. "Banning the Bomb in Outer Space." *International Security,* 5:3 (Winter, 1980/81).

Halsted, Thomas A. "Why No End to Nuclear Testing?" *Survival,* 19:2 (March/April, 1977).

Issraelyan, Victor L. and Flowerree, Charles, C. *Radiological Weapons Control: A Soviet and U.S. Perspective.* Occasional Paper No. 29. Muscatine, Iowa: The Stanley Foundation, February, 1982.

Kaiser, Karl, et. al. "Nuclear Weapons and the Preservation of Peace: A German Response to No First Use." *Foreign Affairs,* 60:5 (Summer, 1982).

Klein, Jean. "Political and Technical Aspects of Verification." *Arms Control.* 1:3 (December, 1980).

Lundin, S.J. "Chemical Weapons: Too Late for Disarmament?" *Bulletin of the Atomic Scientists,* 35:10 (December, 1979).

Juda, Lawrence. "Negotiating a Treaty on Environmental Modification Warfare." *International Organization,* 32:4 (Autumn, 1978).

Meselson, Matthew, ed. *Chemical Weapons and Chemical Arms Control.* New York: Carnegie Endowment for International Peace, 1978.

Potter, William C., ed. *Verification and SALT: The Challenge of Strategic Deception.* Boulder, Colorado: Westview Press, 1980.

Ramberg, Bennett. *The Seabed Arms Control Negotiations: A Study of Multilateral Arms Control Conference Diplomacy.* Denver, Colorado: University of Denver Monograph Series in World Affairs, Vol. 14, 1978.

Robinson, J.P. Perry. "The Negotiations on Chemical Warfare Arms Control." *Arms Control,* 1:1 (May, 1980).

Snow, Donald. "Over the Strategic Horizon: Directed Energy Transfer Weapons and Arms Control." *Arms Control Today,* 9:10 (November, 1979).

Stares, Paul. "Outer Space: Arms or Arms Control." *Arms Control Today,* 11:6 (July/August, 1981).

Stockholm International Peace Research Institute (SIPRI):

Chemical Weapons Destruction and Conversion: Current Disarmament Problems. London: Taylor and Francis, 1980.

Strategic Disarmament, Verification, and National Security. London: Taylor and Francis, 1977.

Weapons of Mass Destruction and the Environment. London: Taylor and Francis, 1977.

Survival. "Chemical Arms Control: Documentation," 18:6 (November/December, 1976).

Vayrynen, Raimo. "The Seabed Treaty Reviewed." *World Today*, 34:6 (June, 1978).

York, Herbert and Greb, Allen G. *The Comprehensive Nuclear Test Ban*. Santa Monica, California: California Seminar on Arms Control and Foreign Policy, 1979.

VI. WORKS ON REGIONAL ARMS CONTROL ISSUES

Acimovic, Ljubivoje. "CSCE and the Non-Aligned States." *Survival*, 18:3 (May/June, 1976).

Adeniran, Tunde, and Stoffer, Howard. "African Arms Control: A New Perspective." *Stanford Journal of International Law*, 17:1 (Winter, 1981).

Astor, David and Yorke, Valarie. *Peace in the Middle East: Super Powers and Security Guarantees*. London: Corgi, 1978.

Barton, John H. and Imai, Ryukichi. *Arms Control II: A New Approach to International Security*. Cambridge, Massachusetts: Oelgeschlager, Gunn, and Hain, Publishers, 1981.

Bertram, Christoph. "Implications of Theater Nuclear Weapons in Europe." *Foreign Affairs*, 60:2 (Winter, 1981/1982).

Brent, Mark and Kincade, William H. "NATO Decides: New Arms and Arms Control In Europe." *Arms Control Today*, 10:2 (February, 1980).

Coffey, Joseph I. *Arms Control and European Security: A Guide to East-West Negotiations*. New York: Praeger Publishers, 1977.

Davis, Lynn E. "A Proposal for TNF Arms Control." *Survival*, 23:6 (November/December, 1981).

Epstein, William. *A Nuclear-Weapon-Free Zone in Africa*. Occasional Paper No. 14. Muscatine, Iowa: The Stanley Foundation, 1977.

Evron, Yair. *The Role of Arms Control in the Middle East*. Adelphi Paper No. 138. London: International Institute for Strategic Studies, Autumn, 1977.

Feldman, Shai. "A Nuclear Middle East." *Survival*, 23:3 (May/June, 1981).

Freedman, Lawrence. "The Dilemma of Theatre Nuclear Arms Control." *Survival*, 23:1 (January/February, 1981).

García Robles, Alfonso. *The Latin American Nuclear-Weapon-Free Zone*.

Occasional Paper No. 19. Muscatine, Iowa: The Stanley Foundation, May, 1979.

Guilhaudis, Jean Francois. "Nuclear Free Zones and Zones of Peace: The Regional Approach to Disarmament Within 'Non-Nuclearised Regions.' " *Arms Control,* 2:2 (September, 1981).

Haas, Richard "Naval Arms Limitation in the Indian Ocean." *Survival,* 20:2 (March/April, 1978).

Hyland, William G. "Soviet Theater Forces and Arms Control Policy." *Survival,* 23:5 (September/October, 1981).

Jabber, Paul. *Not By War Alone: Security and Arms Control in the Middle East.* Berkeley, California: University of California Press, 1981.

Keliher, John G. *The Negotiations on Mutual and Balanced Force Reductions: The Search for Arms Control in Central Europe.* New York: Pergamon Press, 1980.

Kincade, William H.; Yinger, Nancy V.; and Duffy, Gloria C., eds. *Approaches to East-West Arms Control.* Washington, DC: The Arms Control Association and the International Institute for Strategic Studies, 1979.

Lellouche, Pierre. "SALT and European Security: The French Dilemma." *Survival,* 22:1 (January/February, 1980).

Makins, Christopher J. "Negotiating European Security: The Next Step." *Survival,* 21:6 (November/December, 1979).

Prendergast, William B. *Mutual and Balanced Force Reduction: Issues and Prospects.* Washington, DC: American Enterprise Institute, 1978.

Ranger, Robin. "An Alternative Future for MBFR: A European Arms Control Conference." *Survival,* 21:4 (July/August, 1979).

Record, Jeffrey. *Force Reductions in Europe: Starting Over.* Cambridge, Massachusetts: Institute for Foreign Policy Analysis, 1980.

Redick, John R. "Regional Restraint: U.S. Nuclear Policy and Latin America." *Orbis,* 22:1 (Spring, 1978).

de Rose, Francois. "European Concerns and SALT." *Survival,* 21:5 (September/October, 1979).

Sharp, Jane. "Four Approaches to an INF Agreement." *Arms Control Today,* 12:3 (March, 1982).

Yoder, Amos. *Chinese Policies Toward Limiting Nuclear Weapons.* Occasional Paper No. 22. Muscatine, Iowa: The Stanley Foundation, March, 1980.

VII. DOCUMENTATION OF THE UNITED NATIONS

Because the volume of UN documentation is substantial, there is space only for a few references in this bibliography. Each UN forum produces its own set of documents with separate classification numbers and acronyms.

The second UN Special Session on Disarmament was actually the twelfth special session of the General Assembly since the founding of the United Nations. Other special sessions have addressed different economic and political topics. The Committee on Disarmament in Geneva submitted a special report to the SSOD–II which was classified as A/S–12/2. This document contains the text of the draft Comprehensive Programme of Disarmament. The Disarmament Commission's report to the special session was classified as A/S–12/3. The work of the Ad Hoc Committee of the SSOD had the classification, A/S–12/AC.1/ . . . etc. The *Concluding Document* of the special session was first a draft report of this committee, A/S–12/AC.1/L.5 and Add. 1–4 (four addenda). The General Assembly accepted the report as the *Concluding Document,* which was subsequently classified as A/S–12/32.

The regular session of the UN General Assembly in fall 1981 was the 36th such session. The Committee on Disarmament submitted its annual report to this session as A/36/27. These reports also enter the official records of the General Assembly; the classification of the CD's report therefore also became GAOR, 36th Session, Supplement No. 27. A number of other reports written by the Secretariat were submitted to the General Assembly at this session but did not become official records. These received only one classification. For example, the Secretary-General's *Report on Confidence-Building Measures* became A/36/597.

At both the SSOD–II and the 36th session of the General Assembly, the proceedings of plenary meetings are recorded verbatim and are given the designation, PV, for provisional verbatim. Unlike other committees of the Assembly, which have only SR, or summary, records, the First Committee focusing on disarmament issues has verbatim records. During the 36th session of the Assembly, meetings of the Committee occurred from September 16 to December 4, 1981, and their records were classified as A/C.1/36/PV.1–53.

On each agenda item during a session of the General Assembly, the First Committee prepares a report of its work, which contains one or more draft resolutions which it is recommending to the full Assembly. In 1981, for example, for the item "General and Complete Disarmament," the report was classified as A/36/756. One of the twelve draft resolutions, for example, dealt with confidence-building measures. It was adopted without a vote by the General Assembly and was classified as General Assembly Resolution 36/97 F.

The UN Centre for Disarmament, in the UN Secretariat, prepares a number of publications, some of which are reports to the General Assembly that are subsequently published; others are written specifically for public distribution. See for example: (1) *Comprehensive Study on Confidence-Building Measures,* Sales Publication No. 82. IX. 3.; (2) *Study on the Relationship Between Disarmament and Development,* 82. IX.; (3) *Study on the Relationship Between Disarmament and International Security,* 82. IX. 4.; (4) *Comprehensive Study on Nuclear Weapons,* 81. I. 11.; (5) *Study on All the Aspects of Regional Disarmament,* 81. IX. 2.; and (6) *Study on the Reduction of Military Budgets,* 81. I. 9. In addition, a series titled "Disarmament Fact Sheets" and the *UN Disarmament Yearbook* are published by the Department of Public Information and the Centre for Disarmament.

INDEX

Afghanistan, 47, 49, 60, 62, 63, 105, 111, 136, 180, 192

Africa, concerns about verification, 138; ethnic partitions and boundary disputes in, 122; guerrilla war in, 122, 123; North Africa, 188; nuclear-free zone in, 55; sub-Saharan, 18; 102, 129, 133, 180, 193

Albania, 37, 42

Algeria, 126, 140

Amin, Idi, 134. *Also see* Uganda

Angola, 117, 123, 135

Antartica, Treaty of, 9-11, 44, 99

Anti Ballistic Missile Treaty (ABM) (1972), 74

Anti-nuclear rallies, 177

Anti-satellite weapons (ASAT), 44, 97

Arab states, 17, 124, 131, 138

Argentina, attitude to Latin American nuclear-free zone, 131; invasion of Falklands, 113, 122, 127, 130, 166

Arms control, as stabilizing element, 183; and the strategic balance, 43; bilateral, 54, 56, 91; meaning of, 118, 119; measures, 183; negotiations, size of, 73; objectives of, 15, 182, 198; relation between power and rhetoric in, 54; verification, 68, 69; 7, 9, 11, 18, 23, 25, 31, 38, 39, 44, 50, 52, 53, 59, 60, 65, 69, 182. *Also see* multilateral arms control

Asia, 25, 26, 82, 102, 133. *See* individual countries

Asia, East, 18, 192, 206. *See* individual countries

Asia, South, 38, 55, 134, 156. *See* individual countries

Asia, Southeast, 65, 106, 111, 188, 192, 194. *See* individual countries

Aspen Institute, 53

Associated Measures (AM's), 198, 201

Australia, 149

Ayacucho Declaration (1974), *See* Latin America

Balance of power, 117, 126, 134

Bangladesh, 133

Belgium, 85, 87

Bhutan, 38

Biafra, 134

Biological Weapons Convention, amendment to, 26; review conference on, 44; US Senate approval of, 13; 8, 13, 19, 25

Black Sea, 48

Bloomfield, Lincoln P., 53

Brazil, 84, 121, 126, 130, 131, 133, 134, 187, 196

Brezhnev, Leonid I., 49, 105, 218

Britain, *See* United Kingdom

Bulgaria, 128

Bundy, McGeorge, 107

Cambodia, 49, 50, 133, 136

Canada, deuterium uranium reactors (CANDU), 159; free riding by, 87; nuclear imports, 149; 64, 65. *Also see* Trudeau, Pierre

Carter Administration, anti-plutonium campaign, 154; approach to arms transfer limitations, 190; "damage limitation" strategy of, 109; "deep cuts" proposal of, 66; idealism of, 41; nuclear non-proliferation policy of,